"*By the Hand of Providence* skillfully examines the faith-based core beliefs of the revolutionaries—and convincingly refutes the contention that George Washington was an uncommitted Christian or a deist."
—Edward G. Longacre, historian, author of *Cavalry of the Heartland* and *Worthy Opponents*

"Fascinating. . . . Gragg shows the decisive importance that Americans of the 1770s and '80s attributed to the providential intervention of God in the momentous events of the Revolution."
—Dr. Steven Woodworth, author of *This Great Struggle: America's Civil War* and *While God Is Marching On: The Religious World of Civil War Soldiers*

"Rod Gragg has done it again! A page-turner that reads like a novel! I found myself not only wanting to devour the next page, but praying for our nation, 'O Lord, do it again.' "
—Dr. Harry Reeder III, senior pastor, Briarwood Presbyterian Church, Birmingham, Alabama, and author of *The Leadership Dynamic*

How Faith Shaped
the American Revolution

BY THE

HAND OF

PROVIDENCE

ROD GRAGG

HOWARD BOOKS
A Division of Simon & Schuster, Inc.

NEW YORK NASHVILLE LONDON TORONTO SYDNEY NEW DELHI

Howard Books
A Division of Simon & Schuster, Inc.
1230 Avenue of the Americas
New York, NY 10020

First Howard Books hardcover edition June 2012

HOWARD and colophon are trademarks of Simon & Schuster, Inc.

For information about special discounts for bulk purchases,
please contact Simon & Schuster Special Sales at 1-866-506-1949
or business@simonandschuster.com.

The Simon & Schuster Speakers Bureau can bring authors
to your live event. For more information or to book an event,
contact the Simon & Schuster Speakers Bureau at 1-866-248-3049
or visit our website at www.simonspeakers.com.

Designed by Jaime Putorti

Manufactured in the United States of America

10 9 8 7 6 5 4 3 2 1

Library of Congress Cataloging-in-Publication Data

Gragg, Rod
  By the hand of providence : how faith shaped the American revolution / Rod
Gragg.
    p. cm
  Includes bibliographical references and index.
  1. United States—Church history—To 1775. 2. United States—History—
Revolution, 1775–1783—Religious aspects. 3. Christianity and politics—United
States—History. I. Title.
  BR520.G735 2011
277.3'07—dc22
                        2011016811

ISBN 978-1-4165-9630-1
ISBN 978-1-4516-2352-9 (pbk)
ISBN 978-1-4391-8276-5 (ebook)

For Kylah, Sophia, Jaxon, and Gracie

The hand of Providence has been so conspicuous in all this, that he must be worse than an infidel that lacks faith, and more than wicked, that has not gratitude enough to acknowledge his obligations. . . .

—George Washington, 20 August 1778

CONTENTS

INTRODUCTION

George Washington hoped that Americans would never forget God's role in the American Revolution. "I am sure there never was a people who had more reason to acknowledge a divine interposition in their affairs, than those of the United States," he stated during his first term as president, "and I should be pained to believe that they have forgotten that agency, which was so often manifested during our Revolution, or that they failed to consider the omnipotence of that God who is alone able to protect them." It was a theme that Washington stressed frequently during and after the Revolutionary War. Repeatedly, he believed, God had intervened to rescue the American cause—what he called "the sacred Cause of Freedom"—from disaster and defeat. American liberty and independence, he believed deeply and stated often, had been achieved by "the hand of Providence." [1]

Washington was not alone in his thinking. When the Revolutionary War ended in an American triumph, there was a widespread belief among the American people and their leaders that God was responsible for the victory, and that the establishment of the United States of America was providential. When the Continental Congress received the news of the British surrender at

Yorktown, which signaled an end to the war, they responded by assembling in a Philadelphia church for a worship service. Soon afterward, Congress officially recommended that Americans everywhere observe a nationwide day of "public thanksgiving and prayer" for the American victory. "Whereas," the Congressional prayer day resolution declared, "it hath pleased Almighty God, father of mercies, remarkably to assist and support the United States of America in their important struggle for liberty against the long continued efforts of a powerful nation; it is the duty of all ranks to observe and thankfully acknowledge the interpositions of his Providence in their behalf. Through the whole of this contest, from its first rise to this time, the influence of divine Providence may be clearly perceived in many signal instances. . . ."[2]

Such public demonstrations of faith were routine for the Continental Congress, which regularly called for national days of "humiliation, fasting, and prayer" and days of "public thanksgiving and prayer" throughout the Revolution. As aptly observed by a twentieth-century Library of Congress historian, "both the legislators and the public considered it appropriate for the national government to promote a nondenominational, nonpolemical Christianity." In doing so, Congress reflected the Judeo-Christian worldview on which Colonial America was established and which prevailed as the common consensus throughout America at the time of the Revolution. A Bible-based faith was not only the underlying foundation of eighteenth-century American thought and culture, it was also the motivation that propelled American Patriots into the Revolution and sustained them in its darkest days.[3]

A familiar slogan of the Revolution, which was preached from America's pulpits, endlessly reprinted in newspapers and pamphlets and emblazoned on American battle flags, stated simply, "Resistance to Tyrants is Obedience to God." It succinctly reflected the pervasive, deeply held belief in American culture that obedience to the Higher Law of God as revealed in the Bible took precedence over the law of man whenever the two conflicted. At the time of the Revolution, many Americans believed, the British King and Parliament were attempting to suppress the American people's God-given or "inalienable" rights, and thus were also attempting to usurp the authority of God's Higher Law. American pastor Abraham Keteltas spoke for countless American Patriots when he preached that the Revolution was, in reality, the "cause of heaven against hell—of the kind Parent of the universe against the prince of darkness."[4]

Even the British recognized the faith-centered foundation of American resistance. In the opening days of warfare, a prominent member of Parliament who was sympathetic to America's plight tried unsuccessfully to make his fellow parliamentarians understand that Americans generally saw their quest for freedom as righteous resistance to ungodly tyranny. "Religion, always a principle of energy, in this new people is no way worn out or impaired . . . ," he said. "The people are Protestants; and of that kind which is most adverse to all implicit submission of mind and opinion. This is a persuasion not only favorable to liberty, but built upon it." Recognizing the powerful influence of American ministers in favor of independence—especially Presbyterians— another British statesman concluded, "Cousin America has run off with a Presbyterian parson. . . ."[5]

The heart of Revolutionary America was reflected in even more memorable comment by a veteran of the Revolution who was interviewed at age ninety-one. His name was Levi Preston. In 1775, he had been a "Minute Man"—a soldier in the Massachusetts militia—and had been engaged in the opening battle of the war. Although old and stooped when interviewed in 1842, his mind was sharp and his memories were vivid. At one point his youthful interviewer pressed him to explain American motivation for the Revolution. Why were Americans willing to fight for freedom and independence? Were they motivated by the democratic philosophers of the day—by "reading Harrington or Sidney and Locke about the eternal principles of liberty?" The ancient warrior looked up and replied, "Never heard of 'em. We read only the Bible, the Catechism, Watts's Psalms and Hymns, and the Almanack."[6]

The Continental Congress expressed that same faith-centered heart, when—in an open letter to the American people—it described the Revolution in biblical terms:

> *America, without arms, ammunition, discipline, revenue, government or ally, almost totally stript of commerce, and in the weakness of youth, as it were with a "staff and a sling" only, dared "in the name of the Lord of Hosts," to engage a gigantic adversary, prepared at all points, boasting of his strength, and of whom even mighty warriors were greatly afraid."*

As did David in the biblical account of his battle with Goliath, America prevailed against the might of the British Empire to win its freedom and independence, and to become—in the words of George Washington—a place of refuge "for the oppressed and needy of the earth." It did so firmly founded on the Judeo-Christian worldview—as a nation of people motivated, disciplined, and inspired by a Bible-based faith.[7]

It is a remarkable history, and it is uniquely American. Yet amid the distractions and clutter of the twenty-first century "information age," it is largely neglected and generally unknown to modern Americans. Washington hoped, he wrote, that future generations would always look back to the American Revolution and see how the struggle, the triumph, and the birth of the United States of America were so critically influenced by faith. To do otherwise, he believed, was inconceivable. "The hand of Providence has been so conspicuous in all of this," he concluded, "that he must be worse than an infidel that lacks faith, and more than wicked, that has not gratitude enough to acknowledge his obligations. . . ."[8]

CHAPTER ONE

"By the Providence of Almighty God"

The red-coated regimental bands played "God Save the King" as the victorious British army marched into the conquered American capital. It was Friday morning, September 26, 1777, and Philadelphia had fallen to the enemy. Continental forces had engaged in valiant and bloody combat to defend the city, but had been unable to stop the British advance. Now the lead regiments of General William Howe's fifteen-thousand-man army marched unopposed into Philadelphia on the same cobblestone streets recently abandoned by ragtag American troops. A week earlier, the delegates to the Continental Congress had packed up and left with as much dignity as possible, to reassemble first in Lancaster then farther away in York. Hosts of fearful Philadelphians had also fled—many with more haste than dignity. "Today many teams loaded with furniture and people [were] flying from Philadelphia," penned an eyewitness. "Coaches, chaises and wagons loaded with fugitives [were] passing without intermission." Wrote another: "Every face you see looks wild and pale with fear and amazement, and quite overwhelmed with distress." [1]

Accompanied by their triumphant tunes, the British army filed through Philadelphia's streets unopposed—as if on parade—its ranks broken only when a soldier here and there stepped aside to hurriedly gulp a cup of cider offered by Loyalist bystanders. Accompanying the red-coated British regulars were two battalions of German Hessians—mercenary troops hired by the British government to help suppress the Revolution. Although recognized on both sides as well-drilled troops, the Hessians were infamous for their brutality. Now they marched down Philadelphia's streets "with the swing and swagger of an invading army." The British army was experienced and well equipped—arguably the best military force in the world—and the victorious troops exuded confidence and discipline as they marched through Philadelphia, which was the largest city in America. Upon orders, they kept their battle flags encased and out of sight to avoid needlessly provoking the conquered Philadelphians. Such restraint appeared unnecessary, however: the city's patriots were either gone or were staying indoors, and the files of British troops were met by crowds of cheering Loyalists. The American capital appeared thoroughly conquered.[2]

Two weeks earlier, at the Battle of Brandywine, this same British army had defeated a last-ditch American defense, inflicting almost twice as many casualties as it incurred. Soon afterward, at what would become known as the "Paoli Massacre," the British army had demonstrated its deadly efficiency with a surprise nighttime bayonet assault on sleeping Continental troops near the town of Paoli, Pennsylvania. Scores of surprised and confused American soldiers had fallen to British bayonets. "[They] were running about, barefoot, and half-clothed, and in the light of their own fires," a Hessian sergeant would later boast. "We killed three hundred of the rebels with the bayonet. I stuck them myself like so many pigs, one after another, until the blood ran out of the touch-hole of my musket."[3]

Upon his capture of Philadelphia, General Howe established

a huge camp at Germantown on the city's outskirts, and posted troops in force throughout the city. Artillery batteries were erected on the city's riverfront, and infantry were placed at key points. Among these sites was the Pennsylvania State House—"Independence Hall"—where little more than a year before, members of America's Continental Congress had passed the Declaration of Independence. Now one of the delegates' worst fears had become reality: the British had captured the seat of the new national government, including the building and chamber where American independence had been debated and declared. Independence Hall—the new nation's landmark of freedom—would soon become a prison hospital for captured American soldiers. In distant Europe, monarchs and military commanders learned of the capture of the American capital and assumed that the Revolution was over. Great Britain, they believed, had won the war.[4]

They were wrong. Defying all odds, the American cause would survive. Repeatedly, American forces would suffer battlefield calamities that should have ended the Revolution in a British victory. General George Washington's army was repeatedly forced to retreat. Other American armies were defeated and scattered. Principal American seaports and cities fell to the enemy. New York City was occupied by the British for seven years. The national capital was captured and Congress was forced to flee. At various times throughout the war, American forces teetered on the edge of disintegration—poorly armed, inadequately equipped, sometimes near starvation—while facing the military superpower of the day. Yet Continental forces repeatedly survived, and would eventually prevail against all odds.[5]

For generations to come, historians would continue to examine the War for Independence, reanalyzing the astonishing events leading to the American victory. Time after time, British leaders were perplexed by America's unexpected survival, and were stunned by the eventual outcome. How did it happen? George Washington had an answer, which he continuously restated in letters and speeches during and after the war. The success of American arms, Washington believed, was due to nothing less than what he called the "astonishing interpositions of providence"—the sovereign intervention of Almighty God. "To the Great ruler of events, not to any exertions of mine, is to be ascribed the favorable termination of our late contest for liberty," Washington would pronounce at war's end. "I never considered the fortunate issue of any measure adopted by me in the progress of the Revolution in any other light than as the ordering of kind Providence."[6]

Washington was not one to make such statements lightly. He was a Virginia low-church Anglican whose expressions of faith were generally quiet, reserved, and carefully reverent. "We must . . . place a confidence in that Providence, who rules great events," he once observed in a typical commentary, "trusting that out of confusion he will produce order, and, notwithstanding the dark clouds, which may threaten at present, that right will ultimately be established." The "dark clouds" that preceded the American Revolution had gathered largely during Washington's lifetime, and he had been personally involved in a remarkable number of those critical events. They were extraordinary preparation for the singular role of leadership he would assume—and he did not consider the Revolution or his preparation for it to be accidental.[7]

Washington's faith in the sovereignty of God—"Providence" in the vernacular of his day—was a universal belief in eighteenth-century America. From Massachusetts to Georgia, "the idiom of religion penetrated all discourse, underlay all thought, marked all observances, gave meaning to every public and private crisis," according to historian Patricia Bonomi, a twenty-first-century expert on Colonial America. American political thought at the time of the Revolution, twentieth-century

Jewish historian Abraham I. Katsh would observe, reflected "the deeper meaning and higher purpose of a constant regard for principles and religious ideas, based on a profound sympathy for the Scriptures. . . ." The renowned historian Merle Curti would agree. "The Christian tradition," he would note, "was the chief foundation stone of American intellectual development [in the Colonial era]. Whatever differences in ways of life and whatever conflicts of interest separated the country gentry and great merchants from the frontiersmen, poor farmers, artisans, and small shopkeepers, all nominally subscribed to Christian tenets and at least in theory accepted Christianity as their guide."[8]

From the beginning, America was forged in faith—the Judeo-Christian worldview of the Bible. In 1607, when the first successful English colony in North America was established at Jamestown, Virginia, its royal charter declared the colony's mission in part to be the "propagating of Christian Religion." Although many of Jamestown's early colonists showed more interest in gold than God, even rowdy Jamestown reflected a biblical faith. A chaplain held services in a crudely constructed church, and settlers were expected to attend prayer services twice daily, two worship services on the Lord's Day and regular communion. When the colonists fell into near mutiny over Jamestown's "Common Store" system—a socialistic policy that equally rewarded those who worked and those who loitered—Captain John Smith implemented a compulsory work program based on the New Testament admonition "if any would not work, neither should he eat."[9]

A few years later, Virginia governor Thomas Dale enacted a code of laws founded on biblical principles: "I do strictly commaund and charge all Captaines and Officers . . . to have a care that the Almightie God bee duly and daily served, and that they call upon their people to heare Sermons, as that also they diligently frequent Morning and Evening praier themselves by their owne exemplar and daily life, and dutie herein, encouraging others thereunto. . . ." Although harshly enforced, Dale's faith-based laws provided the discipline needed for the colony to survive. In 1619, Virginia's newly established House of Burgesses—America's first legislative assembly—established a precedent with faith-based self-government. The first session of the House of Burgesses was held in Jamestown's log church, its first official act was an opening prayer, and among its first legislative actions were statutes requiring church attendance on the Lord's Day, and mandating that Sundays be kept "in holy and religious order." Two years later, Virginia's constitution dedicated the colony to "the Advancement of the Honour and Service of God, and the Enlargement of His Kingdom." [10]

Thirteen years after Jamestown was founded in Virginia, another English colony was established in America with an even stronger faith-based foundation. It was Plymouth Colony, established on the coast of modern Massachusetts by the people who would become known as the Pilgrims. The driving force of the one hundred–plus colonists who landed near Cape Cod in 1620 were thirty-five "Separatists"—so named because they had separated themselves from the Anglican Church of England, believing that every local church should be independent and self-governing. Early Separatist leaders had been executed in England, and sect members had suffered ridicule, threats, and persecution. After temporary self-exile in Holland, a group of Separatists put together a plan for a colony in the New World, obtained a charter, were joined by a larger group of non-Separatists, and set out across the Atlantic aboard the *Mayflower*—bound for the northern reaches of Virginia. [11]

They missed. Stormy weather drove them far to the north, and there—in what would become New England—they planted a faith-based colony in the wilderness. "Being thus arrived in a good harbor and brought safe to land," Pilgrim leader William Bradford would report, "they fell upon their knees & blessed the God of heaven, who had brought them over the vast & furious ocean. . . ." They also immediately drafted a founding document for governing their colony—the Mayflower Compact. As the Virginians had done with the House of Burgesses, the Pilgrims based their government on biblical precepts. The opening line of the Mayflower Compact—"In the name of God, Amen"—acknowledged the God of the Bible as the authority for law and culture in the Pilgrims' New World colony.[12]

The Compact stated the motivation that had driven the Plymouth colonists to risk all to establish a new life in a new land: "Having undertaken for the Glory of God, and Advancement of the Christian Faith, and the Honour of our King and Country, a Voyage to plant the first Colony in the northern Parts. . . ." Through this founding document, the Pilgrims pledged to "covenant and combine ourselves together into a civil Body Politick," and to establish and obey "just and equal laws . . . for the general Good of the Colony." It was a mighty precedent for the construction of American law and culture. While humbly acknowledging fidelity to king and country, the Mayflower Compact clearly recognized the biblical precept that all authority—even that of a king—was granted by the grace of God, and was subordinate to the "Higher Law" of Scripture.[13]

In 1630, shiploads of English Puritans followed the example set by their Pilgrim cousins and began arriving on the wooded shores of Massachusetts. The Puritans were so named because they wanted to purify the Church of England of what they deemed to be unbiblical doctrines and practices. By the early seventeenth century, England was officially Protestant, and so were most of its people. The Protestant Reformation had come to England during the reign of the mercurial King Henry VIII, who at first persecuted Protestants, then, when it suited his self-serving purposes, turned against the Catholics and established the Protestant Church of England—the Anglican Church.[14]

In 1517, a century before the Pilgrims' journey, Martin Luther, a Roman Catholic priest in Germany, had sparked the Protestant Reformation by calling for the Church to return to key biblical doctrines many Christians believed had been distorted or abandoned in the early Middle Ages. He reaffirmed salvation by faith in Jesus Christ alone rather than by faith and works, and upheld the authority of Scripture over church tradition and church leadership, including papal authority. Church officials in Rome excommunicated Luther, but the Reformation flooded Western Europe with a Bible-centered revival—and a political transformation. With its emphasis on the authority of Scripture as the Higher Law, the Reformation persuaded countless commoners that every person, whether a prince or a pauper, was of equal value to God. It also spread the belief that God's law, as revealed by Scripture, superseded man's law—including the authority of princes, queens, and kings.[15]

The Reformation and its emphasis on the authority of Higher Law was suppressed by three of the four leading world powers— Spain, Portugal, and France. In England, however, the Reformation and its biblical doctrines took root and flourished. The first published translation of the Bible in English gave the common people of England personal access to the Scriptures—and the country was transformed. "The whole moral effect . . . was simply amazing," English historian John Richard Green would later conclude. "The whole nation became a church."[16]

By the early 1600s, many people in England weighed everything according to a biblical worldview—including government. Already, they cherished individual rights and a representative form of government—the legacy of the canon law of Christianity and the English Constitution it had inspired. The English Reformation inspired the English people with an even greater commitment to Higher Law and the God-given rights of the individual. Most committed of all were the Puritans, who believed in "covenant theology." Scripture revealed that God had established covenants with his people through the ages, they believed, and government therefore should be a contract—a covenant— between the governing and the governed. Covenant theology held that even kings and queens were subject to God's Higher Law and were biblically obligated to recognize the God-given right to individual life and liberty.[17]

Covenant theology and the Puritan desire to "purify" the Church of England—the official government denomination— were not popular with English monarchs. Neither was the Puritan belief that all people were equal before God. King James I vowed to "harry them out of the land, or else do worse," and his son and successor, King Charles I, permitted Anglican officials to persecute them. Puritan preaching was restricted, their books and tracts were banned, and many Puritans were whipped, tortured, branded, or imprisoned. Facing increased persecution, scores of Puritans prayerfully chose to follow the Pilgrims to America. Between 1630 and 1640—in what became known as the Great Migration—more than twenty thousand Puritans immigrated to Massachusetts Bay Colony, bringing with them the seeds of Bible-based liberty.[18]

Although far from perfect, the Puritans' Massachusetts Bay Colony was based on biblical principles and became an influential model for other colonies. Many of the fundamental rights that would be championed by America's founding fathers, such as representative self-government, regular elections, and respect for private property, were inspired by the Puritans. The Judeo-Christian worldview became the foundation for American law and culture, as expressed, for example, in the 1643 Articles of Confederation of the United Colonies of New England: "Whereas we all came into these parts of America with one and the same end and aim, namely, to advance the Kingdom of our Lord Jesus Christ and to enjoy the liberties of the Gospel in purity with peace. . . ."[19]

At times, some Colonial Americans appeared to forget the persecution they and their ancestors had suffered in the Old World and repeated the same sins in the New World. But the New was not the Old, and religious intolerance would not last in the Bible-based culture of Colonial America—too many colonists were unwilling to stand for it. Instead, gradually, steadily, there arose an American tradition of religious tolerance, based on the Gospel of Jesus Christ. It was advanced by such people of faith as Roger Williams in Rhode Island, William Penn in Pennsylvania, Cecilius Calvert in Maryland, and countless unnamed American colonists who rejected religious persecution. Colonial Americans eventually established laws and government that reflected biblical values and principles while allowing full freedom of faith and conscience for all. The foundation of American liberty was the Judeo-Christian worldview, and a keystone in that foundation was religious freedom.[20]

Colonial America was overwhelmingly Protestant. Jewish communities were sprinkled throughout the Thirteen Colonies, and a minority Catholic community was clustered in Maryland, but Colonial America was marked by a multitude of Protestant denominations. The Church of England was the official state church in Colonial America, but by the dawn of the eighteenth century, Anglicans were clearly outnumbered by members of the so-called dissenter denominations—Congregationalists, Presbyterians, Baptists, Lutherans, Dutch Reformed, Quakers, and others. Colonial America was distinguished by a variety of denominations, some of which were at times competitive, but it was overwhelmingly united by the commonly-shared Judeo-Christian worldview. With its unique combination of Bible-based faith and freedom, America was a land like no other.[21]

By the early 1700s, however, some feared America's heritage of faith was growing dim. Biblical principles continued to shape American law and culture, but some feared America's foundational faith was fading, undermined by prosperity in the cities and a scarcity of clergy and churches on the frontier. "Church discipline was neglected, and the growing laxness of morals was invading the churches," reported a New England pastor. "The difference between the church and the world was vanishing. . . ."[22]

Then came an event that transformed Colonial America, re-stored its biblical foundation, united its people, and left the culture awash in faith on the eve of the Revolution. Known as the Great Awakening, it was an epic-sized revival of Christianity that swept floodlike through Colonial America. It began in full in the summer of 1743, with a solemn, unemotional sermon delivered by the Reverend Jonathan Edwards at a Congregationalist church in Enfield, Connecticut. A brilliant scholar and theologian who would later become president of Princeton University, Edwards preached a sobering call to salvation through Jesus Christ. A wave of conversions swept through the congregation, then through the region, all of New England, and eventually all of the Thirteen Colonies. It was further fueled by the preaching of English evangelist George Whitefield—the most famous preacher in the world at the time—whose Gospel message attracted crowds numbering in the thousands.[23]

As Colonial America approached the Revolution and nation-hood, the hearts and minds of the American people were rein-forced and molded by the biblical doctrines that were revived through the Great Awakening. Under its pervasive influence, they overwhelmingly rejected the humanistic worldview of Europe's Age of Reason—the Enlightenment deism, rationalism, and athe-ism that was becoming faddish among some at the time. The Judeo-Christian worldview remained America's consensus phi-losophy, and on that foundation America's founding fathers would establish a new nation that was forged in faith. The Bible thus re-mained the guidebook for life, law, and government, and the local church became a "school of democracy," teaching the biblical principle that life and liberty are intended as God's gift of grace to all. Americans did not believe that God existed for America, but that America should exist for God.[24]

A citizen's first responsibility, Colonial Americans generally believed, was to live righteously according to biblical standards of morality. A biblical faith was the foundation of responsible citizenship, they believed. "[He] who neglects his duty to his Maker," observed Abigail Adams, the wife of John Adams, "may well be expected to be deficient and insincere in his duty towards the public." A government's first responsibility, Americans also believed, was to govern righteously according to the Word of God, for it was from God, not man, that genuine liberty originated. "They looked up to Heaven as the source of their rights, and claimed [those rights] not from the promises of kings, but from the parent of the Universe," observed David Ramsay of South Carolina, who was a member and President pro tempore of the Continental Congress.[25]

Ramsay, who became a noted American historian, would later describe the political mind-set and motivation of the typical American at the time of the Revolution:

> *The political creed of an American colonist was short but substantial. He believed that God made all mankind originally equal: That he endowed them with the rights of life, property, and as much liberty as was consistent with the rights of others. That he had bestowed on his vast family of the human race, the earth for their support, and that all government was a political institution between men naturally equal, not for the aggrandizement of one, or a few, but for the general happiness of the whole community. Impressed with sentiments of this kind, they grew up, from their earliest infancy, with that confidence which is well calculated to inspire a love for liberty, and a prepossession in favor of independence.*

On the eve of the Revolution, Americans generally respected the preeminence of God's Higher Law, and expected those in authority to abide by it—even king and Parliament.[26]

CHAPTER TWO

"For Such a Time as This"

Nineteen-year-old George Washington was deathly ill. It was November of 1751, and Washington lay bedridden at a plantation outside Bridgetown on the island of Barbados. He had traveled from Virginia to the Caribbean with his older half brother Lawrence, who was attempting to cure a serious case of tuberculosis with a sojourn in a warm climate. The long cruise and mild winter in Barbados had done nothing for Lawrence Washington's health, and young George had contracted smallpox. It was the killer disease of his age—a scourge that took the life of twenty percent of its sufferers and left legions of survivors blind. For almost a month, he languished in bed, at one point near death, and appeared poised to disappear into history. Finally, the crisis passed. George Washington survived with nothing more than a few pockmarks and immunity to smallpox, which would protect him in the future as the disease felled his soldiers by the thousands. Washington's recovery was one of numerous narrow escapes—all of which he would attribute, in his words, to "the miraculous care of Providence."[1]

Washington, like other Americans of the eighteenth century, grew up in a culture founded and centered on the Judeo-Christian worldview. His great-great-grandfather was an Anglican minister—the Reverend Lawrence Washington—whose son John emigrated from England to America in 1656. John Washington settled in Westmoreland County, Virginia, on a peninsula between the Potomac and Rappahannock rivers. John's grandson Augustine, or "Gus" as Washington's father was known, was a moderately successful planter, land trader, and part owner of an iron furnace. He was a widower with three children when he married Mary Ball, who gave him six more—of whom Washington was the first. He was born in Westmoreland County, but as a small boy moved with his family to a modest plantation called Ferry Farm, which was located on the Rappahannock River opposite Fredericksburg, Virginia. Washington was living there at age eleven when his father unexpectedly died.[2]

After his father's death, Washington divided his childhood between time at home with his mother at Ferry Farm, and long periods with his half brother Lawrence in Westmoreland County. Lawrence lived on a sprawling, pastoral plantation, Mount Vernon, which overlooked the Potomac River near Alexandria, Virginia. His father's death ended plans for Washington to attend college in Great Britain like his older brothers. His education was limited to about seven years of tutoring and a brief stint under an Anglican minister at a small academy in Fredericksburg. Whatever educational limitation he experienced, however, was likely offset by his exposure to the privileged life of a gentleman planter at Mount Vernon. There, at an impressionable age, Washington was trained in "the courtly manners and customs of the best English culture."[3]

Nor, apparently, was his spiritual training neglected. He was raised in churchgoing households, studied the Anglican Book of Common Prayer, and, judging by his frequent references to Scripture, developed a genuine familiarity with the Book of Books. "Washington, from his youth to the close of life, was a conscientious observer of the 'Lord's Day,' " observed an early biographer, "and considered it a duty, when at all practicable, to attend divine service on that day." Given road conditions and travel distances in rural Virginia in his day, "when practicable" was seldom weekly on a consistent basis. His mother, however, habitually read to him from Biblically based books on character, and reportedly led him to memorize key passages from the Bible, including Mordecai's momentous question to Esther: "Who knoweth whether God hath not given thee this reputation and esteem for such a time as this?"[4]

Young Washington also absorbed a series of maxims promoting character. "Associate yourself with Men of good Quality if you Esteem your own Reputation," one such proverb advised, "for 'tis better to be alone than in bad company." The advice came from a book titled *Rules of Civility and Decent Behavior in Company and Conversation*, which the youthful Washington apparently studied conscientiously—he meticulously copied it. Authored by Catholic Jesuits, it offered Biblically based counsel on developing good character. "A man ought not to value himself [because] of his Achievement or rare Qualities, his Riches, Titles, Virtue or Kindred," the book advised. "Let your Conversation be without Malice or Envy," it counseled, "and in all causes of Passion admit Reason to Govern." Young Washington laboriously copied the admonitions, and sought to live by them—including one that became characteristic of his personality: "When you speak of God or His attributes, let it be seriously and [with] reverence."[5]

In adulthood, George Washington emerged as a man whose personal theology, character, and actions were securely founded on a biblical faith. He was a sincere, low-church Anglican of Virginia's plantation gentry. Unlike New England's seventeenth-century Puritans, or the Presbyterians and Baptists of his day, he was reserved in his verbal declarations of faith, although his writings were consistently laced with biblical allusions and expressions of the Judeo-Christian worldview. According to those closest to him, Washington believed that actions, not words, were the most meaningful expressions of faith. "For no man," he once wrote, "who is profligate in his morals, or a bad member of the civil community, can possibly be a true Christian. . . ." Observed his granddaughter Nelly Custis: "He was a silent, thoughtful man. . . . I never *witnessed* his private devotions. I never *inquired* about them. I should have thought it the greatest heresy to doubt his firm belief in Christianity. His life, his writings, prove that he was a Christian."[6]

As an adult, he became increasingly active in church affairs, took to carrying a small copy of the book of Psalms in his coat pocket, and routinely recorded what he perceived as the work of God in his life. His principal biographer, Douglas Southall Freeman, concluded that Washington's faith matured significantly with his years. "He indulged in no theological disquisition and he wrote no homilies," Freeman wrote, "but as he served the church, he developed new reverence for its Head, and as he lengthened his own journey of life, he had to conclude that a Guide directed his path." By the time of the Revolution, Freeman reported, "Washington was distinctly more religious . . . and he was more frequently mindful of Providence."[7]

As a youth, Washington yearned to join the British navy, and the influential Lawrence tried to help him embark on a naval career while a teenager. Washington's mother would not hear of it, depriving the British navy of a potential officer and sparing Washington for greater achievement. In 1748, when he was sixteen—tall, muscular, intelligent, and decisive—Washington joined a surveying team for a trek to Virginia's rugged western frontier. As they felled trees and cut through thickets to make their surveys, Washington and his companions encountered an Indian war party returning from a raid. Although they outnumbered the surveyors, the warriors allowed the surveying team to continue on unharmed. On the same expedition, Washington survived a freak accident: his straw bedding caught fire while he was asleep. Before his clothing could become enflamed, one of the other surveyors awakened and doused the blaze. The close calls were among the first in an extraordinary number of narrow escapes Washington experienced throughout his life—escapes that he attributed to divine intervention.[8]

He returned from his 1748 surveying adventure filled with zeal for the rigors and adventures of outdoor life. So motivated, he plunged into survey books and, little more than a year later, was appointed a county surveyor while still in his teens. The job put him in the wilds of western Virginia, where he learned the ways of life in the field and acquired skills that would serve him well as a future military commander. It was during this period of his life that he also survived smallpox in Barbados. While the visit to the Caribbean left Washington immune to the disease, the trip did nothing to cure Lawrence, who died shortly after the brothers returned to Virginia.[9]

Lawrence's death removed the second father figure from George's life, but it also left him as the eventual inheritor of Mount Vernon—the plantation on the Potomac that he loved so deeply. All of his life, Washington would aspire to the planter's life at Mount Vernon. Duty came first, however, and Washington would spend most of his life away from home, immersed in the highest levels of public service. In 1753, at age twenty-one, he was commissioned major and district adjutant of Virginia colonial troops by acting governor Robert Dinwiddie, filling a post that Lawrence had held. It placed him in a position of leadership, required him to teach himself military drill and tactics, and for the first time placed him in command of troops. More perilous events awaited him, and would train him for the future even as he repeatedly escaped their dangers.[10]

The first came in 1753. The French, old and bitter enemies of the British, were reportedly building military posts on the rim of the distant Ohio Country on lands claimed by Virginia. Washington was chosen by Virginia's governor to lead a small party of frontiersmen to a French post on the faraway Ohio River. There he would present an official ultimatum to the French commander, advising him to withdraw his troops from lands claimed by Virginia. Washington successfully made the long and hazardous wintertime trek through the wilderness, then learned that to find the ranking French officer he had to go farther north—almost to Lake Erie. That done, he returned with the French officer's reply, tramping through snow-covered forests, canoeing down icy rivers, and portaging around ice jams. He narrowly escaped death when a renegade Indian shot at him at close range, and barely escaped drowning and frostbite when he tumbled off a log raft into an ice-clogged river.[11]

A year later, the governor promoted the twenty-two-year-old Washington to lieutenant colonel in command of 150 Virginia volunteers, and sent him north again to reinforce a British frontier post on the Ohio River at modern-day Pittsburgh. As he led his troops through the rugged wilderness, he received word that the French had captured the British post and renamed it Fort Duquesne. Realizing his force was too small to recapture the post, Washington halted in the wilderness at a place called Great Meadows and established a small fortification that he named Fort Necessity. He planned to wait there until reinforcements arrived from Virginia, but he learned that a body of French troops was approaching through the forest. Assuming he was under attack, he led about forty men in a bold surprise assault on the French force, which turned out to be a thirty-five man reconnaissance party led by a French-Canadian officer named Joseph Coulon de Jumonville. In a fierce fifteen-minute battle, the French were defeated and Jumonville was killed.[12]

On July 3, 1754, a superior French force from Fort Duquesne attacked Washington's troops at Fort Necessity. After a ten-hour battle, with his troops low on rations, Washington accepted French surrender terms that allowed him and his men to return to Virginia. He did not realize that the French-language surrender terms he signed claimed that he had "assassinated" the commander of the French reconnaissance force—a "confession" that the French would use to justify the French and Indian War. Back home in Virginia, he was not blamed for the defeat at Fort Necessity, and the colony's legislature instead publicly praised him for "gallant and brave behaviour." The young officer had survived a battlefield loss that could have ended his military career—and he learned valuable lessons about command.[13]

A year later, the government in distant London decided to make a forceful stand against the French on the American frontier as the French and Indian War unfolded. General Edward Braddock and fourteen hundred British regulars were dispatched to march against the French stronghold of Fort Duquesne. Washington meanwhile—exhausted from his Fort Necessity expedition and frustrated by a reorganization of Virginia's military—had resigned his command and was trying to pursue the planter's life at Mount Vernon. After seriously pondering his options, however, Washington petitioned the commanding general for a command in the campaign. Aware of Washington's familiarity with the campaign's area of operations, Braddock made the young officer an aide on his command staff. With this, Washington was rescued from obscurity and given an important position in events already shaping the future of America.[14]

General Braddock was a sixty-year-old desk officer with little field experience. Washington reportedly advised him to adopt frontier tactics on the march. If so, Braddock disregarded the advice. The British army lumbered through the dark forests with little or no reconnaissance for most of its march. On July 9, 1755, after an exhausting day's march, Braddock's army neared Fort Duquesne—and was ambushed by a force of French and Indians who fought frontier-style from cover. Cornered in the open road, Braddock's army was slaughtered. More than nine hundred British troops were killed or wounded, making the battle of the Wilderness or Braddock's Defeat, as the engagement came to be called, the worst defeat the British had ever suffered in North America. Washington tried to restore order amid the carnage, but the British ranks melted in bloody chaos.[15]

General Braddock was mortally wounded, and when his panicky British troops refused to assist their fallen commander, it was Washington who had the general moved to the rear. When Braddock died, Washington took charge of the burial. To prevent the enemy from discovering the grave site, Washington had his commander buried on the Wilderness Road and then marched the retreating British troops over the site to obliterate all traces of the grave. That night, before leaving, Washington took over for the wounded British army chaplain and conducted a funeral service for Braddock by lamplight. It was also Washington who led the retreat out of the wilderness and back to safety.[16]

Once more, George Washington had survived a deadly encounter unhurt. Two-thirds of the expedition's officers had been killed or wounded, and Washington reported that he was the only officer in Braddock's presence who escaped the battle unharmed. Two horses, however, had been shot out from under him, and he later counted four holes where bullets had passed through his clothing. Nothing less than an act of God had spared his life, Washington believed. At age twenty-three, he had now survived a freak fire, smallpox, Indian ambushes, battle with the French, near drowning—and the worst British defeat in North America to date. Others might attempt to explain Washington's extraordinary survival as a combination of chance and circumstances. Not Washington. He was convinced then and for the rest of his life that he had been spared by God's sovereign grace. "I now exist and appear in the land of the living," he wrote his brother John, "by the miraculous care of Providence, that protected me beyond all human expectation. . . ."[17]

His military career had also survived potentially crippling blows—the surrender of his troops at Fort Necessity and his association with Braddock's disastrous defeat. Instead of viewing

Washington critically, however, his fellow Virginians proclaimed him a hero. So did Virginia's governor and the colony's legislature. At age twenty-three, he was promoted to colonel and given command of Virginia's seven-hundred-man colonial militia. With such a huge responsibility, Washington learned much that would serve him as a military leader in the future. Like Washington, others now openly attributed his survival and achievements to the providence of God. The Reverend Samuel Davies, a future president of Princeton University and Virginia's most prominent Presbyterian minister, made the point publicly. "As a remarkable instance of this," he said in a sermon to Virginia militia troops, "I may point out to the public that heroic youth, Colonel Washington, whom I cannot but hope Providence has hitherto preserved in so signal a manner for some important service to his country." [18]

Washington spent the next two years strengthening Virginia's militia and protecting the colony's frontier from Indian raids. He also signed on for another campaign against distant Fort Duquesne in 1758. This time the campaign was commanded by an experienced British officer and 6,500 British and American troops—including George Washington, who was promoted to brigadier general of colonial troops. As the expedition neared Fort Duquesne, the French abandoned the post, bringing a measure of relief to the Virginia frontier. His duty in the French and Indian War provided invaluable experience for Washington. Through trial and error he had learned the principles of successful command, how to persevere when victory proved elusive, and how to make do with inadequate ammunition, equipment, rations, and troops. He had seen firsthand the disastrous results that could strike an under-strength army, improperly trained troops, and an incautious commander. He had also taken the measure of the British officer corps and found its members at times arrogant and impetuous. Likewise, he had learned that the British army was not invincible. At the battle of the Wilderness, he confided to a contemporary, the British regulars "broke and ran as Sheep before the Hounds." He would not forget these lessons—he had repeatedly endured deadly conditions to learn them.[19]

In 1758, Washington concluded that his military duty was finally done and went home to marry Martha Dandridge Custis—whom Washington called "Patsy." She was an attractive twenty-seven-year-old widow, whose late husband, Daniel Parke Custis, had been a prominent Virginia planter and landowner. The wedding took place on January 6, 1759. Martha brought two small children—a son and a daughter—to her new marriage, and Washington accepted them as his own. He would later adopt his step-granddaughter, Eleonor Parke "Nelly" Curtis and her brother, George Washington Parke Curtis, but he and Martha would have no biological children. For the next decade and a half, George Washington lived his ideal profession. The gentleman planter of Mount Vernon grew wheat, oats, corn, tobacco, and other crops, conducted scientific crop and livestock experiments, and practiced crop rotation and soil conservation methods that were advanced for his time.[20]

He was also a slave owner. Like other Virginia planters, he owned scores of slaves, and for much of his life was untroubled by the fact. Over time, however, like some other prominent slave owners of his day—Benjamin Franklin and Thomas Jefferson, for instance—he developed misgivings about slavery. Eventually his attitude toward slavery shifted entirely, and he reportedly came to loathe the institution. Slavery was an unjust moral evil, he concluded, and his will granted freedom to his slaves when Martha died. One of his greatest desires, he would eventually declare, was "to see some plan adopted, by which slavery in this country may be abolished by slow, sure, and imperceptible degrees." Throughout his lifetime, he attempted to improve Mount Vernon, adding to its acreage, and waging the planter's ongoing struggle to keep the plantation profitable.[21]

His pleasures included the gentleman's pastimes of fox hunting, fishing, billiards, and ballroom dancing. He also served as an Anglican vestryman in his local parish. Although his reserved nature did not lend itself to dinnertime theological discussions, Washington served as a church lay leader, collected published sermons, privately fasted at times, and in his letters made frequent references to his lifelong belief that God repeatedy intervened in his life and in the life of the nation—what he called the "astonishing interpositions of providence." By his own admission, he believed that God had repeatedly spared him for a purpose, and that God also had a divine plan for America. Throughout his lifetime, Washington would continue to acknowledge his faith in the God of the Bible, and would consistently profess his dependence on the "blessings of His providence," during dark and deadly days. As he pursued the life of a Virginia planter with his new family in the early 1760s, those dark days were rapidly approaching.[22]

In 1763, the French and Indian War ended in a world-changing British victory. France was forced to cede Canada and all its territorial claims east of the Mississippi River to Great Britain, and Britain became the dominant power controlling North America. The war in America was an epic triumph for Great Britain, but it came at a great price: the British government was left deeply in debt. As Britain withdrew troops from the thirteen American colonies at war's end, a bold Ottawa leader named Pontiac unleashed a deadly Indian uprising—Pontiac's Rebellion—in the lightly protected Ohio Country. British military outposts on the faraway frontier were attacked, troops were massacred and American colonists on the frontier were endangered. The uprising was eventually suppressed, but London officials realized that huge numbers of British troops would be necessary to secure the American frontier. How could Britain's financially strapped government raise the funds necessary to protect the frontiers of its American colonies?[23]

King and Parliament agreed on a solution: new laws would be imposed on the Americans to raise revenue for the London government. First, to eliminate the Indian threat in the Ohio Country—and the cost of fielding more troops—Parliament enacted a law that closed America's western frontier to settlement. Known as the Proclamation of 1763, it prohibited Americans from moving west of the Appalachian Mountains, and settlers already living in the Ohio Country were ordered "forthwith to remove themselves." Under the new British policy, America's Indian tribes were to be left alone to fight one another for control of the frontier, instead of battling British troops, and colonists were advised to settle in Canada instead of Ohio. For the first time since 1607, America's westward expansion was officially halted. To most Americans, the Proclamation of 1763 was a misguided attempt by the British Parliament to restrict the growth and influence of the American colonies. It reinforced the suspicion held by many Americans that the London government valued the Thirteen Colonies chiefly for their natural resources and as a market for English goods.[24]

A year later, Parliament imposed the American Revenue Act, known as the "Sugar Act" in the colonies. It placed duties on sugar and molasses, outlawed the importation of foreign wines and rum, and placed taxes on a variety of manufactured foreign wares that were commonly imported into America from countries other than Great Britain. Within a year came the Quartering Act, which required cities and towns in the American colonies to garrison and supply British troops as needed. British officers could commandeer inns, taverns, or unoccupied buildings to quarter troops, and the Colonial legislatures were ordered to pay for supplies, rum, and beer issued to those troops. As a result, discontent swelled in the Thirteen Colonies. The most controversial new law of all, however, was the Stamp Act of 1765.[25]

It was the first direct tax on the American colonies, which had no voice in the issue because they were not represented in Parliament. The Stamp Act levied taxes on a wide range of paper-related products used in America—newspapers, licenses, pamphlets, playing cards, almanacs, even college diplomas. Stamp Act officials were appointed to oversee taxation, and violators were threatened with prosecution. Such taxation without representation in Parliament was an attack on American freedom, many colonists believed. Many also suspected that the Stamp Act was merely the first in a series of direct taxes on Americans that would be imposed by the Mother Country without American representation in Parliament. The new laws, especially the Stamp Act, drove a giant wedge into what was already a widening fissure between Britain and the American colonies.[26]

The colonists were generally loyal to the Mother Country and its king, even though the vast majority had not been born in England and were decidedly more American than English. For generations, the Thirteen Colonies had been largely ignored by the British government; "happy neglect," one historian would call it. Americans had come to view the colonies as almost autonomous—part of the British Empire, but quasi-independent, based on the royal charters granted by the king when most of the colonies were founded. If the colonies occasionally were needed to contribute to the national treasury, such aid had been requested by the king, not Parliament, and His Majesty had done so through the colonial legislatures where Americans did have political representation. In the 1760s, however, "happy neglect" was replaced by a succession of new taxes and legal restrictions—even though Americans had no voice in Parliament. Pennsylvania publisher Benjamin Franklin spoke for many when he declared that Parliament "had really no right at all to tax them" and was guilty of "compulsion over persuasion."[27]

The Stamp Act outraged most Americans. From Massachusetts to Georgia, the cry of "No taxation without representation!"
swept through the colonies. Protests were staged. Riots broke
out. Government offices were ransacked. Stamp Act officials
were heckled and harassed—some of them tarred and feathered
by unruly mobs. A few Americans turned to violence, but many
more turned to their pastors. On the eve of the Revolution, the
most influential profession in Colonial America was the clergy.
"The corporate and collective action of the American clergy was
a mighty force in politics," British historian George Otto Trevelyan would observe, "but the influence of the individual minister must be accounted as more important still. That influence . . .
extended over every department of daily life." In time of crisis,
Americans flocked to their churches to receive biblical direction
from the pulpit. They read sermons in the newspapers, passed
around printed versions of them, and discussed the sermon topics
in the workplace, marketplace, and fields. While some pastors
counseled unquestioning submission to London—particularly
those pastors in the Church of England—many more denounced
taxation without representation as a violation of God-given or
"inalienable" rights.[28]

Throughout Colonial America, countless pastors advised
their congregations that they had a biblical duty to resist the
Stamp Act as governmental tyranny. The most influential sermon
of the day came from Congregationalist minister Jonathan
Mayhew of Boston, whose discourse was printed and distributed
throughout America. "All commands running counter to the declared will of the Supreme Legislator of heaven and earth are
null and void, and therefore disobedience to them is a duty, not
a crime," Mayhew told his congregation. They congregation had
"learned from the Holy Scriptures," he said, that "the Son of God
came down from heaven to make us free indeed, and . . . 'where
the Spirit of the Lord is, there is liberty.' " His Bible-based view
was generally shared by Americans—and their political leaders.[29]

Taxation without representation was an assault on liberty, most Americans believed. It was an attempt by Parliament and king to usurp authority that belonged only to God and thus violated Higher Law. The same belief underscored the action taken by Virginia's House of Burgesses in May of 1765, when it became the first colonial legislature to officially oppose the Stamp Act. The Virginia Resolves, as the legislature's action would become known, declared that taxation without representation violated "the liberties, privileges, franchises, and immunities" granted by Virginia's covenant-style royal charter. The author of the Virginia Resolves was twenty-eight-year-old Patrick Henry, a backcountry freshman legislator who was influenced by the teaching of Presbyterian minister Samuel Davies. If the Stamp Act were not resisted, Henry argued, it would eventually "destroy British as well as American Freedom."[30]

Other colonies' legislatures followed Virginia's example and denounced the Stamp Act. The Massachusetts legislature responded to the crisis by inviting legislative delegations from the Thirteen Colonies to hold a Stamp Act Congress. Nine colonies accepted the invitation and sent delegates to an assembly in New York City in October of 1765. The Stamp Act Congress adopted a resolution called the Declaration of Rights and Grievances, which declared that Parliament had no right to tax the colonies without granting Colonial representation. A clergyman's congress was also organized by Presbyterian and Congregationalist ministers to develop a strategy for church members to defend religious and political freedom in America. Parliament paid no attention to either, but a precedent had been established: Americans had convened a congress.[31]

They also organized a boycott of English goods. Stung by America's fierce political resistance and besieged by British merchants affected by the boycott, Parliament and King George III relented and repealed the infamous Stamp Act in 1766. Colonial America was swept by celebration—but only briefly; even as it re-

pealed the Stamp Act, Parliament passed what was called the De-
claratory Act, which bluntly asserted that Parliament reserved the
right to place any laws it so desired on Colonial America "in all
cases whatsoever." Within a year, Parliament enacted a series of
new taxation laws called the Townshend Acts, which placed taxes
on paper, lead, glass, and tea. Again America's preachers took the
lead in denouncing the new laws; Americans organized another
boycott; and Colonial legislatures protested taxation without representation. Again the British Parliament relented under pressure
and rescinded the tax—on everything but tea. "I will never think
of repealing it," vowed British prime minister Frederick, Lord
North, "until I see America prostrate at my feet."[32]

As tensions between the colonists and the royal government
grew, Boston emerged as the flashpoint of the conflict. There
in March of 1770, British troops opened fire on an unruly mob,
killing five people and unifying Americans in outrage over what
became known as the "Boston Massacre." Relations between the
colonies and the Mother Country continued to deteriorate. In
1773, Parliament increased colonial resentment by enacting the
Tea Act, which was designed to assist the politically connected
East India Tea Company by establishing a monopoly that would
put American competitors out of business. In December of that
year, protestors outfitted in mock Indian costumes marched to
the Boston docks and dumped ninety thousand pounds of English tea into Boston Harbor. The "Boston Tea Party"—as the
protest became known—infuriated King George III, who called
on Parliament to punish Massachusetts.[33]

Parliament did so—enacting a series of laws that became
known in colonial parlance as the "Intolerable Acts." The acts
closed the port of Boston to commercial shipping. They also outlawed town meetings, prohibited Colonial courts from trying
British officials, gave British army officers authority to seize any
unoccupied structures they desired for quartering troops, and ordered future members of the Massachusetts legislature to be ap-

pointed by the king. To back up its punishment, London sent British troops to Boston and replaced Massachusetts's civilian governor with a military ruler, General Thomas Gage. "The die is now cast," George III vowed; "the colonies must either submit or triumph."[34]

The colonists of Massachusetts were not intimidated, and neither were the rest of the American people. At a Boston town meeting in May of 1774, the people of Massachusetts went on record denouncing the Intolerable Acts as "injustice, inhumanity and cruelty" that endangered all of "North America and her liberties"—and they issued a dramatic public "appeal to God and the world" that was circulated throughout the Thirteen Colonies. The plight of Massachusetts unifed the American people in protest—a protest fueled from the pulpit by America's preachers. Amid the crisis, Americans came to believe that Parliament—and King George III—were tyrannically attempting to subvert God-given, inalienable rights. "This liberty hath God not only given, but entailed on all men," pronounced Massachusetts pastor Nathaniel Whitaker in a typical sermon, "so . . . should any state, through fear, resign this freedom to any other power, it would be offensive to God."[35]

In Virginia, the House of Burgesses—which had been the first American legislature to denounce the Stamp Act—again took the lead, in opposition to the Intolerable Acts. The Virginia legislators officially declared that the day on which the port of Boston would be forcibly closed—June 1, 1774—should be observed throughout Virginia as a day of "fasting, humiliation and prayer." Crafted by a gifted young wordsmith named Thomas Jefferson, the resolution urged Virginia's colonists to "implore the Divine Interposition for averting the heavy Calamity, which threatens Destruction to our civil Rights, and the Evils of civil War; to give us one Heart and one Mind firmly to oppose, by all just and proper Means, every Injury to American Rights. . . ." Virginia's royal governor responded by ordering the legislators to disband and go home. Instead they passed another resolution, this one calling for the creation of a continental congress that would represent "the united interests of America."[36]

Twelve of the Thirteen Colonies agreed to send delegates—Georgia was preoccupied with an Indian uprising—and a time and a place were set for the convening of the First Continental Congress: Philadelphia in September. Creation of the Continental Congress, which would prove critical to the birth of the American nation, were triggered by an act of faith—the vote by the Virginia House of Burgesses to declare a day of prayer and fasting. Despite the objections of the colony's royal governor, the legislators publicized their prayer and fasting resolution in the colony's newspapers so that the people of Virginia could participate. On June 1, 1774, countless did, dropping all other duties to attend church and engage in "fasting, humiliation and prayer." Among them was George Washington, who penned in his diary: "Went to church and fasted all day."[37]

CHAPTER THREE

"A Kind of Destiny"

George Washington arrived at church in a "grave mood," a fact that might have gone unnoticed in his home congregation, but he was not at home. This Sunday morning—May 29, 1774—he was in Williamsburg, where he had been serving in the House of Burgesses. Washington had been one of the House members who passed the resolution declaring a day of prayer and fasting for the beleaguered colonists in Massachusetts, and was part of the assembly that called for creation of a continental congress. When the assembly ended, he had remained in Williamsburg on business over the weekend. Throughout his life, it was Washington's practice to attend church while traveling, and he did so this Sunday, worshipping at the imposing Bruton Parish Anglican church—which routinely set aside pews for visiting members of the legislature.[1]

Washington attended two worship services that Lord's Day, the regular Sunday morning service and an afternoon prayer meeting. He had sound reasons for his somber mood: the long-gathering "dark clouds" of conflict between the Mother Country and America were rapidly worsening—and he had the training to recognize it. In addition to serving in the Virginia legislature, the forty-two-year-old Washington had served as a local judge in Alexandria for more than a decade. That and his military experience gave him keen insight into unfolding events. He disapproved of the destructive nature of the Tea Party protest, but he fully supported Massachusetts's resistance to London's assault on American liberty—and he was gratified by the creation of a continental congress. What did he pray at Bruton Church that famous fast day? No one knows, but the peril facing Colonial America had to be on his mind.[2]

On Wednesday, June 1, 1774, Washington and other members of the House of Burgesses lined up in a procession behind the legislature's mace, and marched under a cloudless summer sky back to Bruton Parish Church. There they officially observed the day of prayer and fasting they had recommended to their fellow Virginians. They listened dutifully to a sermon by the chaplain of the House of Burgesses, the Reverend Thomas Price. The chaplain preached from a text in the Old Testament book of Genesis, noting how God had judged the sin of Sodom, and reminded his congregation of the question Abraham asked God: "Wilt Thou also destroy the righteous with the wicked?" He emphasized the Lord's answer—"I will not destroy it for ten's sake"—in an obvious call for Americans to live in obedience to the Bible. Throughout the colony, Virginians observed the fast day in solidarity with the colony of Massachusetts, praying, fasting, and attending church assemblies. At one worship service, the traditional closing—"God save the king!"—was replaced with a new prayer: "God preserve all the just rights and liberties of America!"[3]

A month later, in his home congregation at Pohick Church, on Sunday, July 3, Washington discussed the escalating crisis with his fellow church members. King and Parliament were determined to make the American colonies submit to government authority, he believed, even in violation of taxation without representation. Should the British "push matters to extremity,"

Washington grimly predicted, "more blood will be spilt . . . than history has ever yet furnished instances of in the annals of North America." A grave threat now loomed over America. Yet, recalling the biblical account of God's judgment on the Egyptian Pharaoh of the Exodus, Washington professed to believe that "the finger of Providence is in it, to blind the eyes of our enemies. . . ." To stand in defense of American liberty was a moral obligation, he believed. "Ought we not, then," he asked a friend, "put our virtue and fortitude to the severest test?"[4]

On August 31, 1774—a sweltering summer day—George Washington mounted his horse at Mount Vernon and took to the road. He was accompanied by two other riders, Patrick Henry and Edmund Pendleton, who were fellow members of the seven-man delegation selected to represent the Colony of Virginia at the First Continental Congress. Ahead lay a five-day journey on dusty lanes through Virginia, Maryland, and Pennsylvania, ending in Philadelphia. Henry and Pendleton, lawyer-legislators in the House of Burgesses, had joined Washington at Mount Vernon the night before departing. They had dined at Washington's table, talked politics, spent the night, and then left together for the Continental Congress. "I hope you will all stand firm," Washington's wife, Martha, reportedly urged Henry and Pendleton. "I know George will."[5]

Washington and his colleagues arrived in Philadelphia on September 4, 1774. The First Continental Congress, composed of delegates from twelve colonies, convened at Carpenters' Hall the next day. On the second day of deliberations, when Congressional unity appeared strained by disagreements, the delegates voted to open future sessions with prayer, beginning the next day. Chosen for the task was a prominent Anglican clergyman, the Reverend Jacob Duché of Philadelphia's Christ Church. He opened deliberations with prayer and the passage of Scripture scheduled for that day in the Anglican prayer book. It was Psalm 35: "Plead my cause, O LORD, with them that strive with me: fight against them that fight against me. . . . Let them be confounded and put to shame that seek after my soul; let them be turned back and brought to confusion that devise my hurt."[6]

The psalm, which had been printed in the prayer book long before, was obviously appropriate for the tense crisis facing America—and so was Pastor Duché's prayer:

> *O! Lord, our heavenly father, King of Kings and Lord of lords: who dost from thy throne behold all the dwellers upon earth and reignest with power supreme & uncontrouled over all kingdoms, empires and governments, look down in mercy, we beseech thee, upon these our American states who have fled to thee from the rod of the oppressor and thrown themselves upon thy gracious protection, desiring henceforth to be dependent only on thee. . . .*[7]

The Congressional devotional "filled every Bosom present," according to Massachusetts delegate John Adams. Pastor Duché became America's first Congressional chaplain and the delegates went back to work reunified. The First Continental Congress met for less than two months, but took several important actions to defend the American people's inalienable rights to "life, liberty and property." Before adjourning on October 26, the delegates voted to reconvene the Congress in Philadelphia in May of 1775 if further Congressional action were necessary.[8]

It would be: In early 1775, Parliament rejected a Congressional attempt at reconciliation and declared Massachusetts to be in a state of rebellion. On April 19, British troops sent from Boston to destroy a stockpile of militia munitions confronted a band of militiamen on the village green at Lexington. Someone fired a shot, and the British opened fire, killing eight Americans and wounding ten. The British moved on to Concord and engaged the militia again—this time suffering three dead and nine wounded in their own ranks. They located and set fire to a store of militia ammunition, but on their return march to Boston they were repeatedly attacked by the Massachusetts militia, whose numbers swelled as word of the fighting spread through the countryside. Fighting Indian-style from the cover of wooded ridges along the road, they inflicted severe casualties on the Redcoats, who limped back to Boston. The opening fire at Lexington—made famous as "the shot heard 'round the world"—ignited the American War for Independence.[9]

When the Second Continental Congress convened a month later, the sentiment for American independence was noticeably stronger among its delegates, and so was Congressional unity. "There never appeared more perfect unanimity among any set of men than among the Delegates," Virginia delegate Richard Henry Lee would later recall; "indeed . . . all are directed by the same firmness of union and determination to resist by all ways and to every extremity." Few delegates were more determined to resist than returning delegate George Washington. In a private letter to his brother John Augustine Washington, he had clearly stated his commitment to American independence, stating that "it is my full intention to devote my Life and Fortune to the cause we are engaged in, if need be." At the Second Congress, he began wearing his red and blue colonel's uniform from the French and Indian War—which was a reminder of his opposition to British aggression, as well as his experience as a military commander. To the delegates, it was also a reminder that in military affairs, George Washington was almost certainly the most knowledgeable man in Congress.[10]

On June 15, 1775, the Continental Congress appointed Washington general and commander-in-chief of "all the continental forces raised or to be raised for the defence of American liberty." Although still officially attempting reconciliation with the king and Parliament, the delegates understood that war was already under way, and believed an intercolonial force—a continental army—must be organized and placed under an experienced, competent commander. In Boston, thousands of militia troops now surrounded the city and besieged the British garrison posted there. More bloodshed was expected any day. Some contended that the militia troops at Boston should have a New England commander, but John and Samuel Adams of Massachusetts believed a Southern-born commander would signal unity—and that Washington was the best choice. The other delegates agreed, and the vote for Washington as commander-in-chief was unanimous.[11]

"I do not think myself equal to the command," Washington told Congress—but he accepted the post and volunteered to serve without pay. It was George Washington's reputation for competence and character as much as his unsurpassed field experience that compelled his selection by Congress. "I can now inform you that the Congress have made a Choice of the modest and virtuous, the amiable, generous and brave George Washington Esqr., to be the General of the American Army," John Adams wrote his wife. "He is a modest man," agreed fellow Virginian Roger Atkinson, "but sensible & speaks little—in action cool, like a Bishop at his prayers." Said Connecticut delegate Silas Deane: "the more I am acquainted with [him], the more I esteem him."[12]

"You may believe me, my dear Patsy," Washington privately wrote his wife, ". . . as it has been a kind of destiny, that has thrown me upon this service, I shall hope that my undertaking of it is designed to answer some good purpose. . . ." What was on his mind as he wrote those lines? Did he recall the surveying expeditions that had trained and toughened him in the Virginia backcountry? His dangerous duties on the Virginia frontier? The sight of General Braddock's bloodied body lowered into a makeshift grave? The seasoning experience he had gained as a judge and legislator? His many narrow escapes and the Bible stories his mother had read him in preparation for such a time as this? "I shall rely, therefore," he wrote, "confidently, on that Providence which has heretofore preserved, and been bountiful to me. . . ."[13]

·············◦◦◦◦◦ ◦·◦· ◦ ◦◦◦◦◦◦·············

Thirty-five hundred miles across the Atlantic, in Great Britain, meanwhile, George Washington's chief adversary went about his royal duties, committed to the destruction of America's rising revolution. King George III would prove to be a determined foe—he was accustomed to getting his way and usually did. He was the official head of the Church of England and appears to have taken that role more seriously than did his two predecessors, but his view of higher law contrasted sharply with Washington and most Americans. George III's personal theology was insepa-rably linked to the "divine right of kings." It was a common belief among the monarchy of Europe, and King George's predecessors had fiercely defended it. Scripture advised "every soul to be sub-ject to the higher powers," and to adherents of the divine right of kings—including George III—that meant accepting the ways and whims of the monarchy as God's will.[14]

George William Frederick—King George III—was a member of the House of Hanover. Like his two successors, George I and II, he was descended from a family of German no-blemen who came to rule England through a peculiar series of events. In 1714, Great Britain's Queen Anne died after a twelve-year reign. She had been repeatedly pregnant, had suffered nu-merous miscarriages and stillbirths, and the children who had survived birth had all died before any could assume the throne. At her death, Queen Anne still had no heir. According to the 1701 Act of Settlement, which was enacted by the English Parliament to ensure a Protestant monarch, the British throne passed to George I—a nobleman from the German state of Hanover, who was a descendant of King James I.[15]

King George I—the great-grandfather of George III—

arrived in Britain with two mistresses; his wife Sophia was imprisoned for adultery at the time. He spoke little English, conducted royal business in French, and spent so much time in Germany that the post of British prime minister had to be created to run the nation. He happily left affairs of state to the first holder of that post, the politically astute Robert Walpole, who ran the country in the king's absence. The monarch suffered a fatal stroke in 1727, following a binge of overeating en route to Germany, and his son ascended to the throne as King George II. Although he had a thick German accent, the second King George did speak English, but he too left much of the royal decision making to Walpole. Personally courageous, he was the last British ruler to lead troops in battle, and Great Britain increased its reach as a world power during his reign.[16]

George II also seemed to prefer Germany to Britain, however, and in a fit of anger over things English, he once exclaimed, "Devil take the whole island." British satirist William Thackeray once described him as "that godless old King yawning under his canopy [in a worship service] as the chaplain before him is discoursing . . . about righteousness and judgment. Whilst the chaplain is preaching, the King is chattering in German almost as loud as the preacher; so loud that the clergyman . . . actually burst out crying in his pulpit. . . ." Like the first George, he was indifferent to Christianity, and reportedly allowed Prime Minister Walpole (who was said to spend his own Sundays "boozing . . . over beef and punch") to take steps to discourage revival in England. He detested his oldest son, Prince Frederick, who was the father of George III, and was relieved when Frederick died from respiratory failure after being injured by an errant cricket ball. "I have lost my eldest son," George II declared, "but I was glad of it." Although he had given his grandson little attention over the years, he was pleased that the boy, and not his father, had become next in line for the throne.[17]

In the absence of his father, who died when George III was

twelve, the future British king of the American Revolution was raised by his mother. Princess Augusta was the daughter of German nobility, and she trained young George to rule with authority. A forceful, shrewd woman who was detested in court circles for her ambitious scheming, she was both overindulgent and domineering, and exercised rigid control over her son. His grandfather the king ordered him enrolled in a disciplined regimen of study in preparation for rule, but his mother allowed him to spend days loitering in bed, and raised him to adopt an attitude of self-importance. As an adolescent, he was shy, introverted, friendless, and given to bouts of pouting. His tutors praised him for high morals, but also noted that his "kind heart" could change quickly to display sullen, obstinate anger. "He has great command of his Passions and will seldom do wrong," one member of the court noted, "except when he mistakes wrong for right. . . . "[18]

Under the German Georges before him, political power had shifted significantly from king to Parliament, and George's mother was determined to see it shift back to her son and his court, once he was crowned. "George, be king!" she reminded him repeatedly. Under her influence, the future king was raised in a court household marked by constant suspicion, gossip, and intrigue. "She kept her household lonely and in gloom, mistrusting almost all people who came about her child," a British biographer observed. "His mother's bigotry and hatred he inherited with the courageous obstinacy of his own [Germanic] race." He remained zealously obedient to his mother—even in affairs of the heart. When he fell in love with his cousin, a fifteen-year-old court beauty named Sarah Lennox, his mother stated her disapproval and thus quashed the potential romance.[19]

On October 25, 1760, after consuming his customary morning cup of hot chocolate, young George's grandfather—King George II—collapsed and died in the royal bathroom. George III inherited the throne at age twenty-two. One of his first acts was to marry. A king needed a queen, his mother believed, and so she arranged a marriage to a seventeen-year-old German nobleman's daughter—Princess Charlotte of Mecklenburg-Strelitz. Summoned from Germany, the teenage princess battled seasickness on a stormy voyage across the North Sea by pounding a harpsichord and singing aloud. She was a "homely little bride," according to one observer, and young George III reportedly "shrank from her gaze" at their first meeting. Princess Charlotte, however, was endowed with a diplomat's savvy, keen intelligence, and an extraordinary ability to bear children. The couple's long marriage would produce fifteen children, including future kings George IV and William IV.[20]

On September 22, 1761, in a lavish official coronation ceremony at London's Westminster Abbey, the Anglican archbishop of Canterbury formally placed a bejeweled crown on the king's head amid a flourishing of trumpets and cheers of "God save the king." Despite his childhood indolence, he proved to be an energetic ruler, arose early each day, and was attentive to royal duties. In his prime, he was tall, slender, and ruddy-faced—handsome, many said—and almost always appeared well groomed in public. He traveled little, perhaps due to his childhood seclusion, and probably saw less of the world than any British monarch of his century. He enjoyed horse racing and hunting, loved the theater, enthusiastically supported the arts, and was so obsessed with anything related to agriculture that he became famous in Britain as "Farmer George."[21]

By the time George Washington was appointed commander-in-chief of the Continental Army, King George III had ruled fifteen years. Over time, public admiration for him in the Mother Country was diminished by reports of his less attractive traits and peculiar behavior. He was "not cheered in the streets," a British historian would tactfully write; in fact, his public appearances were sometimes greeted with jeers and catcalls. Although he usually conducted himself with dignity in public, the king could be surprisingly coarse and undignified in private. Supporters called him "high-principled" but others described him as arrogant, rude, and spiteful. Any disagreement—no matter how diplomatically explained—might provoke the royal ire. "Those who were not for him, were against him," said a key advisor.[22]

Some described him as a "born schemer" who was constantly involved in duplicity of some type. "He bribed, he bullied [and] he exercised . . . a vindictive resolution," observed a critic. Throughout his reign, George III's primary focus never shifted: he was determined to build royal power, not yield it. He came to detest England's majority political party, the Whigs, whom he blamed for the shift in authority from the Crown to Parliament. He aligned himself with the opposing Tory party, and waged continuous political warfare against the Whigs, fueling decades of political strife that wearied politicians and the public alike. He was a confrontational leader rather than a consensus builder, opponents charged. Others said he was simply a poor ruler.[23]

His decision making was also likely affected by a rare behavioral disorder, diagnosed by modern medical professionals as a form of the neurological disease *acute porphyria*. Symptoms of the illness include abdominal disorders, muscle pain, hallucination, and disorientation. Twentieth-century tests on strands of the king's hair would also reveal traces of a form of arsenic that was used to powder wigs in George's day, which may have worsened the effects of his disease. Behind closed doors at Windsor Palace, according to court gossip, the king sometimes paced relentlessly back and forth, talking incessantly. At other times he would remain seated while he rocked from side to side in an agitated manner, rattling on in a monologue and compulsively ending each sentence by repeating, "What? What?" Decades later, in his old age, sequestered in the care of his queen, he would reportedly roam the palace halls "addressing imaginary parliaments, reviewing fancied troops, holding ghostly Courts."[24]

Molded by his self-directed upbringing, motivated by his belief in the divine right of kings, and affected at times by his illness, King George III was determined to prevail in what became a contest of wills with his American subjects. "I do therefore here in the presence of Our Almighty Lord promise that I will remember the insults, and will never forgive . . . ," the king once vowed aloud in response to criticism. It was *he* and no other, he believed, who ruled the British Empire by the will of God. "I must look upon all who would not heartily assist me as bad men, as well as bad subjects," he proclaimed. "I wish nothing but good, therefore every man who does not agree with me is a traitor and a scoundrel." Far away in the Thirteen Colonies, meanwhile, increasing numbers of American "traitors" had decided that defense of God-given inalienable rights took precedence over allegiance to the king.[25]

Ultimately, that was the theme of the Declaration of Independence: King George III had usurped the authority of Higher Law to suppress the inalienable rights of "life, liberty and the pursuit of happiness." In 1775, the Congress unsuccessfully attempted reconciliation with the king, then passed a prelude to the Declaration of Independence—the Declaration of the Causes and Necessities of Taking of Arms. God had prepared the American people for such a time as this, it declared: ". . . Providence would not permit us to be called into this severe controversy, until we were grown up to our present strength . . . and possessed of the means of defending ourselves." It was upon God, it proclaimed, that the American people and their leaders now depended:

> *With an humble confidence in the mercies of the supreme and impartial Judge and Ruler of the Universe, we most devoutly implore his divine goodness to protect us happily through this great conflict, to dispose our adversaries to reconciliation on reasonable terms, and thereby to relieve the empire from the calamities of civil war.*[26]

Likewise, when the Declaration of Independence was adopted by the Continental Congress a year later, on July 4, 1776, it too clearly reflected Colonial America's foundational belief in the Higher Law of Scripture. Drafted by Thomas Jefferson, edited by a Congressional committee that included John Adams and Benjamin Franklin, and amended by the full Continental Congress, it was intended to unify the American people, who would have to live by it and, in many cases, die for it. Therefore, it intentionally reflected the Judeo-Christian worldview on which American culture, law, and government were founded—the consensus belief system held by Colonial Americans.[27]

"I did not consider it as any part of my charge to invent new ideas altogether . . . ," Jefferson would later note. "The general principles on which the fathers achieved independence, were the only principles in which that beautiful assembly of could unite," according to John Adams. "And what were these general principles?" he would later explain. "I answer, the general principles of Christianity . . . and the general principles of English and American liberty. . . ." Thus the Declaration of Independence was laced with the language of Bible-based faith, and reflected—in the words of the twentieth-century Jewish historian Abraham Katsh—"a profound sympathy with the Scriptures."[28]

"When in the Course of human events," stated the Declaration's preamble, "it becomes necessary for one people to dissolve the political bands which have connected them with another, and to assume among the powers of the earth, the separate and equal station to which the Laws of Nature and of Nature's God entitle them, a decent respect to the opinions of mankind requires that they should declare the causes which impel them to the separation." In referring to "the Laws of Nature and of Nature's God," the Declaration reflected the tradition of English law and its foundation on the Higher Law of the Bible. It thus acknowledged the authority of God over mankind, that the rights of man were derived from God, and imprinted by him on the human heart as "Natural Law"—the revelation of God as seen in the natural order of his creation.[29]

The faith-based references in the Declaration reassured the people of Colonial America that they were defending God-given or "unalienable" rights. "We hold these truths to be self-evident," proclaimed the Declaration, "that all men are created equal, that they are endowed by their Creator with certain unalienable Rights, that among these are Life, Liberty and the pursuit of Happiness." *This* was the "sacred Cause of freedom"—which the founders and the American people believed was reflected in Natural Law, revealed and confirmed by the Bible, followed by the canon law of the early Church, promoted by the Reformation, transmitted by America's forefathers to a New World and now proclaimed as the foundation of a new nation.[30]

To morally justify its action—that of declaring American independence—the Continental Congress officially appealed to "the Supreme Judge of the World for the rectitude of our intentions," thus declaring itself right before God. Since the Stamp Act crisis, American pulpits had condemned the British government for suppressing inalienable rights and usurping the authority of God, and had proclaimed resistance to tyranny as a Bible-based duty. The Declaration of Independence put forth the same argument, asserting that "when a long train of abuses and usurpations, pursuing invariably the same Object, evinces a design to reduce them under absolute Despotism, it is their right, it is their duty, to throw off such Government, and to provide new Guards for their future Security."[31]

Finally, the Declaration of Independence ended just as it began—with recognition of the existence and authority of Almighty God: "And for the support of this Declaration, with a firm reliance on the protection of divine Providence, we mutually pledge to each other, our Lives, our Fortunes and our sacred Honour." When the Declaration of Independence was adopted, one who was *not* present was Commander-in-Chief George

Washington, who had long before left to assume his command in the field. No one's life, fortune, or sacred honor was more at stake than his, however; and few leaders would more openly and often declare a "firm reliance on the protection of divine Providence" than Washington.[32]

CHAPTER FOUR

"The Lord Fighteth for Them"

The letter was sent to an old colleague who had become a new enemy. It was written by George Washington, and the recipient was General Thomas Gage—the commander of all British troops in North America. Washington and Gage had once served together during the French and Indian War. Now, in the summer of 1775, the two faced each other as enemies. Washington wrote Gage from Boston, where he had traveled from Philadelphia with a small group of staff officers promptly after receiving his new command from the Continental Congress. He had hurried to Boston to take command of the New England militia, which would become the nucleus of the Continental Army, and which was in a tense standoff with Boston's British garrison.[1]

By the time he reached Boston, the standoff had erupted in warfare—the battle of Bunker Hill. On June 17, 1775, the British army had assaulted Patriot positions on high ground overlooking Boston—on Breed's Hill, actually, although the battle would be named for nearby Bunker Hill. To the surprise of British commanders, the Americans had proven far tougher opponents than they had expected. It had required three British assaults and the loss of more than a thousand men to defeat the Americans, and, despite their loss, American forces still surrounded Boston. In the wake of the battle, Washington received reports that the British army had jailed captured American troops, treating them as rebels and criminals rather than as prisoners of war.[2]

Washington addressed the issue by letter with his former friend and new enemy, General Gage. If captured American officers had to endure such mistreatment, Washington warned Gage, so would captured British officers. "If Severity and Hardship mark the Line of your Conduct," he wrote, "(painful as it may be to me) your Prisoners will feel its Effects." In reply, Gage accused Washington of disloyalty to king and country, and vowed that any American who jailed a British officer would suffer "dreadful consequences"—with no mercy except from God.[3]

Gage's threatening letter—particularly his reference to God—provoked a telling response from Washington. He dispatched a terse reply standing by his earlier warning, and pointedly addressing Gage's reference to the Almighty. It was American liberty—not royal abuse of authority—that Washington believed rested on God's truth. "May that God," wrote Washington, "judge between America, and you. Under his Providence, those who influence the Councils of America, and all the other Inhabitants of the united Colonies at the Hazard of their Lives are determined to hand down to Posterity those just and invaluable Privileges, which they received from their Ancestors."[4]

Washington's letter was a significant reflection of his command style—and the quiet, underlying faith he demonstrated throughout the war. He turned to his thirty-four-year-old military secretary, Colonel Joseph Reed, to help draft the letter. Reed was a committed churchman who attended Philadelphia's Pine Street Presbyterian Church, and was a close friend of Presbyterian minister John Witherspoon, who was a member of the Continental Congress. Washington's faith-centered response to

General Gage and his clearly stated belief that Providence guided the American cause was typical: throughout the war Washington would make similar statements both publicly and privately. Few American military commanders of any era would match Washington's record for attributing military success to God, or—as he put it—"the Supreme being to whom alone can be attributed the signal successes of our Arms." His faith was also reflected in his distinctive command style.[5]

Despite its proven ability to fight, the army he inherited at Boston in many ways resembled an armed mob. Camps were dirty and unsanitary. Some officers allowed soldiers to treat them with casual disrespect. Others misused their rank and abused their troops. Few officers were experienced, and even fewer soldiers had received professional military training. The army was short of rations, ammunition, and equipment, and troop enlistments were expiring for many men. Despite such serious challenges and limitations, Washington effectively rebuilt and improved the army he had inherited, even while facing a formidable enemy. In contrast to the disdain for the common soldier that was typical of many military professionals of his day, Washington displayed a deep personal interest in the welfare of his troops, and was also devoted to discipline—character traits that defined his leadership and reflected his biblical worldview.[6]

He issued orders prohibiting the looting of civilian property and punished offenders. "It is our business to give protection and support to the poor, distressed inhabitants," he advised his troops, "not to multiply and increase their calamities." He also enforced punishment on troops who slept on guard duty, engaged in drunkenness, or displayed disrespect to officers. Knowing that inactivity could quickly erode army discipline, he kept his troops busy while in camp: camp streets were regularly swept, trash was removed, duties were routinely performed, and troops were drilled regularly. Meanwhile, he beseeched Congress for arms, equipment, rations, and longer terms of enlistment—and issued orders designed to improve morality and spiritual discipline in the army.[7]

At age forty-three, George Washington was an impressive figure—almost six feet, four inches tall, graced by a muscular build, and noted for a dignified military bearing. His commanding presence, however, came less from his appearance than from his conduct: he was renowned for the caliber of his character, which obviously molded his command style as well as his personal life. Washington's famous character, which would make him the object of admiration for generations of Americans, was a reflection of his personal faith—particularly his reliance on the sovereignty of God, which he consistently described as "divine providence."[8]

Eighteenth-century Americans knew exactly to whom Washington was referring when he spoke of "Providence"—the God of the Bible. The leading dictionary of the day defined *providence* as "the care of God over created beings; divine superintendence." It was a common and respectful reference to the Judeo-Christian doctrine that God created the world and superintended the events of humankind, and that all developments—even those that appeared to be disastrous—ultimately had a good purpose for believers. This doctrine, sometimes described as "the sovereignty of God," was summarized in a verse familiar to eighteenth-century Americans, which was found in the New Testament book of Romans: "And we know that all things work together for good to them that love God, to them who are the called according to his purpose."[9]

Despite his formal and reserved nature—and his low-church Anglican heritage—Washington repeatedly referred to God and expressed his faith in official orders and public statements. "I now make it my earnest prayer," he officially stated at one point, "that God . . . would dispose us all, to do Justice, to love mercy, and to demean ourselves with that Charity, humility and pacific temper of mind, which were the Characteristicks of the Divine Author of our blessed Religion. . . ." He officially urged the men of his army to behave "as becomes a Christian soldier," and called on them to display the "Character of [a] Christian." He also spoke of "the Almighty," publicly referred to "the Lord, and Giver of Victory," acknowledged "the Supreme Author of all Good," attributed military success to "the Almighty ruler of the Universe," officially called for thanksgiving to "the supreme disposer of Human events," and respectfully referred to "the omnipotence of that God who alone is able to protect" America.[10]

His most frequent reference to God was in the term *Providence*. He referred to "the finger of Providence," spoke of "the providential aids" of "that Almighty Being who rules over the Universe," wrote of "the providence of Almighty God" and "the favorable interpositions of his providence." He described favorable developments as "a most Providential event" and as "Providential circumstances," expressed gratitude for "the ordering of kind Providence" and the "smiles of Providence," declared that "there is a good Providence which will never fail to take care of His children," proclaimed his dependence on "the same All-wise Providence," acknowledged his reliance on "the care of an indulgent Providence," attested that "it is the duty of all Nations to acknowledge the providence of Almighty God," and repeatedly stated his conviction that America's future would be determined by "the hand of Providence."[11]

As was common in eighteenth-century America, Washington's personal faith was consistently expressed in his professional life. He issued orders encouraging his troops to attend Sunday worship services in camp, ordered camp duties to be lightened, and forbade military reviews and avoided troop inspections on the Lord's Day. Regular participation in Sunday worship services by his troops, he announced at one point, "will reflect great credit on the army in general, tend to improve the morals, and at the same time, to increase the happiness of the soldiery, and must afford the most pure and rational entertainment for every serious and well disposed mind."[12]

When the Continental Congress voted to provide each regiment with a chaplain, Washington urged his officers to find chaplains who were genuinely strong in faith and character. "The Colonels or commanding officers of each regiment are directed to procure Chaplains . . . of good Characters and exemplary lives," he ordered, and the troops were instructed to "pay them a suitable respect and attend carefully upon religious exercises." Soon after he took command at Boston, the Congress officially proclaimed a day of "public Humiliation, Fasting and Prayer." In response, Washington ordered his troops to "attend Divine Service, at the accustomed places of worship" even if they had to go armed and ready for battle. "The General orders that Day to be religiously observed by the Forces under his Command," Washington declared, "exactly in the manner directed by the proclamation of the Continental Congress."[13]

As he strove to instill Judeo-Christian morality and discipline in the army, Washington even attempted to end the age-old soldier practice of profanity. "The General is sorry to be informed," he stated in a general order, "that the foolish, and wicked practice of profane cursing and swearing . . . is growing into fashion; he hopes the officers will, by example, as well as influence, endeavour to check it, and that both they and the men will reflect, that we have little hopes of the blessing of Heaven on our Arms, if we insult it by our impiety, and folly; added to this, it is a vice so mean and low, without any temptation, that every man of sense, and character, detests and despises it." Washington knew the rowdy, undisciplined mob he had inherited at Boston faced a mighty challenge—defeating the heralded British army—and he believed it would take more than military discipline to do it.[14]

He issued orders calling on his troops to follow the same Bible-based standards that governed and motivated most Americans in his day. Soon after taking command, he officially urged one of his commanding officers to encourage a "true Christian spirit" among the troops. Later he issued a general order reminding the soldiers of his army that the "blessings and protection of Heaven are at all times necessary, but especially so in times of public distress and danger." God could not be expected to provide those "blessings and protection," his order implied, if Americans in uniform did not conduct themselves with biblical standards of morality. "The General hopes and trusts," he declared, "that every officer and man, will endeavour so as to live, and act, as becomes a Christian soldier defending the dearest Rights and Liberties of his country."[15]

Washington repeatedly stated his belief that success and survival of the army and the nation could occur only through God's intervention—which he referred to as "frequent Favors from divine providence." He believed he witnessed those "frequent favors" in events both large and small. When a ship bearing a cargo of flour for the British army fell into the hands of hungry Continental troops, Washington concluded, "I cannot but consider this as a most Providential Event. . . ." When America won a battlefield victory, he credited it to "the interposition of Providence." He viewed America's quest for independence as a sacred cause—"the sacred Cause of Freedom," he called it. Throughout the Revolutionary War, he steadfastly believed the cause would eventually prevail. He was committed to do all in his power to achieve victory through the force of arms, but—as he repeatedly stated—he believed American independence would become reality through the "remarkable Interposition of Providence."[16]

Keeping his army equipped, fed, and in the field was a mighty task. When he took command of the assembled New England volunteers outside Boston in 1775, Washington had to mold an army from thousands of hard-fighting but undisciplined men.

He was constantly plagued by troop shortages in both the regular Continental Army and in the state militias, and the size of his army alternately shrank and swelled as old enlistments ended and new ones began. Congress and the states were often strapped for funds. Soldiers frequently served with no pay, meager rations, and ragged uniforms. Troops were promised back pay and the reward of free land upon victory, but that was scant motivation; Washington's army remained in the field despite death and deprivation because so many soldiers believed in the cause of American independence—and because of the inspiration they drew from their commander-in-chief.[17]

"The fate of unborn Millions will now depend, under God, on the Courage and Conduct of this army," Washington announced to his troops early in the war. "Our cruel and unrelenting Enemy leaves us no choice but a brave resistance, or the most abject submission; this is all we can expect—We have therefore to resolve to conquer or die: Our own Country's Honor, all call upon us for a vigorous and manly exertion, and if we now shamefully fail, we shall become infamous to the whole world." As he would do throughout the war, he urged each soldier to serve with courage and a sacrificial attitude—and to trust God for the ultimate victory. "Let us therefore rely upon the goodness of the Cause," he stated, "and the aid of the supreme Being, in whose hands Victory is, to animate and encourage us to great and noble Actions. The Eyes of all our Countrymen are now upon us. . . ."[18]

A number of key "Countrymen" shared his belief in "the Sacred cause of Freedom" and encouraged his faith. "The Supreme Director of all events has caused a wonderful union of hearts and counsels to subsist among us," enthused Connecticut governor Jonathan Trumbull in a congratulatory message to Washington upon his appointment as commander-in-chief. "May the God of the armies of Israel shower down the blessings of His divine providence upon you, give you wisdom and fortitude, and cover your head in the day of battle!" the governor wrote. Connecticut's Trumbull was himself an invaluable blessing to Washington—at one point, he was the only Colonial governor to support the Patriot side. Trumbull, a devout Christian, funneled the resources of his state into Washington's army, providing indispensable support in the opening years of the war. "Now, therefore, be strong and very courageous," he wrote Washington early in his command, repeating God's admonition to Joshua on the eve of battle.[19]

Washington no doubt needed such encouragement: he encountered one frustration after another as he attempted to besiege British forces at Boston, while trying to organize his army and direct overall American military strategy. Despite his faith and determination, he suffered occasional dark moments during the worst of war. "Could I have foreseen what I have, and am likely to experience," he confided to a friend in late 1775, "no consideration on earth should have induced me to accept this command." Such gloom was infrequent, however; Washington repeatedly recorded his confidence that God in his sovereignty would eventually provide an American victory. "How it will end, God in his great goodness will direct," he wrote. "I am thankful for his protection to this time."[20]

For eight months in 1775 and 1776, he conducted a stalemate siege against the British army at Boston, unable to mount a serious attack due to lack of troops, weapons, and artillery. "If I shall be able to rise superior to these and many other difficulties," he wrote in January of 1776, "I shall most religiously believe, that the finger of Providence is in it, to blind the eyes of our enemies. . . ." That same month, events unfolded that led him to believe he was indeed witnessing "the finger of Providence" at work.[21]

In late January of 1776, Washington's young artillery commander, Colonel Henry Knox, arrived in Boston with more than fifty desperately needed pieces of heavy artillery. The guns had been captured at Fort Ticonderoga and other British posts in New England, then arduously hauled by oxen-borne sleds

over snow-covered passes and roads for more than three hundred miles. It was an extraordinary achievement. So was the
way Washington deployed the guns. Using prefabricated heavy
timber frames, 360 ox carts and a 1,200-man workforce, he had
his engineers erect a powerful artillery battery atop Boston's
Dorchester Heights in a single night. By daylight, American artillery commanded the British positions below.[22]

The British commander-in-chief, General Gage, had been
replaced by General William Howe, who was a capable, experienced forty-five-year-old career army officer. On the morning of March 5, Howe looked up at Dorchester Heights and was
shocked to see American artillery trained on his garrison. "The
rebels have done more in one night than my whole army could do
in months," he reportedly exclaimed. The British artillery could
not be elevated high enough to bombard Dorchester Heights,
and British warships in Boston Harbor were as vulnerable as the
British army. General Howe ordered an infantry assault against
the new American gun emplacements, but reconsidered when
he recalled the horrible British casualties at Bunker Hill. Then a
severe, unexpected winter storm struck Boston and made the assault impossible. Howe believed he had no choice: on March 17,
1776, British forces evacuated Boston.[23]

Washington had won—the British had been forced to abandon their strategic American post, and they sailed away for
Canada. Another commander might have ordered a raucous celebration, at least at army headquarters. Not Washington. He
calmly ordered an advance force to secure the city, but chose not
to lead it in person. Instead he went to church. It was Sunday, and
Washington made a point of attending an afternoon worship service at a local meetinghouse. An army chaplain—the Reverend
Abiel Leonard—presided over the service. For his sermon text,
he chose a passage from the Old Testament book of Exodus. It
was a verse that surely struck Washington as appropriate at this
moment of triumph, for it praised "the aid of the supreme being"

to whom Washington so often attributed victory. "And . . . the Egyptians said, Let us flee from the face of Israel," the chaplain read, "for the Lord fightenth for them against the Egyptians."[24]

········∘·◦·◦·◦·∘········

Four months after the red-coated "Egyptians" left Boston, troopships packed with British soldiers appeared off New York City, which General Howe had chosen as his new base. British strategy now called for crushing the Revolution in the northern colonies from headquarters in New York, and doing likewise in the southern colonies by capturing a southern seaport as a base. The port targeted as a base in the South was Charleston, South Carolina. The city was attacked in June of 1776. The British commander, General Henry Clinton, launched a powerful army-navy assault against Fort Sullivan, a thirty-one-gun fortification of logs and sand on Sullivan's Island, which bordered Charleston Harbor. The British expected a quick and easy victory, boasting that two British warships could take both the fort and Charleston. Their boast seemed supported by military logic: the fort had been hastily constructed, and was so low on ammunition that only twenty-six of its guns could be fired. The British had not two warships but eight—and one ship alone was supplied with more artillery than the entire American fort.[25]

General Clinton skillfully deployed his forces: the warships would bombard Fort Sullivan with a crossfire while infantry assaulted the fort from an undefended adjacent island. Everything appeared to favor the British—until a series of surprising events undermined their attack. First, Clinton had poorly reconnoitered his landing site and unexpectedly deep water kept the British infantry from fording a creek onto Sullivan's Island, which forced them to abandon the ground assault. Meanwhile, three British warships crucial to the naval bombardment ran aground within easy range of the fort and were severely raked by American artillery. Before an incoming tide set them free one had to be set afire and destroyed. The British naval fire, meanwhile, was unable to penetrate Fort Sullivan's log earthworks, which were constructed of spongy local palmetto trees.[26]

With his gun crews so protected, the fort's commander, Colonel William Moultrie, directed an effective return fire that inflicted serious damage on the attackers: the British suffered more than two hundred casualties compared to thirty-seven among the South Carolinians. It was a surprising setback for General Clinton, who finally admitted defeat and aborted the attack on Charleston. It had been a costly operation for the British, and some in the ranks were relieved to see it end. "By God, we are glad of it," a British sailor exclaimed to his shipmates, "for we never had such a drubbing in our lives."[27]

America needed a victory, and Washington needed some good news—the war elsewhere had taken a turn for the worse. In midsummer of 1776, a major American military campaign in Canada collapsed, while the British campaign to capture and occupy New York City steadily moved toward a successful conclusion. General Howe had arrived in New York Harbor in late June with more than thirty thousand well-trained and superbly equipped British troops and Hessian mercenaries, supported by a large fleet of warships armed with twelve hundred pieces of naval artillery. To oppose this British juggernaut, Washington had nineteen thousand poorly armed Continental and militia troops, limited artillery, no cavalry and no navy. He had skillfully moved his army from Boston and had surrounded New York City with entrenchments—but his troops were no match for the British this time and he knew it. He intended to defend New York to the best of his ability, but his main goal was simply to keep his army from being destroyed until the tide of war somehow shifted to the side of America. To do so, Washington admitted, he depended on "the hand of Providence."[28]

He encouraged his troops to do the same—to stay focused on what he saw as God's sovereign role in America's "sacred cause."

When Congress recommended a day of "fasting, humiliation and prayer" in May of 1776, Washington notified his troops of the Congressional recommendation to "supplicate the mercy of Almighty God, that it would please him to pardon all our manifold sins and transgressions, and to prosper the Arms of the United Colonies. . . ." To accompany the Congressional resolution, Washington issued a general order to his troops. "The General commands all officers, and soldiers, to pay strict obedience to the Orders of the Continental Congress," it read, "and by their unfeigned, and pious observance of their religious duties, incline the Lord, and Giver of Victory, to prosper our arms." [29]

Washington's army was in the trenches around New York City when he learned that the Continental Congress had passed the Declaration of Independence. In response, he ordered his troops to assemble in formation within sight of British positions across the harbor. The Declaration of Independence was then read aloud to the army—along with an official admonition by Washington: "The General hopes this important Event will serve as a fresh incentive to every officer, and soldier, to act with Fidelity and Courage, as knowing that now the peace and safety of his Country depends (under God) solely on the success of our arms." It was the same day—July 9, 1776—that Washington called on his troops to be soldiers of faith: "The blessing and protection of Heaven are at all times necessary but especially so in times of public distress and danger," his orders proclaimed. "The General hopes and trusts, that every officer and man, will endeavour so to live, and act, as becomes a Christian soldier defending the dearest Rights and Liberties of his country." [30]

Despite Washington's best efforts—and his faith in the "interposition of Providence"—his army took a battering in the summer and fall of 1776, and was repeatedly forced to give ground to superior British forces. At the Battle of Long Island on August 27,

Washington's army suffered a serious defeat, incurring more than fourteen hundred casualties. General Howe and the British conducted a masterful campaign, while Washington twice committed tactical mistakes that could have led to the annihilation of his outnumbered army. Under Washington's command, American forces were defeated, demoralized, reduced in strength, driven off Long Island, and forced to abandon New York City. General Howe triumphantly occupied the city in September of 1776, making it the British command center for military operations in America.[31]

Washington's forces appeared increasingly powerless before the British army, and the cause of American independence and nationhood seemed dangerously imperiled. However, while General Howe successfully occupied New York City, he failed to destroy Washington's army, despite the huge numerical superiority of British forces. Throughout the New York campaign, he inexplicably missed repeated opportunities to crush American forces and end the Revolution—a failure that would puzzle students of the campaign for centuries to come. The survival of Washington's army, a twentieth-century historian would conclude, "makes one marvel for an explanation."[32]

In the face of overwhelming odds, Washington and his beleaguered army had survived, and were still fit to fight. The Revolution would continue, and "the Sacred cause of freedom" remained alive. The American defeats and his own mistakes in generalship would prove to be a valuable learning experience for Washington. As for the survival of his army—others might be perplexed by it, but not Washington. He gave the credit to God. "The singular interpositions of Providence in our feeble condition," he would later recall, "were such, as could scarcely escape the attention of the most unobserving. . . ."[33]

One of the "interpositions" to which Washington might have been referring occurred in August, following the battle of Long Island. Eleven thousand troops, the bulk of Washington's army, had been driven from their Long Island lines and pinned against the banks of the East River opposite Manhattan. Instead of delivering a deathblow to American forces as some of his commanders urged, Howe unexpectedly halted his advance and deployed the British army for a siege. Washington meanwhile directed a well-executed evacuation across the river, using a flotilla of small boats oared by troops who were former fishermen and sailors from Massachusetts.[34]

It was a dangerous exercise—"a military operation to try the skill and courage of veterans," an American army officer would later attest. If detected by the British while withdrawing across the river to Manhattan, the Americans would have been vulnerable to attack and destruction. As the disembarkation began, however, a heavy fog unexpectedly drifted in and settled over the East River, cloaking the operation for hours. The evacuation went undetected by the British, and except for a handful of stragglers and two pieces of heavy artillery that were mired in mud, the entire American force was rescued. "Every atmospheric condition aided the patriots," a twentieth-century military historian would conclude. "Providentially for us," an American soldier would report, "a great fog arose, which prevented the enemy from seeing our retreat from their works. . . ."[35]

Another unlikely set of events that aided the American cause occurred after Washington's army was forced to withdraw from New York City. In November of 1776, British forces captured Fort Washington, a key American fortification north of New York, and soon afterward took Fort Lee across the Hudson River in New Jersey. The captures cost Washington another three thousand troops and irreplaceable ordnance and equipment, and appeared to be a double military disaster. The losses, however, actually became an American advantage. "Both disasters were unrecognized blessings," twentieth-century Washington authority John C. Fitzpatrick would conclude. "They freed the Continental Army from responsibility for fixed fortifications, in which it had small chance . . . and made it a mobile, maneuvering force." Soon the army's new mobility and Washington's skillful maneuvering would yield critically important victories.[36]

But first Washington had to escape British forces that pursued his army as it withdrew across New Jersey. He did so skillfully, directing a brilliant strategic retreat through New Jersey, and eventually taking his army across the Delaware River into Pennsylvania. His army had been defeated. It was reduced in numbers. Troop morale had fallen. Even so, the army had survived to fight again, and Washington remained confident of ultimate victory. Why? "The fortitude with which he met overwhelming difficulties was based upon his faith," Fitzpatrick would observe. "Defeats were merely temporary setbacks and victories were merely longer or shorter steps toward final success." Forced to retreat from New York to Pennsylvania, left with an army that was ragged and reduced—and still threatened by a powerful and victorious enemy—George Washington weighed his options and vowed, "I will not, however, despair. . . ."[37]

CHAPTER FIVE

"The Sacred Cause of Freedom"

On a Sunday morning in January of 1776, twenty-nine-year-old pastor John Peter Muhlenberg stood before his congregation for the last time. His church was located in the backcountry hamlet of Woodstock, Virginia, and churchgoers had traveled from the hills and hollows of the Shenandoah Valley in such numbers that they packed the church pews shoulder to shoulder and spilled outside into the churchyard. It was largely a Lutheran congregation, composed mainly of German immigrants, and they came to church this Sunday in such large numbers because they had heard that their respected young pastor was leaving, and they wanted to hear him explain why.[1]

Muhlenberg was a gifted preacher, the son of the best-known Lutheran minister in Colonial America, and had made the little Woodstock church the center of a thriving backcountry ministry. He was also a prominent regional political leader, the head of the local Committee of Safety, a member of the Virginia House of Burgesses, and friends with two of Virginia's most famous Revolutionary leaders—Patrick Henry and General George Washington. When he mounted the church pulpit this Sunday, he was attired in his black clergyman's robe, and he stood ramrod straight before his congregation—a posture he had perhaps acquired as a militia soldier in his youth. His sermon text this day, he announced, was found in the Old Testament book of Ecclesiastes, chapter 3: "To everything there is a season, and a time to every purpose under heaven. A time to be born and a time to die; a time to plant and a time to pluck up that which is planted; A time to kill, and a time to heal. . . ."[2]

He was compelled to leave the ministry of the Woodstock church, Muhlenberg proclaimed, because he had accepted a new call. In "the language of Holy Writ," he explained, "there was a time for all things," including "a time to fight"—and for him that time had now come. He had accepted a colonel's commission in Eighth Virginia Militia, he told the congregation, and would soon be leaving to serve in America's fight for freedom— along with any recruits who wished to join him. That said, he pronounced a benediction, stepped away from the pulpit and dropped his clergyman's robe—revealing the full uniform of a Virginia militia officer. The congregation reportedly rose as one and burst into a fervent chorus of "Ein feste Burg ist unser Gott"—"A Mighty Fortress Is My God." Pastor Muhlenberg, who was destined to become one of George Washington's most valued brigadiers, marched off to war accompanied by a parade of more than three hundred recruits.[3]

Such was the influence of American pastors at the time of the Revolution. No profession was more influential than the clergy, including America's political leadership, and just as they had done during the Stamp Act crisis, countless American preachers called on their congregations to resist what they decried as British tyranny. "The cause we are engaged in is the cause of God; and you may hope for his blessing and fight under his banner," Connecticut pastor Nathaniel Whitaker told his congregation in a typical discourse. "Love itself implies hatred to malevolence. . . . True benevolence, is therefore, exercised in opposing those who seek the hurt of society. . . ." Whitaker was a Presbyterian, but support for American liberty and independence was not limited to the "dissenter" denominations—the Presbyterians, Congregational-ists, Baptists, Lutherans, Dutch Reformed, and others outside the Church of England.[4]

As members of Britain's official state church, American Angli-cans were divided over the Revolution, although most supported it. Included among them were more than half the signers of the Declaration of Independence, who were Anglican. America's An-glican clergy were far more divided than the laity: ministers were required to take an oath to the king as well as the Church of England, and supporting the American cause was a struggle of conscience for many. Some became Loyalists, some tried to be neutral, and some fled to Britain. Others decided that the Higher Law of Scripture outweighed the obligation of their oath, and sided with the Revolution despite their personal risks. Anglican rector David Griffith of Virginia spoke for many of his fellow ministers—and their Anglican congregations—when he preached that "the cause of truth and justice is the cause of God, and . . . his mighty arm is irresistible."[5]

Even some Quakers supported the Revolution, despite the Quaker tradition of pacifism. Many complied with the advice of Quaker leaders in England who urged neutrality, and were treated with suspicion by Patriot leaders. Others, however, sup-ported independence, and some even joined the American army. Colonial leader John Dickinson, who represented Pennsylvania in the Continental Congress, was raised as a Quaker, and while he declined to vote for the Declaration of Independence, he accepted a brigadier's commission in an American militia brigade. Briga-dier General Nathanael Greene, one of Washington's ablest com-manders, had also grown up in a Quaker family, although he left the Friends to join the military. Aging Quaker leader Elizabeth Shipley of New Jersey expressed her support for the Revolution in a deathbed proclamation issued in 1777. "Hold out, Americans," she reportedly proclaimed, "your cause is good, and God will give you your country."[6]

Colonial America's small population of Roman Catholics, located mainly in Maryland, generally supported the American cause as well, despite public criticism of English Catholicism by the Continental Congress. When the British Parliament officially recognized the Catholic Church in Canada as part of the Quebec Act of 1773, the Continental Congress had responded with an open letter to the English people that accused the Roman Church of spreading "impiety, bigotry, persecution, murder and rebellion through every part of the world." Such pronouncements ceased as Congress attempted to raise the sympathies of Canadians toward American independence and enlist the military support of Catholic France. Among the signers of the Declaration of Independence was America's most prominent Catholic, the scholar and political leader Charles Carroll of Maryland. Like Carroll, most American Catholics apparently believed that an independent America—even if overwhelmingly Protestant—offered greater religious freedom than Great Britain.[7]

That view was echoed by America's tiny Jewish community, estimated at fewer than three thousand, which rallied to the Patriot cause with influence far beyond its numbers. "They have supported the cause, and have bravely fought and bled for liberty. . . ," the president of Philadelphia's Jewish congregation would attest of his people at war's end. Indeed, Haym Salomon, a Jewish merchant and financier in Philadelphia, donated a fortune to the nearly bankrupt American government, financially shored up Washington's army at critical time, and personally supported soldiers, officers, and members of the Continental Congress. By some accounts, he poured more than six hundred thousand dollars into the American war effort and was left "practically penniless" at the time of his death in 1785. Even more important to the Revolution than men and money, was the motivation of Colonial America's consensus philosophy—the Judeo-Christian worldview—which reflected the Old Testament or Hebrew Bible as well as the New Testament. "Covenant Theology"—the belief that a nation or a people would be "prosperous or afflicted, according to their general Obedience or Disobedience" to God—which was professed by countless patriot Americans, was also rooted in the Old Testament or Hebrew Bible.[8]

No one was more fervent in support of the Revolution than the members of America's Reformed or Calvinist denominations—the Congregationalists, Presbyterians, Baptists, Dutch Reformed, German Reformed, and others. While a few Congregational congregations were drifting toward Unitarianism, most Calvinist denominations in Colonial America remained firmly committed to Bible-based doctrines as defined by the sixteenth-century French-Swiss theologian John Calvin. The core doctrines of Calvinism and the Protestant Reformation were the sovereignty of God, the authority of Scripture, and the belief that personal salvation comes by faith alone in Jesus Christ through God's grace. Whether a king or a commoner, every person was subject to the authority of God, according to Scripture—and Calvinists therefore believed that everyone was of equal value to God. Biblical principles such as these reinforced Colonial Americans' widely held respect for God-given or inalienable rights.[9]

Respect for the authority of Scripture called for obedience to the Higher Law of the Bible whenever it conflicted with man's law, the Calvinist denominations believed, even if it meant resisting king and Parliament. "For earthly princes lay aside their power when they rise up against God," John Calvin wrote, "and are unworthy to be reckoned among the number of mankind. We ought rather utterly to defy them than obey them." Under the influence of the Great Awakening, most Colonial Americans and their political leaders had been taught the preeminence of Higher Law at home and church since childhood, and many believed the king and Parliament were violating Higher Law by subverting God-given rights to life and liberty.[10]

Even among their fellow Calvinists, few people in Colonial America could match the Revolutionary fervor of America's Presbyterians. Many of them were descendants of the English Puritans and Presbyterians who had battled King Charles I a century earlier in the English Civil Wars, and they had inherited a distrust of English royalty. Others were descendants of French Huguenots. Deeply aware that the French monarchy had directed the slaughter of thousands of Huguenots in 1572, they were generally suspicious of all royalty. Though scattered in limited numbers throughout Colonial America, the Huguenots were highly influential. Members of Congress, judges, military officers, and leaders in numerous other fields were descended from Huguenots who were slaughtered for their faith in France or forced to flee the country. Many American Huguenots had thus inherited a serious commitment to Higher Law and a willingness to defend inalienable rights.[11]

Other American Presbyterians had been born in Scotland or were the children or grandchildren of Scots immigrants, and possessed a clannish suspicion of English authority from an era of religious repression by the English monarchy. By far, however, the great majority of American Presbyterians were the people known as "Scots-Irish" or "Scotch Irish." Some were descendants of Scots who had fled to Ireland to escape a famine in Scotland in the 1690s, but most were descended from Scots who had relocated to the Ulster province of Northern Ireland generations earlier. In the early seventeenth century, England's King James I had colonized Catholic Ulster with tens of thousands of Scots Presbyterians, along with smaller numbers of English Anglicans. The king hoped to suppress Irish rebellion in the region and reward Scots supporters, but the effort ignited decades of bloody fighting between Irish Catholics and the Scots Presbyterians—including a massacre of some four thousand Protestants in 1641.[12]

Finally, in the early eighteenth century, the Scots-Irish, or "Ulster Scots" as some called them, began immigrating to Colonial America from northern Ireland—and they came in massive numbers. Between 1717 and 1770, more than a quarter-million Scots-Irish fled to the American colonies, and the vast majority of them were Presbyterians. Unlike the Puritans, Quakers, and Catholics, they did not initially settle in a single region or colony, although many were drawn to the Appalachians, which reminded them of Scotland in terrain and climate. Instead the Scots-Irish—like the Huguenots—settled throughout the Thirteen Colonies, but they did so in large numbers, becoming a powerful influence throughout Colonial America.[13]

America's Scots-Irish Presbyterians believed that civil liberty and religious liberty were inseparable, and that the loss of one would almost certainly lead to the loss of the other. "The knowledge of God and his truths, have . . . been chiefly, if not entirely, confined to those parts of the earth where some degree of liberty and political justice were to be seen," proclaimed Dr. John Witherspoon, who was the Presbyterian president of Princeton University, as well as a delegate to the Continental Congress. Their well-known support for the Revolution sometimes made Presbyterians and their churches favorite targets for the British. An English naval officer, for example, when bombarding a seaside community on the New England coast, reportedly took special delight in doing harm to local Presbyterian. "Now, my boys," he was said to have shouted," we will aim at the damned Presbyterian church . . . one more shot and the house of God will fall before you!" The targeted church survived, however, and so did American Presbyterianism, which unwaveringly fueled Patriot resistance at home, in the pulpit, and on the battlefield.[14]

Despite their religious and cultural differences, Colonial Americans—Protestant, Catholic, and Jewish—were united by their common identity and by the biblical perspective they shared. Already America was a "melting pot" of people—still predominantly English, but seasoned with Scots, Irish, Germans, Dutch, French, Africans, and others. Beneath this New World garden of cultures, however, America was unified by the bedrock foundation of the Judeo-Christian worldview. "Those Europeans who came to settle in America were preponderantly Christians, nominally, habitually, or devoutly," twentieth-century historian Clarence Carson would observe. "The few who were not were probably theists and people of the Book, i.e., Jews. They were Christians whose churches and sects were known by such varied names as Baptists, Brownists, Moravians, Quakers, Presbyterians, Congregationalists, and Catholics. Though it was their differences which stood out at the time over which they wrangled, they nonetheless shared a basic outlook which transcended their differences and evidenced their common heritage."[15]

In the Judeo-Christian culture of Colonial America, the impact of the clergy's leadership was enormous. "There was hardly a day of the week, to say nothing of the Sabbath," historian Patricia Bonomi would note, "when colonial Americans could not repair to their churches for some occasion or other, all of which gave a certain tone to everything they did. . . ." The influence of the clergy went far beyond their Sunday worship services. Well-publicized theological debates drew audiences numbering in the hundreds, and popular preachers sometimes attracted thousands to outdoor venues. Even greater was the influence of printed sermons, which were routinely published in leading newspapers and mass-printed in pamphlets called "broadsides." Bible-based literature—sermons, devotionals, homilies, theological discourses—constituted the largest single classification of published works in Colonial America, outnumbering the total combined works of science, law, and history. Colonial America was a faith-centered society; its pastors led the way—and they overwhelmingly supported the Revolution.[16]

Defending God-given "unalienable Rights" was a biblical obligation for all peoples, Colonial America's clergy often preached. The concept of liberty, proclaimed one Philadelphia pastor, when "traced to her true source, is of heavenly extraction." Massachusetts minister William Gordon agreed, urging his flock to go forward "without murmuring or complaining" to defend American liberty. "The important day is now arrived that must determine whether we will remain free," he said, "or, alas! be brought into bondage, after having long enjoyed the sweets of liberty." Philadelphia pastor John Ewing agreed. "As to our civil rights and privileges," he said, "to suffer others to invade them with impunity is to concur in the subversion of all society and civil government."[17]

Colonial America's political leadership understood the powerful influence of the American clergy. In Philadelphia to attend the Continental Congress, Massachusetts's John Adams was delighted, he wrote his wife, to see that the city's pulpits "thunder and lighten every sabbath" in support of American liberty. So important were clergymen that the Continental Congress officially urged American ministers to "use their Pastoral Influence to work in the disposition of the people" on behalf of the Revolution. In 1776, Congress hired two ministers, Elihu Spencer and Alexander McWhorter, to raise support for the American cause in the Colonial backcountry, knowing that potential recruits viewed "their Spiritual pastors with great respect and that truths from their mouths come with redoubled influence upon their minds."[18]

With eighteenth-century Britain drifting toward a more secularized society, many British leaders missed the importance of the pulpit in Colonial America. Others, however, were more observant, and if they did not respect the Patriot pulpit, they at least feared it. The American Revolution was in reality "a religious war," one British official advised his superiors in London. Referring to the black robes commonly worn by American clergymen of the day, another described America's preachers as a "black regiment" that wielded the equivalent power of an army. The "Yell of Rebellion," he concluded, resounded from pulpits throughout the American colonies. "Your Lordship can scarcely conceive," wrote a Loyalist leader to a British nobleman, "what Fury the Discourses of some mad Preachers have created in this Country."[19]

Some Britons, accustomed to a single national church, expected America's heralded diversity of Christian denominations to eventually unravel the American cause in sectarian discord. They did not realize that the glue that cemented American unity was its Bible-based foundation—the Judeo-Christian worldview. "Although Americans entered the revolt against Britain in several ways, their religion proved important in all of them, important even to the lukewarm and indifferent," twentieth-century historian Robert Middlekauff would observe. "It did because, more than anything else in America, religion shaped culture—values, ideals, a way of looking at and responding to the world—which held them together in the crisis and upheaval of war."[20]

From Massachusetts to Georgia, America's preachers in great numbers unleashed the power of the pulpit in support of the American cause—and they made a major impact. Early in the conflict, an estimated one-third of Americans remained loyal to king and Parliament, and even more were reluctant revolutionaries. Many of these, however, were swayed to the American cause by Patriot preachers, who sounded the biblical justification for resistance from their pulpits. In South Carolina, the Reverend William Tennent III issued such a convincing call at one service that his male worshipers collectively volunteered for military duty on the spot. New England pastor John Cleaveland reportedly recruited every able-bodied man in his congregation for military service, then went to war with them. So did Pennsylvania preacher John Craighead, who was reprimanded in mid-sermon by a worried mother who resented his call to duty. "Stop, Mr. Craighead," she protested. "Yer always preaching to the boys about it, but I dinna think ye'd be very likely to go yerself." The pastor responded by joining the army—with a crowd of menfolk from his church.[21]

In New England, a group of ministers organized a Solemn League of Covenant to support American liberties. Massachusetts minister John Clark not only preached resistance but also converted his house into a community political center. Everywhere, American ministers joined Committees of Correspondence, published pro-independence articles, and provided leadership in a variety of ways—but mainly they preached. Their sermons reminded Americans of the biblical justification for resistance to British misrule—and the obligation of believers to oppose genuine tyranny. "How cruel and unjust is [Britain's] conduct, in carrying on this bloody war, to ruin and enslave us," preached the Reverend Abraham Keteltas, a New York Presbyterian, in a sermon typical of the day. "Our cause," he proclaimed, "is the cause of truth against error and falsehood; the cause of righteousness against iniquity; the cause of the oppressed against the oppressor.... America will be a glorious land of freedom, knowledge and religion—an asylum for the distressed, oppressed and persecuted virtue. [You] contend not only for your own happiness, for your dear relations, for the happiness of the present inhabitants of America, but you contend for the happiness of millions yet unborn."[22]

Colonial clergymen delivered their pulpit salvos with the impact of mass media. While frontier churches might not see a minister but once a month, pastors in Colonial America's cities and towns routinely preached three sermons a week—twice on Sunday and once in midweek. By one estimate, the typical churchgoer in New England heard no less than seven thousand sermons in his or her lifetime. Three types of sermons—fast day sermons, thanksgiving sermons, and election sermons—were especially influential in Colonial America. In fast day sermons, preachers called on their congregations to fast, pray, and repent of personal and national sins as they beseeched God for victory. "Do we join piety to our prudence and fortitude," asked a typical fast day sermon, "do we confess and repent of our sins . . . become a holy people, and make the most high our confidence? [Then] we may hope that he will be on our side; and 'if the Lord is for us, what can man do to us?' "[23]

Thanksgiving sermons encouraged believers to give thanks to God for the success and survival of American independence and liberty or simply for the blessings of living in America—a land that many preachers believed was predestined by God for a special future. Like the Jews of the Bible, Americans in some ways were a "chosen people," many pastors proclaimed, and if they humbled themselves in gratitude to the Lord, they would become the inheritors of God's blessings in a new nation. "We are ready to anticipate those happy times, when these days of tribulation shall be at an end," declared one pulpit discourse, "when our brethren shall return from the high places of the field, when we with them shall sit under our own vines and fig-trees quietly enjoying . . . the fruits of our own hard labor, and . . . tranquility and liberty flourish. Here shall dwell uncorrupted faith the pure worship of God, unawed, uninterrupted."[24]

Election sermons usually preceded election days and imposed a biblical application on the issues of the day. A classic election day sermon was delivered by Jonathan Edwards a generation before the Revolution. It not only established a model for such sermons but also set a standard in Colonial America for evaluating those in authority. Mankind would "scarce be able to subsist in the world," Edwards taught, if God had not established civil government "to keep men from destroying each other." Just as pastors were ministers of God, Edwards believed, so were civil rulers, who were granted authority by God to do what was right according his Word. Like selfless and devoted human fathers, civil servants were to protect those in their care from external attacks and internal disorder. "When he that is in authority," Edwards pronounced, "is not only a man of strong reason and great discerning to know what is just, but is a man of strict integrity and righteousness . . . [he] is one that has a strong aversion to wickedness, and is disposed to use the power God has put in his hands to suppress it . . . he will be faithful to God, whose minister he is [and] to his people for good. . . ."[25]

The opposite of righteous leaders, Edwards preached, were "sordid and vile" leaders, who would "take advantage of their authority or commission to line their own pockets with what is fraudulently taken or withheld from others. When a man in authority is of such a mean spirit, it weakens his authority, and makes him justly contemptible in the eyes of men. . . ." Following the Intolerable Acts, Jonathan Edwards's model of a civil minister who was "faithful to God [and] to his people" was seldom applied to King George III. As the wages of war spread throughout America, increasing numbers of Americans and their pastors ranked the King with history's "wicked tyrants and oppressors." George III was no longer "the father of his people," declared one sermon, but had become their "destroyer." His "Britannic Majesty," asserted another, was obsessed "by a mad desire to take by compulsion what would otherwise be cheerfully given." Eventually the king even came to be denounced as the "the Prince of Darkness" by some pastors, who called for "victory over the beast and his image."[26]

"Courage, my brave American soldiers," a Pennsylvania preacher counseled assembled Patriot troops early in the war; "if God be for you, who can be against you? Equip yourselves, and to be equipt for this warfare—put on, gentlemen, the gospel armour—have your feet shod with its preparation—for your helmet, salvation—for your shield, faith—and be girded with truth—this, Sirs, is a gospel uniform, that well becomes the Christian soldier. . . ." A Massachusetts minister urged the soldiers gathered before him to face the enemy on the battlefield the way they would resist a spiritual attack from Satan. "May we take to ourselves the whole armour of God," he urged, quoting from the book of Ephesians, "that we may be able to stand against the wiles of the devil, and quench all his fiery darts."[27]

As warfare widened and American casualties mounted—along with civilian suffering—many Patriot Preachers attempted to infuse the American cause with a Bible-based backbone. "The clergy made it their business to see that staunch patriots, and shrewd men of affairs, were returned to Congress," historian George Trevelyan would note, "that the ranks of the local Company were replenished with recruits; and that whoever had once enlisted should stay with the colours until his time was up." For eighteenth-century Americans, the knowledge that a man would have to face his local pastor if he deserted could be a powerful inducement to remain in the ranks. According to Trevelyan, a "farming lad who tired of campaigning, and was tempted to return home without leave, knew well that—even if his sweet-heart forgave him, and his father was secretly glad to have him back for the hay-harvest—he should never dare to face the minister."[28]

For some clergy, preaching was not enough. Like Pastor Muhlenberg, they went to war with the men of their congregations—some as officers and soldiers, and some as chaplains. Thirty-one-year-old David Avery, a Yale alumnus, left his Vermont pastorate to become a chaplain in the Continental Army. Converted at a George Whitefield appearance during the Great Awakening, he had studied for the ministry under the Reverend Eleazar Wheelock, the founder of Dartmouth College, and was a former missionary to the Oneida Indians. As an army chaplain, he ministered to his troops even on the battlefield, and lost an eye in combat. Massachusetts minister Thomas Allen reportedly stood on a log in earshot of British lines and attempted to preach to the enemy—until his rhetoric was answered by gunfire. "Now give me a gun," he announced, and joined the battle. Few volunteers, clergy or otherwise, matched the patriotic spunk displayed by the Reverend Benjamin Pomeroy: at age seventy-one, he fought as a soldier at the battle of Bunker Hill, then joined the army as a chaplain despite his advanced years.[29]

Some pastors paid a high price for their leadership. British troops resented their influence and burned or desecrated many church buildings. Other churches were commandeered for use as British stables or hospitals, and Patriot preachers were routinely harassed. A Connecticut pastor arrested by British troops in New York for possessing Continental currency was publicly punished. "He was this morning obliged to chew up all the money," reported a Loyalist newspaper, "and declare, in the presence of a large assemblage of the people, that he will not again pray for the Congress or their doer of dirty work, Mr. Washington. . . ." When British troops occupied Long Island during the New York campaign, the Reverend Ebenezer Prime, a seventy-five-year-old pastor and Patriot leader, was forced to flee his church, which was deliberately desecrated. A few years later, when the pastor died, his followers buried him in the churchyard cemetery, prompting the local British commander to tear down the church, desecrate the cemetery, and pitch his tent over the preacher's grave—so, he reportedly boasted, that he might daily "tread over the old rebel."[30]

Presbyterian minister Charles McKnight, a prominent New Jersey pastor and Patriot leader, was seized by British troops while preaching near Monmouth. His church was burned and he was put in prison, where he died. Chaplain Daniel McCalla, a Pennsylvania pastor and educator, joined the ill-fated American invasion of Canada in 1776. Captured with other American troops at the battle of Three Rivers in Quebec, he was declared a "rebel parson" and incarcerated in deplorable conditions aboard a British prison ship. Although eventually freed and restored to his ministry, he suffered from a "protracted disease" for the rest of his life. Also locked up on a British prison ship was the thirty-year-old Reverend Moses Allen, a pastor-turned-chaplain, who was captured at the battle of Savannah. Desperate to escape the deadly conditions aboard the floating prison, Allen jumped ship and attempted to swim ashore, but drowned. The prison ship's British commander had Allen's body dumped in a swamp, declaring that "the rebel preacher deserved only a traitor's grave."[31]

The Reverend James Caldwell left his pastorate in Elizabeth-town, New Jersey, to serve in the Continental Army as a chaplain and commissary officer. While he was away, his wife was shot and killed by a British soldier who saw her at her window and mistook her for a sniper, and his home and church were burned. Caldwell came home to tend to his terrorized children, then returned to the army, which was engaged at the battle of Springfield. When American troops began running low on ammunition wadding, Caldwell hurried to a nearby church and returned with a stack of the Isaac Watts hymnal. He went down the firing line passing out hymnbooks, and as the soldiers tore out pages for wadding, he repeatedly shouted, "Now put Watts into them, boys!" [32]

Perhaps the most notorious treatment of an American chap-lain befell the Reverend John Rosbrugh, a Presbyterian minis-ter in New Jersey. A portly, good-humored man unaccustomed to life in the field, Rosbrugh insisted on joining the army with the men of his congregation, even though he was fifty years old and had five children. When the British advanced on Trenton, New Jersey, he became separated from his brigade. Realizing that he had been left behind and enemy troops were approach-ing, he hurriedly tried to escape—but stumbled into a patrol of Hessian troops. He offered to surrender, but one of the soldiers struck him in the face with a sword, knocking him to his knees. Realizing that the enemy troops intended to kill him, the chap-lain began praying aloud for God to forgive them. Undeterred, the Hessians bayoneted him to death, then robbed and stripped him. One of the soldiers was later seen waving Rosbrugh's stolen watch, bragging that he had killed "a damned rebel minister." [33]

Grounded on the Judeo-Christian worldview, motivated by bibli-cal justification, and inspired by their preachers, Americans went to war convinced that they were defending a righteous cause. Their foundational faith was revealed in the banners they carried into battle. Volunteer troops from Connecticut and Massachusetts went to war under battle flags bearing the mottos "An Appeal to Heaven" or "An Appeal to God." So did warships commissioned by Massachusetts and Pennsylvania. Troops from Pennsylvania fought under a flag bearing a slogan that became a familiar battle cry of the Revolution: "Resistance to Tyrants is Obedience to God." [34]

Colonial America's foundational faith was also expressed in the music of the Revolution. Much of the music of the Revolutionary era was borrowed from popular British tunes, and some ballads were satirical, and anything but inspirational. Many songs, however, featured lyrics that clearly reflected Colonial America's Judeo-Christian worldview. One of the most popular tunes of the day, "The Liberty Song," celebrated the unity of faith and values shared by the American people:

> *Then join hand in hand brave Americans all,*
> *By uniting we stand, by dividing we fall;*
> *In so righteous a cause let us hope to succeed,*
> *For Heaven approves of each generous deed.* [35]

The Revolutionary era tune, "American Hearts of Oak," clearly expressed the widespread American view that the war was about a British attempt to suppress America's inalienable rights, and that the Providence of God would protect the American people:

> *They tax us contrary to reason and right,*
> *Expecting that we are not able to fight;*
> *But to draw their troops home, I do think would be best,*
> *For Providence always defends the oppressed.* [36]

"The Thanksgiving Hymn," another wartime song, also reflected the God-centered national consensus that defined eighteenth-century American culture:

With one accord we'll praise the Lord,
All glory to Him give.
To whom all praise is due always,
For He is all in all;
George Washington, that noble one,
On His great name doth call.
Our Congress too, before they do,
Acknowledge Him supreme;
Come let us all before Him fall,
And glorify His name.[37]

The era's most popular song, sung by Patriot soldiers and civilians alike, was a rousing tune called "Chester," which was written by eighteenth-century American composer William Billings, and was said to be the favorite marching song of Washington's army. It too contained an obvious expression of biblical based values and reflected the common American conviction that God's Higher Law superseded the laws of king and Parliament. America's cause, the lyrics boldly stated, was providentially "inspir'd" and would thus prevail against Great Britain's "galling chains."

Let tyrants shake their iron rod,
And slavery clank her galling chains;
We fear them not; we trust in God—
New England's God forever reigns.

When God inspir'd us for the fight,
Their ranks were broke, their lines were forc'd;
Their ships were shatter'd in our sight,
Or swiftly driven from our coast.

What grateful offering shall we bring?
What shall we render to the Lord?
Loud hallelujahs let us sing,
And praise his name on every chord.[38]

In songs, slogans, sermons, and the printed word, the Judeo-Christian foundation of Colonial American culture fueled the American Revolution. "Brothers! We are necessitated to rise, and forced to fight," declared a typical pamphlet of the day. "We think our cause is just; and therefore hope that God will be on our side. We do not take up the hatchet and struggle for honor or conquest; but to maintain our civil constitution and religious privileges; the very same for which our forefathers left their native land and came to this country. . . ." As Americans turned out to bear arms in defense of their liberties, they also turned out in great numbers to pray, motivated by their personal faith, encouraged by their pastors, and called to their knees by their political leaders. Just as the Continental Congress recommended days of public prayer, fasting, and thanksgiving, so did colonial, provincial, and, later, state assemblies.[39]

Typical was the proclamation issued by South Carolina's provincial congress in 1775: in order to defend themselves, it advised, South Carolinians should become "diligently attentive in learning the use of arms," organize themselves into militia companies—and also observe a "day of fasting, humiliation and prayer." The date for the day of prayer was set by the lawmakers. The resolution also recommended that "ministers of the gospel throughout the Colony . . . prepare and deliver suitable discourses upon this solemn occasion. . . . [and that] every member of the present Congress, who may be in town, do meet at the Commons House of Assembly, and proceed from thence in a body, to attend divine service in St. Phillip's Church. . . ."[40]

In 1776, Connecticut's General Assembly officially appealed "to that God who knows the secrets of our hearts," and vowed to resist British "oppression and injustice" with "such means as God in his providence hath put in our power for our necessary defence and protection." The provincial congress of Georgia officially called on Georgia's colonists to defend the "rights and liberties which God and [the English] Constitution gave them." Likewise, the Rhode Island General Assembly declared that "it becomes our highest duty, to use every means which God and nature have furnished us, in support of our invaluable rights and privileges. . . ." Similar sentiments came from county and town assemblies. Assembly delegates in Albemarle County, Virginia, for example, publicly committed "to join with our fellow subjects . . . in executing all those rightful powers which God has given us," and in Westminster, New York, delegates to a county assembly vowed to sacrifice their "lives and fortunes, to the last extremity, if our duty to God and our country requires the same."[41]

When America's legislative leaders called for days of prayer and fasting and days of thanksgiving and prayer, their actions reflected the Judeo-Christian worldview of the American people—and the leadership of America's clergy. As the Revolution swept across the new nation, Patriot clergy supported the call to arms as a biblically permissible act of self-defense. Based on interpretation of Scripture by St. Augustine and the 1646 Westminster Confession of Faith, Patriot clergy overwhelmingly declared the American Revolution to be a "just war"—a concept that America's political leadership well understood. To be a just war, the conflict had to be a defensive war—conducted to defend a people from certain destruction or clear evil. It had to be declared by a lawful authority—such as the Continental Congress—waged for "a just and necessary" cause—in the words of the Westminster Confession of Faith—and with a just goal that would not produce greater evil or disorder than the threat that needed to be eliminated. It should be conducted only when all other means of resolution had failed, and waged with respect and mercy for noncombatants. Finally, a just war ended when peace was obtained. Pennsylvania pastor David Jones expressed the belief of countless clergy and their congregations when he defended the Revolution as a just war. "In some cases," he counselled, "it is the only mode that is left to obtain justice."[42]

The American war effort at times exhibited the brutality that often typified armed warfare, but it was remarkable not for its excesses, but for the lack of them. From the outspoken zeal of America's Presbyterians to the quiet but invaluable contribution of Jewish patriot Haym Salomon, the American Revolution was borne by a nation of people united by biblical values, and influenced by a clergy committed to God-given inalienable rights. That common cultural worldview was shared alike by the religiously devout, the nominal, and the uninterested, and it infused the Revolution with a moral motivation and a sense of restraint that was lacking in other civil wars and revolutions.[43]

The American Revolution stood in stark contrast to the French Revolution, for instance, although both events occurred in the same age and among people of European extraction. Unlike the American Revolution, the French Revolution was marked by recurring savagery, chaos, political anarchy, the wanton bloodshed of the infamous "Reign of Terror"—and a bitter assault on Christianity. In Paris, Notre Dame Cathedral was transformed into an irreverent "Temple of Reason." The French clergy were reviled rather than revered. The calendar was changed to erase its connection to Christ, and blood from countless victims of the guillotine pooled on the pavement of the Place de la Concorde. Ultimately, the French Revolution produced prolonged lawlessness and the rise of authoritarian rule.[44]

No "Reign of Terror" arose during the American Revolution. No guillotine was erected in Philadelphia. No wave of executions swept the newly established United States—and anarchy never ruled. Instead the American Revolution was a revolt against the abuse of law—a defense of the Higher Law of God against the misrule of man. In this, the American Revolution was unique among revolutions over the ages. United and restrained by Judeo-Christian values and discipline, Americans generally believed they were fighting to defend God-given inalienable rights, and—in the words of George Washington—for "the sacred Cause . . . of Liberty."[45]

CHAPTER SIX

"A Signal Stroke of Providence"

O n Christmas night of 1776, George Washington prepared to take the greatest risk of his military career. If
he failed, the American cause might be smothered in defeat, yet
he decisively took the gamble. After suffering repeated defeats
and forced to retreat across New Jersey from New York to Pennsylvania, he now planned to turn and boldly strike the enemy. In
early December, he had encamped his battle-weary troops on the
Pennsylvania side of the Delaware River. Washington had skillfully eluded British forces dispatched by General Howe and commanded by General Charles Cornwallis, who had bragged that
he would trap Washington like a fox. Cornwallis's army was now
encamped a day's march away across the river near Brunswick,
New Jersey—with heavily manned outposts closer to Washington's army, including one not far across the river at Trenton. For
reasons that would never be fully clear, Howe ordered a halt to
the British advance. Even so, the enemy remained close enough
to unleash a deathblow against Washington's bedraggled troops,
who were weary and demoralized. Fearing the British would cross
the Delaware and seize Philadelphia at any moment, scores of

Philadelphians fled the city, and the Continental Congress voted to temporarily reconvene in Baltimore.[1]

Nothing seemed able to stop the British army. American morale had plummeted. The war appeared near an end. Even members of the Congress appeared resigned to defeat. One of the signers of the Declaration of Independence, Delaware's Thomas McKean—among the staunchest of Patriots—confided to a colleague that if nothing stopped the British momentum, "Congress would be obliged to authorize the Commander in Chief to obtain the best terms that could be had from the enemy." As the twentieth-century military historian William M. Dwyer would observe: "In other words, barring a miracle, the Revolution was over."[2]

But the British did not attack. General Howe instead ordered Cornwallis's army into winter quarters with plans to finish off Washington's army in the spring. Washington, meanwhile, decided to do the unexpected—to attack the British. On Christmas night, with the countryside cloaked in deep snow and bone-chilling temperatures, he intended to lead a surprise attack on a garrison of Hessian troops at nearby Trenton. To do so, he faced a daunting challenge. He had to move thousands of soldiers across the ice-clogged Delaware River on a makeshift flotilla of freight boats and ferries; deploy his army in three assault forces amid snow, sleet, hail, and high winds; surprise and defeat a Hessian garrison composed of brutal, hard-fighting mercenaries—then get his army back across the Delaware to safety before British reinforcements in nearby Princeton could counterattack.[3]

It was a risky gamble. Another defeat for his army might sink the American cause. Yet Washington was willing to take the risk—the army and the country appeared to be teetering on the brink of disaster. Something *had* to be done. In a few weeks when the Delaware was frozen over, he believed, Cornwallis's army would empty its camps, march across the river and capture Philadelphia. At the moment, however, the enemy was overconfident,

tired, inattentive, and within striking distance. Washington organized his six thousand–man army into three columns. He would
personally command the main assault force, which consisted of
about 2,400 troops and eighteen pieces of field artillery. On December 23, he ordered the troops be issued three days' cooked rations, and on Christmas afternoon the army left its camps and
began a march through the snow toward the Delaware River.
"[If] we are successful, which Heaven grant," Washington told
his troops, America might soon have a desperately needed victory.[4]

As he planned his daring action against the Hessians at
Trenton, and he looked upon boatloads of his troops rowing
through the Delaware's ice-encumbered current in the darkness, did Washington remember the words he had spoken earlier in the year to the Massachusetts general assembly? On March
28, 1776, he had addressed the legislators as their guest of honor.
The British had just evacuated Boston, and the legislators, like
most Bostonians, were flush with joy. Accompanied by a parade
of Massachusetts dignitaries, Washington had marched in a procession from the legislative chamber to Boston's First Congregational Church, which met in a sprawling, imposing worship
center called the Old Brick Meeting House. There, seated within
the sanctuary's whitewashed walls, Washington listened to a
sermon delivered by the Reverend Andrew Eliot.[5]

A fifty-six-year-old minister and scholar who had twice declined the presidency of Harvard University, Eliot was pastor of
Boston's New North Church. When others fled Boston during
the British occupation, he had chosen to remain in the city and
minister to his flock. He was an unwavering supporter of the
Revolution, but his allegiances were tempered by his faith: when
a mob ransacked the Loyalist governor's home during the height
of prewar tensions, Eliot intervened to rescue the governor's
personal belongings. Through the worst days of the British occupation, he and one other minister had faithfully continued a

traditional Thursday worship service at his church. When the British were gone, Eliot had the honor of preaching to the victorious General Washington.[6]

He took his sermon from the Old Testament book of Isaiah, chapter 33, which dealt with God's preservation of Jerusalem and the Jewish people in the face of powerful enemies. The application was obvious: God would likewise providentially act to preserve America—viewed as the "new Jerusalem" by generations of Colonial Americans. "Look upon Zion, the city of our solemnities," Eliot read to Washington and the assembled dignitaries. "Thine eyes shall see Jerusalem a quiet habitation, a tabernacle that shall not be taken down; not one of the stakes thereof shall ever be removed, neither shall any of the cords thereof be broken. But there the glorious Lord will be unto us a place of broad rivers and streams. . . . For the Lord is our judge, the Lord is our lawgiver, the Lord is our king; he will save us."[7]

When Washington addressed the Massachusetts assembly, his message was the same as Eliot's—God was guiding the American cause. "That the metropolis of your colony is now relieved from the cruel and oppressive invasions of those, who were sent to erect the standard of lawless domination, and to trample on the rights of humanity, and is again open and free for its rightful possessors, must give pleasure to every virtuous and sympathetic heart," Washington said, "and its being effected without the blood of our soldiers and fellow citizens must be ascribed to the interposition of that Providence, which has manifestly appeared in our behalf through the whole of this important struggle, as well as to the measures pursued for bringing about the happy event."[8]

He ended his address with a strong statement of faith—so strong that future historians would wonder if Washington had recruited a clergyman to compose his speech. If so, it echoed his many observations on the intervention of Providence. Regardless, George Washington's disciplined and deliberate nature ensured that any statement made by him or issued in his name carried his approval. His concluding remarks rang with the tone of a benediction:

> *May that Being, who is powerful to save, and in whose hands is the fate of nations, look down with an eye of tender pity and compassion upon the whole of the United Colonies; may He continue to smile upon their counsels and arms, and crown them with success, whilst employed in the cause of virtue and mankind. May this distressed colony and its capital, and every part of this wide extended continent, through His divine favor, be restored to more than their former lustre and once happy state, and have peace, liberty, and safety secured upon a solid, permanent, and lasting foundation.*[9]

Now, in the bitter cold of Christmas night, 1776, Washington looked to his army and "that Being who is powerful to save" to surprise and defeat the Hessian garrison at Trenton. As his troops boarded boats to cross the Delaware, the weather worsened—snow, sleet, hail, and high winds pounded the troops in what one soldier called "a perfect hurricane." To ferry his army across the Delaware, which was filled with jagged chunks of ice, Washington relied on the aid of Philadelphia boatmen and Colonel John Glover's Fourteenth Continental Regiment—"Glover's Mariners"—the same former Massachusetts fishermen who had aided the army's evacuation from Long Island months earlier. Of the three columns, only Washington and his main force made across the Delaware as planned.[10]

To Washington's benefit, the ferocious winter storm that so assailed his army also made the Hessian garrison at Trenton vulnerable to attack. The Hessian commander, Colonel Johann Rall, was a seasoned combat officer, but he failed to post routine scouting patrols because he was certain that the fierce winter storm made an attack impossible—especially by the Americans. Earlier, he expressed his arrogant disdain for American troops—whom he dismissed as "country clowns." When a junior officer proposed digging defensive entrenchments, Rall waved away the suggestion. "Let them come," he boasted. "We want no trenches. We will go at them with the bayonet." On Christmas night, Rall drank himself into a near stupor and had to be carried to his bed. In the morning, he was awakened to shouts of "Der Feind! Der Feind!"—The enemy! The enemy![11]

Washington's attack was a complete surprise. As the Hessians formed their lines in the streets of Trenton, they were cut down by American artillery and infantry fire. Those who attempted to re-form in the fields outside of town were raked by American fire there too—and one who fell mortally wounded was Colonel Rall. After about an hour and a half of fighting, the Hessians surrendered. They had lost 106 dead and wounded and 918 prisoners, compared to six American wounded and no dead. It was an extraordinary victory for Washington—who escaped across the river with his prisoners. In reaction to the British loss at Trenton, General Cornwallis led a nine-thousand-man army against Washington, who recrossed the Delaware and encamped at Trenton on January 2, 1777. That night, Cornwallis advanced his army to within striking distance outside Trenton, leaving a seven-hundred-man rearguard force at nearby Princeton. He was so confident of victory that he decided to delay his attack until daylight. "We've got the old fox safe now," he boasted. "We'll go over and bag him in the morning."[12]

Washington knew his army was no match for Cornwallis's vastly superior numbers—then a brilliant strategy came to him. He ordered several hundred troops to stay behind and keep the army's campfires lit, creating the illusion that his army was still in place. Meanwhile, with orders given in whispers and artillery wheels muffled by rags, Washington led the bulk of his army on a forced nighttime march around Cornwallis's left flank to make a surprise attack on the British rearguard at Princeton. It was another perilous gamble: if caught on the road by Cornwallis, the much smaller Continental army would be even more vulnerable, and the deep winter mud might easily bog down the march. Instead, an unexpected change in the weather aided the Americans. "For the first time in four consecutive days," historian John Ferling would report, "winter miraculously returned. A hard freeze bore down on Trenton, firming up previously squishy roads, and enabling the Americans . . . to proceed with greater dispatch." Equally unexpected: they encountered no British patrols in their rapid march over the frozen roads. Washington got his army in place in time, and on the morning of January 3, 1777, the Americans struck a mighty blow against the rear of Cornwallis's army at Princeton. Within fifteen minutes, the shocked British rearguard was defeated and in retreat. Taken by surprise, Cornwallis tried to turn back his army and overtake the Americans, but he could not. Instead, he withdrew British forces from southern New Jersey and Washington bivouacked his victorious army at Morristown for the rest of the winter.[13]

In what become known as "the Nine-Day Wonder," the ragged, poorly equipped, ill-fed, and outnumbered Continental Army had risen from the dregs of defeat to score an astonishing double victory. The British high command was stunned: how had Washington and his bedraggled soldiers done it? The American cause had been snatched from near destruction, and war-weary Americans everywhere were newly inspired to keep up the fight. "They deeply believed that the battle of Trenton was a Sign of God's redeeming Providence," historian David Hackett Fischer would conclude, "and proof that the Continental Army was His instrument."[14]

Civilians and soldiers alike praised Washington for the crucial victories—and so did Congress—but Washington knew grim challenges lay ahead, and as usual, he attributed the victories to Almighty God. "Providence has heretofore saved us in a remarkable manner," he wrote a relative after Princeton, "and on this we must principally rely." His private observation echoed a statement he had publicly issued to the army earlier. "The Commander in Chief is confident [that] the Army under his immediate direction, will shew their Gratitude to providence, for thus favouring the Cause of Freedom and America, and by their thankfulness to God, their zeal and perseverance in this righteous Cause, continue to deserve his future blessings." [15]

Washington may have had an even keener appreciation for the "interposition of Providence" due to another narrow escape, which he experienced at the battle of Trenton. At one point in the fighting, he rallied a brigade of retreating militia and led them toward the enemy. Thirty yards from the British line, he ordered them to halt and fire. Obediently, the troops discharged their volley, then braced for the expected return fire from the British. Mounted on horseback, Washington towered above the American battle line only yards from the enemy—an easy, irresistible target. In a roar of flame and smoke, the British unleashed a deadly volley into the American line. Certain his commander would be hit, one of Washington's staff officers covered his eyes, unwilling to watch Washington fall. When the thick white smoke cleared, however, Washington was still in the saddle, unhurt. "Thank God, your excellency is safe," the officer cried aloud, as the British fell back. Then he wept in relief. [16]

By midsummer of 1777, the glow of triumph from the victories at Trenton and Princeton was fading into the dark gloom of looming defeat. General Howe launched a major British offensive that summer. It was designed to deliver a deathblow to the Revolution by isolating New England from the rest of America and simultaneously capturing Philadelphia—the seat of the Continental Congress and the unofficial capital of the fledgling United States. In June, General John Burgoyne led an eight-thousand-man British army southward from Canada into New York's Hudson River

Valley. A politician, gambler, and amateur actor, "Gentleman Johnny" Burgoyne was a competent officer, capable of military brilliance, but also known as "vain, boastful, and superficial, and not a man to depend upon in a tight corner." Burgoyne's offensive began with immediate success. His army quickly drove the American garrison out of Fort Ticonderoga on the border of New York and Vermont, and recaptured the famous fort for the British. Then he continued to aggressively advance southward, heading toward Albany.[17]

General Howe, meanwhile, left New York by sea with an army of fifteen thousand troops and sailed to the Head of Elk on the upper reaches of Chesapeake Bay, landing only fifty miles southwest of Philadelphia. On September 11, 1777, Washington's outnumbered eleven-thousand-man army attempted to halt the British advance southwest of Philadelphia at the battle of Brandywine. The Americans fought hard but General Howe skillfully outmaneuvered Washington, and his army was defeated with more than double the British casualties. Unchecked, the British army moved on Philadelphia, spurring a flood of refugees to flee the capital. The Continental Congress left the Pennsylvania State House—"Independence Hall"—and retreated to Lancaster, then reconvened in York. On September 26, 1777, General Howe's British army marched unopposed into Philadelphia and occupied the city.[18]

A week later, on October 4, in an attempt to retake Philadelphia, Washington launched an attack against the British encampment at nearby Germantown. The attack took the British by surprise, but Washington's complicated battle strategy did not work as he planned, and a dense fog hampered coordination of American forces. The attack failed, Washington's troops again suffered twice as many casualties as their opponents, and the capital remained in British hands. Washington moved his depleted army away from Philadelphia to Whitemarsh and later to Gulph Mills, trying to encamp close enough to the occupied capital to threaten the British without being vulnerable to a surprise attack.[19]

Meanwhile, news of Philadelphia's capture and Washington's defeats at Brandywine and Germantown was carried to Europe. There, knowledgeable military observers concluded that the American cause was lost and that the British would soon put an end to the American Revolution. Instead, Washington's apparent catastrophe unexpectedly aided the American cause. Already, the French government of King Louis XVI was secretly supplying America with desperately needed gunpowder for the war. Now, upon hearing the news of Washington's defeat at Germantown, the French king and his advisors decided that supporting the American war effort against France's age-old enemy was worth the risk. Rather than giving up on the Revolution, Louis XVI concluded that Washington's willingness to attack the British at Germantown so soon after losing at Brandywine was a powerful indicator that America would not be easily defeated. Nothing officially happened immediately, but the news of Germantown—an American defeat—moved French thinking toward the French-American alliance that would prove critical to eventual American victory.[20]

Washington could not know of the increase in pro-American support that his defeat at Germantown had spurred in France; he saw Germantown as another disappointment. Then, he was struck by a new blow on October 15, 1777—one that was accompanied by painful personal disappointment. At his headquarters that day, he received a message from someone he admired, delivered by someone he respected, but bearing information that was both shocking and offensive. It was a lengthy message—fourteen pages—and was discreetly wrapped and sealed. The messenger—who surely had provoked soldiers' stares while being escorted through the picket lines and into the army camp—was an attractive, well-groomed forty-year-old woman. Her name was Elizabeth Graeme Fergusson.[21]

She was a prominent Philadelphia socialite, daughter of an affluent physician, and granddaughter of a former Pennsylvania governor, a woman admired for her piety, charm, and intellect. A poet and writer who had composed a poetic paraphrase of the book of Psalms at age twenty-nine, she was viewed by some as "the most learned woman in America." She lived on a plush country estate outside Philadelphia, had once been engaged to Benjamin Franklin's son, and had personally known and entertained numerous leaders of the Revolution. Now, however, she was married to one of the leading Loyalists in British-occupied Philadelphia—and the message she bore to army headquarters urged General Washington to commit treason.[22]

Washington was stunned by the letter's content, but even more by the identity of its author—the Reverend Jacob Duché. The Continental Congress's first chaplain, Pastor Duché was the Anglican minister whose prayer and Scripture reading had so inspired the First Continental Congress back in 1774. Washington had been present that day, and he no doubt believed the long-ago events were indeed providential, as John Adams had written his wife at the time. Duché's letter apparently did nothing to change his view about the "interposition of providence" at the opening of Congress, but Washington was deeply offended by Pastor Duché's change of heart—and by his message.[23]

In his letter, Duché advised Washington as commander-in-chief to denounce the Declaration of Independence and demand that Congress yield to Great Britain. With "prudence and delicacy," Duché urged Washington, "represent to Congress the indispensable necessity of rescinding the hasty and ill-advised declaration of Independency." If the Continental Congress should reject such an appeal, Duché asserted, "you have an infallible recourse still left; negotiate for your country at the head of your Army." The war could end, Duché wrote, if only Washington would lead the way back to submission to the King and Parliament. "It is to you, and you alone, your bleeding country looks and calls aloud," he pled.[24]

Soon after Howe's army captured Philadelphia, Pastor Duché had found British troops waiting for him at the end of a Sunday morning worship service. He was arrested and jailed for possible treason against the Crown. His Loyalist friends, overjoyed at the occupation of Philadelphia by British forces, urged Duché to recant his support of independence. Under such pressure, Duché suffered a failure of will and agreed to recant. His thinking also may have been affected by a bout of depression and a brain disorder that later manifested itself.[25]

Unquestionably elated to acquire such a prominent turncoat, British authorities granted Duché his freedom. Somehow he became convinced that he could end the bloodshed between America and Britain with a persuasive letter to his old acquaintance General Washington. To get his plea to Washington, Duché had enlisted the aid of Elizabeth Fergusson's Loyalist husband. He, in turn, apparently recruited his wife as an influential courier. The plot, however, did not achieve the effect on George Washington that Duché's Loyalist friends desired. Elizabeth Fergusson would later recall that, after reading Duché's letter while she quietly waited, Washington paced, grim-faced and silent. Finally, he spoke.[26]

Politely but firmly, he reprimanded her and dismissed her with no formal reply to the chaplain. "I should have returned [the letter] unopened," he told her to tell Duché, "if I had had any idea of the contents. . . ." That done, he forwarded the clergyman's letter to Congress with only a terse reference to the distraught man's "ridiculous, illiberal performance." Duché would later regret his actions and would seek Washington's forgiveness, but at the time his defection and call for Washington to give up were shocking. Washington faced a superior enemy who had captured the national capital. His ragged army was defeated and exhausted. The American cause was again in grave jeopardy, and now the Continental Congress's first chaplain was urging him to commit treason.[27]

Instead of languishing in doubt and worry, however, Washington went about his duties with the appearance of a leader who was serenely confident amid the looming peril. It was an extraordinary character trait that marked Washington's behavior throughout the Revolution. Surely he experienced moments of deep despair and frustration, but the behavior that defined his conduct throughout the worst of war was his resolute confidence that the American cause would eventually prevail. Continuously, in his writings, he restated his belief that "the Almighty ruler of the Universe" would intervene "to defend the Cause of the United American States" through what Washington called "the signal Instances of providential Goodness."[28]

Two days after he received Duché's distasteful letter, an unlikely and distant event occurred that again resuscitated the American cause from near destruction. Far to the north near Albany, New York—at a place called Saratoga—General Burgoyne was forced to surrender his much-heralded British army to American forces commanded by one of Washington's subordinates, General Horatio Gates. It was an unexpected and extraordinary victory for the Americans—the first time an entire British army had been surrendered to the ragtag Americans. It was a stunning contrast to the decisive victory that Burgoyne and Howe had expected the British northern invasion to produce. In the words of twentieth-century British historian Sir John Fortescue: "a great blow had been dealt at the reputation of England . . ." Repeatedly, high-ranking British officers and officials asked themselves how it could have happened.[29]

After their initial success at Fort Ticonderoga, Burgoyne's Redcoats had plunged into the wilds of the upper Hudson River Valley, heading toward Albany—and had been swallowed up by the great northern forest. The American wilderness proved to be a far more formidable foe than "Gentleman Johnny" had anticipated. As Burgoyne's army struggled and straggled through the dark forests and dense thickets, it was constantly hounded by ragged but hard-fighting American troops under General Philip Schuyler. The Americans hobbled the enemy advance by felling trees across the line of march, destroying bridges, and piling barriers of boulders on the trail. Repeatedly, they attacked Indian-style from the cover of the forest, and steadily whittled down British numbers. The original British strategy called for General Howe to lead a larger army up the Hudson River from New York City to join Burgoyne's forces. With Howe preoccupied and comfortable in Philadelphia, this did not happen.[30]

Isolated, exhausted, and hungry, Gentleman Johnny's British troops were left in the northern wilds, isolated by an inadequate supply line from Canada, and aggressively pressed by American forces under General Gates, who had been sent by Congress to oppose Burgoyne's army. A former British army officer, Gates was viewed by some contemporaries as an argumentative "snob of the first order," but he was a capable and motivated officer. Assisted by three of Washington's most trusted commanders—General Benjamin Lincoln, General Benedict Arnold, and Colonel Daniel Morgan—and aided by Burgoyne's blunders, Gates scored an astonishing surprise victory over Burgoyne's invading British army.[31]

On August 16, 1777, Burgoyne's force had been seriously weakened when part of it was defeated and captured by an American militia force under Colonel John Stark at the battle of Bennington. On September 19, at the battle of Freeman's Farm, or First Saratoga, Burgoyne won a tactical victory but suffered severe casualties. Then, on October 7, 1777, Gates's forces again engaged Burgoyne's hard-pressed army at Bemis Heights, also known as the Second Battle of Saratoga. Burgoyne set a trap for the American army by training his artillery, European-style, on an open field over which he expected the Americans to advance.

On Daniel Morgan's advice, however, Gates instead launched simultaneous infantry assaults on the British flanks, American-style, through the forest. Despite a fierce defense, the British were again defeated, suffering four times as many casualties as the Americans.[32]

General Howe tardily dispatched a British relief force up the Hudson to reinforce Burgoyne, but it came too late. Reduced to half strength and trapped, Burgoyne's depleted army was forced to surrender at Saratoga on October 17, 1777. To the British, the unimaginable had occurred: they had lost an entire army in the American wilderness. It was the worst British defeat of the Revolution to date—surpassing Trenton and Princeton—and was a stunning humiliation for Great Britain. It was also an unexpected morale raiser for Washington, his army, and the American people. The unlikely victory also encouraged Louis XVI to formally establish the French-American alliance, and thus hastened French support for America.[33]

The rescue of the American cause from seemingly inescapable disaster was nothing short of "amazing," Washington's foremost biographer, Douglas Southall Freeman would conclude. "Then," he would write of Saratoga, "came another of those strange revivals of good fortune that would have justified any army Chaplain in taking as his text the assurance of the Psalmist: 'I will say of the Lord, He is my refuge and my fortress; My God; in him will I trust, surely he shall deliver thee from the snare of the fowler'. . . ." Army chaplains were not the only ones who believed the victory at Saratoga was a gift from God. "This action," exulted a writer in the *Connecticut Courant*, "which resounds so much to the glory of the Great Lord of the heavens, and God of armies, affords the Americans a lasting monument of the Divine power and goodness, and a most powerful argument of love to and trust in God."[34]

George Washington agreed. From his headquarters on October 18, 1777, he issued general orders announcing the surrender of Burgoyne's army at Saratoga. He ordered a thirteen-gun artillery salute followed by a small arms salute by every brigade of his army—but only after the troops were assembled to hear thanksgiving sermons from the army's chaplains. "The Chaplains of the army," he ordered, "are to prepare short discourses, suitable to the joyful occasion to deliver to their several corps and brigades." As was his habit, Washington officially gave God the credit for the victory. "Let every face brighten," he stated, "and every heart expand with grateful Joy and praise to the supreme disposer of all events, who has granted us this signal success." In a private letter to his brother John that same day, Washington described the British surrender as a "Signal Stroke of Providence." He would soon need to remember the "grateful Joy and praise" of the moment—and his trust in "the supreme disposer of all events." Ahead lay another grim and deadly ordeal at a place called Valley Forge.[35]

CHAPTER SEVEN

"By the Hand of Providence"

N o meat! No meat!" The solemn chant drifted through the night like campfire smoke, rolling over the rows of ragged tents that composed the American army's new winter camp. It was a mournful chorus, sounded by thousands of hungry soldiers. One of the army surgeons compared it to the haunting call of a lonely crow. "No meat! No meat!" In the crisp December air, it could be heard clearly in George Washington's headquarters—ringing through the night as an unnerving echo that reminded the general his army was near starvation.[1]

It had been difficult to find a site for winter quarters. After a prolonged search, Washington had chosen a location on Pennsylvania's Schuylkill River—a hilly, forested vale called Valley Forge. It was so named for an old ironworks on the site, and while far from perfect, it offered a reliable water supply, ample woodlands for firewood and building materials for winter huts, and high ground for a natural defensive position. Located twenty miles from Philadelphia, it allowed Washington to pose a continued threat to the British army there while positioning his army between the enemy and the American Congress now meeting at York. Washington's tattered, battle-weary army reached the campsite on December 19, 1777—one day after a nationwide day of "Solemn Thanksgiving and Praise" declared by Congress in recognition of the recent victory at Saratoga.[2]

"Forasmuch as it is the indispensable duty of all men, to adore the superintending providence of Almighty God," the Congress had declared, "to acknowledge with gratitude their obligations to him for benefits received, and to implore such further blessings as they stand in need of; and it having pleased him in his abundant mercy . . . to smile upon us in the prosecution of a just and necessary war, for the defense of our unalienable rights and liberties. . . . It is therefore recommended by Congress . . . that at one time, and with one voice, the good people may express the grateful feelings of their hearts and consecrate themselves to the service of their divine benefactor. . . ." Accordingly, General Washington had ordered the army's chaplains to lead thanksgiving observances among the troops.[3]

By now, however, grim hardship had smothered the glow of the American victory at Saratoga within the ranks of Washington's army. The army's quartermaster and commissary corps had fallen apart, leaving the troops in rags and without adequate rations—sometimes with no food for days at a time. Even the time-honored, soldierly practice of foraging—obtaining food from civilians—was fruitless: British troops had ravaged the countryside during their march to Philadelphia, and what little they missed had been scrounged by the hordes of civilian refugees who had fled the capital. "This is Thanksgiving Day through the whole continent of America," an American officer penned in his diary on December 18, referring to the Congressional observance, "but God knows we have very little to keep it with, this being the Third day we have been without flour or bread, and are living . . . in huts and tents, laying on the Cold Ground. Upon the whole I think all we have to be thankful for is that we are alive and not in the grave with all our friends."[4]

Washington knew better than anyone how easily and how often his army could have been destroyed by superior British forces. Being "alive and not in the grave" was, in fact, a serious cause for thanksgiving. As his army had trudged toward Valley Forge on empty bellies, he had praised their service and sacrifices, while also trying to encourage gratitude to God within the ranks. "The Commander in Chief with the highest satisfaction expresses his thanks to the officers and soldiers for the fortitude and patience with which they have sustained the fatigues of the Campaign," he wrote in a general order to the army. "Altho' in some instances we unfortunately failed, yet upon the whole Heaven hath smiled on our Arms and crowned them with signal success; and . . . by a spirited continuance of the measures necessary for our defense we shall finally obtain the end of our War for Independence, Liberty and Peace." He concluded by reminding the army that they were fighting for what he called a "sacred cause," and promised that he would "share in the hardship, and partake of every inconvenience."[5]

As winter weather befell Valley Forge, the "hardship" increased far beyond mere "inconvenience"—conditions became desperate and deadly. Officers hurried the troops to fell trees and build huts for shelter before their threadbare, field-worn uniforms fell off their bodies and left them unfit for outside duty. The winter of 1777–78 was not unusually harsh at Valley Forge, but every snowfall brought misery to thousands of soldiers who were shoeless and uniformed in rags or nothing at all. Worse than the occasional snow were the winter storms that dumped freezing rain on the miserable, half-starved ranks, turned the camp's mud streets hard with ice, and sent biting winds whipping through the city of log huts.[6]

"I have upwards of seventy men unfit for duty, only for want of the articles of clothing," one officer wrote, "twenty of which have no breeches at all, so that they are obliged to take their blankets to cover their nakedness, and as many without a single shirt, stocking or shoe; about thirty fit for duty; the rest sick or lame, and God knows it won't be long before they will be all laid up, as the poor fellows are obliged to fetch wood and water on their backs, half a mile with bare legs in snow or mud." The army's officers suppressed the cries of "No meat!" as they arose in the camp, fearful they would encourage desertion, but the lack of rations left many soldiers unable to concentrate on anything but their empty bellies.[7]

"The human mind is always poring upon the gloomy side of Fortune, and while it inhabits this lump of Clay, will always be in an uneasy and fluctuating State . . . ," army surgeon Albigence Waldo penned in his diary. "It is not in the power of Philosophy however, to convince a man he may be happy and Contented if he will, with a *Hungry Belly*. Give me Food, Cloaths, Wife & Children, kind Heaven!" By February, more than half of Washington's ten-thousand-man army had fallen ill. Weakened by hunger and exposure, 2,500 died. "I do assure you that there is at least 400 men in the Brigade which I belong to that have not a shoe nor a stocking to put on and more than that number have not half a shirt apiece," a Massachusetts officer wrote. "I have seen the soldiers turned out to do their duty in such poor condition that notwithstanding all the hard heartedness I am naturally possessed of, I could not refrain from tears. It would melt the heart of a savage to see the state we are in."[8]

In British-occupied Philadelphia, meanwhile, conditions were starkly different. "You can have no idea of the life of continued amusement I live in," a young Loyalist woman wrote a refugee friend. "I can scarce have a moment to myself. I am . . . most elegantly . . . dressed for a ball this evening at Smith's where we have one every Thursday. I wish to Heaven you were going with us this evening to judge for yourself." Amply fed and billeted, off-duty British soldiers loitered in the city's taverns or spent their time gambling. Their officers attended parties, concerts, theatricals, and balls, unworried about an attack by the American army, which was rumored to be disintegrating in its winter camp. The only starvation in Philadelphia was among American prisoners of war, who were reportedly so poorly fed by their British captors that they were seen pulling up grass to eat its roots.[9]

At Valley Forge, Washington's soldiers were almost as desperate. At one point, the troops went an entire week without food, and finally reported their desperation to army commanders "in as respectful terms as if they had been humble petitioners for special favors." Washington beseeched Congress for aid. "I am now convinced," he wrote, "that, unless some great and capital change suddenly takes place . . . this Army must inevitably be reduced to one or other of these three things. Starve, dissolve or disperse. . . ." Congress took him seriously and acted promptly, calling on state governments to rush food and supplies to Valley Forge. The question was whether help would come quickly enough.[10]

By the end of February, illness and exposure had put more of Washington's soldiers in the ground than had all the battles since he had taken command. Among the survivors, about one thousand soldiers had deserted, several hundred officers had resigned, and most of the army was too unhealthy or unequipped to fight. At any moment, Washington feared, the great bulk of troops might quit and go home. "According to the saying of Solomon, 'hunger will break through a stone wall,'" one of his commanders advised him. "Three days successively we have been destitute of bread. Two days we have been entirely without meat. The men must be supplied or they cannot be commanded."[11]

While Washington's army languished in smoky huts at Valley Forge, support for the American cause appeared to be ebbing throughout the land. Continental currency—the paper money issued by Congress and the states—proved almost worthless, provoking inflation and discontent among the public. Despite the surprise Continental victory at Saratoga, British armies occupied America's two largest cities, New York and Philadelphia, while the powerful British navy patrolled its coast. Congress had been forced to move from one site to another, and the delegates were still meeting in exile at York, Pennsylvania. The king and Parliament seemed as strong and determined as ever. To many, American victory was a dimming dream, and some leaders feared growing numbers of Americans were losing heart. "The Love of country & public virtue are annihilated," bemoaned one congressman to a friend.[12]

Amid such concerns and the desperate conditions at Valley Forge, Washington learned that some members of the Continental Congress were plotting to remove him as commander-in-chief. The leaders of the cabal reportedly wanted to give Washington's command to General Horatio Gates, the victor of Saratoga, who may have encouraged the scheme with support from a troublesome brigadier general named Thomas Conway. Washington reacted by exposing the secret plan to the full Congress, while leaving his defense to others. His principal commanders closed ranks to publicly support him, and so did the majority of Congress. "All Men acknowledge General Washington's virtue, his personal Bravery, nor do I ever hear his Military abilities questioned," declared Henry Laurens, the president of Congress. Chastened by such overwhelming support for Washington—and by the general's decisive, forthright response—his Congressional critics abandoned their conspiracy to remove him.[13]

For George Washington, the winter at Valley Forge would prove to be the darkest season of the war. "Previously, at every twist of the revolutionary struggle, some essential of successful war had not been available," a leading nineteenth-century historian would conclude, "now at Valley Forge *everything* was lacking." Yet despite the dangers, political intrigue, suffering, and discouragement that befell Washington and his army that season, he prevailed—and he consistently exuded confidence to all around him. He was certain, he stated, that "the officers

and soldiers, with one heart, and one mind, will resolve to sur-
mount every difficulty with a fortitude and a patience, becoming
their profession, and the sacred cause to which we are engaged."
Throughout the prolonged anguish of Valley Forge, he publicly
projected steadfast confidence in the ultimate outcome of that
"sacred cause." [14]

"I could not keep my eyes from that imposing countenance,"
wrote a volunteer French officer of his first meeting with Washington. The general's face, he wrote, was "grave, yet not severe,
affable, without familiarity. Its predominant expression was calm
dignity, through which you could trace the strong feelings of the
patriot, and discern the father, as well as the commander of the
soldiers." Washington's troops shared the foreign officer's admiration: they were devoted to him, and despite the deadly conditions at Valley Forge that winter, surprisingly few deserted.
"I never knew him to utter a Wish or drop an expression," one
would recall, "that did not tend to the good of his Country regardless of his own Interest." The willingness of "those dear,
ragged Continentals" to suffer for Washington and the "sacred
cause," predicted one officer, "will be the admiration of future
ages." Washington's conduct at Valley Forge inspired the army,
the Congress, and, eventually, the country. But what inspired
Washington? What motivated him to persevere—to take the actions that inspired and preserved his troops in the desperation of
Valley Forge? [15]

Throughout the war, Washington the low-church Anglican remained steadfastly confident that the fate of the American
people ultimately rested with what he called "the omnipotence of
that God who is alone able to protect them." He had accepted his
command believing that "the hand of Providence" had preserved
him for "such a time as this." The war had apparently matured
his faith, leading him to rely, as he said, on "the Lord, and Giver
of Victory, to prosper our arms." Biographer Douglas Southall
Freeman, who was as reserved in his comments about Washing-

ton's faith as was Washington himself, would later conclude that prior to the war, Washington "had believed that a God directed his path, but he had not been particularly ardent in his faith. The war convinced him that a Providence intended to save America from ruin." [16]

As his adopted step-granddaughter Nelly Custis would later observe, Washington was "not one of those, who act or pray that they may be seen of men." Washington was careful and deliberate about expressing his faith, and those characteristics, as well as his faith, were consistently demonstrated at Valley Forge. Just as he had called on his troops to display "a true Christian spirit" in times past, he did so again amid the demoralizing hardships of the winter encampment. He kept order in the army by insisting on—as one officer put it—"the exertions of virtuous principles." He ordered the army's chaplains to conduct worship services for the troops regularly "every Sunday at 11 o'clock," and his orders pointedly noted, "It is expected that Officers of all Ranks will by their attendance set an Example to their men." [17]

To keep order in the ranks during the Valley Forge winter, he also exercised the Bible-based discipline he had followed all of his life. While British soldiers in Philadelphia whiled away the winter hours with high-stakes gambling that sometimes provoked animosity within the ranks, Washington's troops were forbidden to gamble away their time, money, and mutual respect. "The Commander in Chief is informed that gaming is again creeping into the Army," noted an order from Washington at Valley Forge; "he therefore in the most solemn terms declares that this Vice in either Officer or Soldier shall not when detected escape exemplary punishment. . . ." Troops were also required to keep a clean camp, preserve an uncontaminated water supply, and maintain all weapons in good firing order. Theft was swiftly punished, and so were officers who abused the troops. [18]

Likewise, Washington issued strict orders to the procurement details that were ordered to round up rations and supplies: they were not to abuse or alienate the common people. "Whatsoever ye would that men should do to you, do ye even so to them," commanded Scripture, and Washington followed that principle, insisting that civilians be treated respectfully and fairly as the army sought supplies from them. Even Loyalists were spared. "He forbade any of the Military, upon severe penalties, from plundering or appropriating the Effects of what are called Tories," noted one of Washington's staff officers, "giving as a Reason, that they had nothing to do in the matter." It was a policy that served him well, reinforcing the loyalty of the common people when the fortunes of war appeared to favor the king's forces, and sometimes softening the resistance of American Loyalists. In contrast, British troops in occupied regions often treated common Americans with arrogance, contempt, and brutality, losing favor and kindling opposition almost everywhere.[19]

As always, Washington put his troops first. He repeatedly beseeched Congress for rations and supplies, but while awaiting aid, he also acted decisively to save his army. He dispatched procurement parties to scour the countryside for food and clothing, while directing a major reorganization of the army's quartermaster and commissary departments. He appointed General Nathanael Greene of Rhode Island, one of his most capable field commanders, to the post of quartermaster general. Greene attacked the army's supply problems as if he were battling the British. Soon, army details were searching for rations, clothing, and footwear as far away as Maryland and Virginia. Herds of cattle were driven in from New Jersey. Boots and saddles were located in Boston. Five thousand muskets were discovered in storage in Albany. Just when the army seemed on the verge of destruction, it was again rescued.[20]

"Today [General Washington] acquainted the Troops . . . that Rations should be raised monthly," surgeon Waldo happily wrote in his journal in early 1778, "that the . . . Troops may be Supply'd with a greater quantity of Provision than they have been of late; and that a Month's Wages extraordinary shall be given to every Officer & Soldier who shall live in Hutts this Winter. Good encouragement this, and we think ourselves deserving of it, for the hunger, Thirst, Cold & fatigue we have suffer'd this Campaign. . . ." Observed General Greene: "God grant that we may never be brought to such a wretched condition again." To avoid a repetition of that "wretched condition," Washington ordered his troops to seriously observe a national day of prayer and fasting called for by Congress in April of 1778 "that it may please Almighty God, to guard us and defend us" in the future. "The General directs that this day *also* shall be religiously observed in the army," he proclaimed, "that no work be done thereon and that the Chaplains prepare discourses suitable to the Occasion."[21]

While guarding and guiding his soldiers with fatherly discipline, Washington also praised them with fatherly appreciation. "It . . . may be said," he wrote at the time of Valley Forge, "that no history now extant can furnish an instance of an army's suffering such hardships as ours has done, bearing them with the same patience and fortitude. To see men without clothes to cover their nakedness, without blankets to lie on, without shoes, (for the want of which their marches might be traced by the blood from their feet,) and almost as often without provisions as with them; marching through frost and snow, and . . . submitting without a murmur, is a proof of patience and obedience which, in my opinion, can scarce be paralleled."[22]

As always, Washington encouraged the army's chaplains to actively minister to his men. Chaplain Israel Evans, a thirty-year-old minister serving a brigade of New Hampshire troops, had preached a Thanksgiving Day sermon back in December that was based on a text from Psalm 115: "Not unto us, O Lord, not unto us, but unto thy name give glory. . . ." Evans was a rugged, soldierlike man of the Word whose faith was as bold as his behavior. A combat veteran with unflinching self-control in the face of fire, he was once sprayed with dirt by an incoming artillery round while standing near General Washington. Calmly, he took off his dirt-covered hat and examined it carefully. "Mr. Evans," Washington joked, "you had better take that home and show it to your wife and children." Evans laughed, and put the dirt-covered hat back on his head.[23]

Chaplain Evans's Thanksgiving Day sermon had been so well received by the New Hampshire troops that it was later printed and distributed to the entire army at Valley Forge. In it, Evans noted how God appeared to have repeatedly intervened in the war on behalf of the American cause. "For these and innumerable instances of public mercy," he told the troops, "we desire most heartily to praise God, and say, 'Not unto us, O Lord, not unto the wisdom of our counselors. . . . Not unto our commanders and armies, though they have behaved themselves so valiantly, and conducted wisely—yet give glory not unto them but unto the name of God, for He it was who taught our Senators wisdom; and girded our soldiers with courage and strength." Evans called on the army to remember that it was "the Lord our God who has fought for us in every successful battle, and has hitherto supported our righteous cause against those who hate us without any just reason."[24]

It was a sermon certain to appeal to Washington's frequently stated belief that God was guiding and guarding America. It also lauded Washington as "a true patriot and most excellent hero"—and a man of faith. "Oh, Americans," Evans declared, "give glory to God for such a faithful hero." Washington read a copy of the sermon, and put aside the duties of command at Valley Forge long enough to write to the chaplain, endorsing the sermon's call to give God the glory for every American success. "I admire, and feel the force of the reasoning which you have displayed through the whole," Washington wrote, "and . . . it will ever be the first wish of my heart to aid your pious endeavors to inculcate a due sense of the dependence we ought to place in that wise and powerful Being on whom alone our success depends. . . ."[25]

Evans was not alone in proclaiming Washington "a faithful hero." Pennsylvania pastor Henry Melchior Muhlenberg, a founder of the Lutheran Church in America, lived near Valley Forge at the time of Washington's winter encampment. He was the father of Brigadier General John Peter Muhlenberg, who now commanded a brigade in Washington's army. "I heard a fine example today," the senior Muhlenberg wrote in his journal in April of 1778, "namely, that His Excellency General Washington rode around among his army yesterday and admonished each and every one to fear God, to put away the wickedness that has set in and become so general, and to practice Christian virtues." Such a public demonstration was rare for Washington, but at critical moments in his life he deliberately set a public example.[26]

Did the pastor receive the report from his brigadier son, who was in a position to witness Washington's actions, or was it merely a camp story? Muhlenberg did not cite a source for the account, but he obviously believed it. "From all appearances," he wrote, "General Washington does not belong to the so-called world of society, for he respects God's Word, believes in the atonement through Christ, and bears himself in humility and gentleness. Therefore, the Lord God has also singularly, yea, marvelously preserved him from harm in the midst of countless perils, ambuscades, fatigues, etc. and has hitherto graciously held him in his hand as a chosen vessel."[27]

Isaac Potts, a young Quaker miller who lived near Valley Forge, reportedly discovered Washington praying alone in the woods near army headquarters. Escaping the bustle of army headquarters for a quiet moment in a secluded glade would not have been an odd action for Washington, a woodsman and former wilderness surveyor, but historians have been unable to document the story from primary sources. It first appeared in an 1800 biography of Washington by Mason Locke Weems. An Anglican minister-turned-bookseller, Weems was shamelessly prone to embellishment and literary invention, which made his work unreliable and cast doubts on the account. The Potts family defended the account as authentic, however, and the description of Washington at prayer—"the commander-in-chief of the armies of the United Colonies on his knees in the act of devotion"—would become an enduring American image, memorialized on monuments and depicted on American postage stamps.[28]

An undeniably reliable record of Washington's faith at Valley Forge would be preserved by words he gave his troops. "While we are zealously performing the duties of good Citizens and soldiers, we certainly ought not to be inattentive to the higher duties of Religion," he stated in a general order in the spring of 1778. "To the distinguished Character of Patriot, it should be our highest Glory to add the more distinguished Character of Christian." Fresh from the hard lessons of Valley Forge, Washington apparently felt compelled to urge his troops to conduct themselves not only as Patriots, but also as men of faith. Always disciplined and deliberate, he would not have issued such a public order had he not purposely intended to make a statement of faith. Again he expressed his conviction that God was guiding and protecting the American cause. "The signal instances of providential Goodness which we have experienced and which have now almost crowned our labours with complete Success," he wrote, "demand from us in a peculiar manner the warmest returns of Gratitude and Piety to the Supreme Author of all good."[29]

By the time he urged his troops to attend to "the higher duties of Religion"—in May of 1778—Washington had seen the desperation of Valley Forge transformed into renewed hope. Looking back at the misery and desperation of winter camp, he believed he saw the sovereignty of God at work. "The determinations of Providence are always wise," he wrote a friend from Valley Forge, "often inscrutable, and though its decrees appear to bear hard upon us at times is nevertheless meant for gracious purposes. . . ." His observation paraphrased a verse from the New Testament: "And we know that all things work together for good to them that love God, to them who are the called according to his purpose." At Valley Forge, Washington believed he saw biblical-style grace providentially befall his army with dramatic results.[30]

Although the "determinations of Providence" did indeed "bear hard" at Valley Forge, Washington's army actually emerged from the ordeal vastly improved as a fighting force. The earlier failure of the army's quartermaster and commissary systems had forced Washington to reorganize both, with dramatic improvements. Instead of destroying morale, sharing the desperate conditions of winter actually built unity within the ranks, and Washington's inspired leadership raised morale. Equally important, a plan by Washington to train his troops with a simplified manual of arms was implemented at Valley Forge with astonishing success—due in large part to the skills of a Prussian freedom fighter, the Baron Von Steuben. A professional drillmaster who had volunteered his services to the American cause, Von Steuben was put to work drilling troops at Valley Forge, and the army was soon transformed. Von Steuben drilled away its amateurish habits and replaced them with a military discipline that matched that of the British.[31]

Thus, instead of dealing death to Washington's army, the ordeal at Valley Forge gave it new birth. In the spring of 1778, a resurgent American army marched out of winter camp, superbly drilled and professionally prepared, determined to face the cream of the British army. "General Washington's Army . . . is amazingly advanced in discipline," reported Henry Laurens, the president of the Continental Congress. The troops exuded a renewed esprit de corps, and appeared confident that they could do battle with General Howe's troops—and win. "If Mr. Howe opens his campaign with his usual deliberation . . . ," predicted an American officer, "we shall be infinitely better prepared to meet them than ever we have been." Washington considered the transformation to be nothing short of a miracle. "The Hand of providence has been so conspicuous in all this," Washington declared in the spring of 1778, "that he must be worse than an infidel that lacks faith, and more than wicked, that has not gratitude enough to acknowledge his obligations."[32]

The spring of 1778 also brought dramatic news that heartened American Patriots everywhere, and altered the course of the war. For more than a year, the French government had been secretly supplying American forces with military arms and equipment to battle France's longtime enemy. The Continental Congress had sent emissaries to encourage France to openly recognize the fledgling United States and openly join the war against Britain, but advisors to Louis XVI, the young French king, had counseled restraint until American forces proved themselves. After reports of the victory at Saratoga and Washington's strong showing at the battle of Germantown, Louis XVI's court was convinced that the Americans would not give up easily—even though their national capital had been lost to the enemy. At year's end in 1777, France announced its recognition of the new nation and its intention to enter into an alliance with the United States.[33]

The alliance was ratified by the Continental Congress in May, and France officially joined the war as an American ally. Throughout the nation, Americans rejoiced at the news—including George Washington. From army headquarters, he issued a general order calling for a day of thanksgiving to God:

> It having pleased the Almighty ruler of the Universe propitiously to defend the Cause of the United American States and finally by raising us up a powerful Friend among the Princes of the Earth to establish our liberty and Independency upon a lasting foundation; it becomes us to set apart a day for gratefully acknowledging the divine Goodness and celebrating the important Event which we owe to his benign Interposition.[34]

The next morning, on Washington's orders, the entire army was assembled, and celebrated the French-American alliance with a thirteen-gun artillery salute, a musket salute and several rounds of "Huzza!" by the troops. The army's chaplains were also ordered to "offer up a thanksgiving and deliver a discourse suitable to the occasion." As historian Douglas Southall Freeman would observe: "As if to acknowledge permanently that the arm of the Almighty had been bared in the deliverance of America, Washington directed that where Chaplains were available, they hold service every Sunday. Until further orders, fatigue parties were not to labor on the Sabbath."[35]

Alarmed at the prospect of fighting America and France simultaneously, George III and Parliament dispatched a peace commission to negotiate with the Continental Congress. The British government now offered to suspend all objectionable laws and taxes imposed on Colonial America since 1763. It was too late, however; Congress had declared independence, and Americans were generally unwilling to revert to colonial status. Washington agreed: "Great Britain understood herself perfectly in this dispute, but did not comprehend America," he wrote. "No! they meant to drive us into what they termed rebellion, that they might be furnished with a pretext to disarm and then strip us of the rights and privileges of Englishmen and Citizens."[36]

In Philadelphia, meanwhile, General Howe was replaced as the British commander in America by General Henry Clinton, a competent and more aggressive officer. Howe had asked for permission to relinquish his command months earlier, but his departure was more than acquiescence by his superiors: both the king and Parliament were frustrated that Washington's army had not been destroyed. Howe, whose mother had been the mistress of King George I, was an able and popular officer, but his style of leadership stood in stark contrast to Washington's. Howe was a man "of coarse mold," according to his leading British biographer, and was renowned for his arrogance, indolence and "notorious" high-living—including a reportedly distracting preoccupation with an American mistress. "He shut his eyes, fought his battles, drank his bottle [and] had his little whore," an American officer observed.[37]

Howe's older brother, General George Howe, who had been killed in the French and Indian War, loved America and had been immensely popular with the American people. To honor his dead brother's affection for the Thirteen Colonies, William Howe had reportedly vowed never to take up arms against America—a promise he broke when he accepted his North American command. Despite his considerable abilities and his extensive experience, William Howe had failed to destroy George Washington's outnumbered army, and some of his contemporaries believed his efforts had been undermined by his personal character. In the spring of 1777 an English wag penned the lines:

> *Awake, arouse, Sir Billy,*
> *There's forage in the plain.*
> *Leave your little filly,*
> *And open the campaign.*[38]

Despite the British army's superiority in numbers and equipment, General Howe had spent the winter of 1777–78 in Philadelphia—preoccupied with rich food, fine wines, dramatic theatricals, and his mistress—without mounting a serious campaign against the weakened, depleted Patriot army encamped at nearby Valley Forge. "What hindered them from dispersing our little army and giving a fatal blow to our affairs . . . ?" Washington would later observe. "After having lost two battles and Philadelphia . . . in what a cruel and perilous situation did we find ourselves in the winter of '77, within a day's march of the enemy, with a little more than a third of their strength, unable to defend our position, or retreat from it, for want of the means of transportation?" Washington would later answer his own question: "I owe it to that Supreme being who guides the hearts of all," he would state, "who has so signally interposed his aid in every Stage of the Contest. . . ."[39]

When General Clinton assumed command of British forces in May of 1778, he did not intend to make the mistakes he blamed on his predecessor, General Howe, and he took prompt action: he abandoned Philadelphia to the Americans. With France now in the war, the British high command believed Clinton should move his field headquarters from Philadelphia back to New York City, where the British would be better able to withstand a French siege. On June 18, after evacuating several thousand Philadelphia Loyalists by ship, Clinton put his army on a forced march across New Jersey toward New York, where he planned to direct a new military offensive against American forces.[40]

Learning of the British evacuation, Washington led his newly trained and reinvigorated army on a rapid march across New Jersey in pursuit of Clinton's forces. On Sunday, June 28, 1778, the Americans caught up with the British rear guard near Monmouth, New Jersey, and ordered an attack. The British skillfully turned back the assault and Clinton ordered a counterattack. General Charles Lee, who commanded the American lead forces, ordered a hasty retreat—but Washington personally took command and checked the British advance. Then, for hours in sweltering heat, the Americans repulsed repeated assaults by the best troops in the British army. Finally, in the late afternoon, Clinton halted his attacks.[41]

That night, he and his exhausted soldiers slipped away and marched to the New Jersey coast, where British troop transports ferried them over to the safety of British-occupied New York. Tactically, the battle of Monmouth was a draw, but Washington saw it otherwise: his troops had stood toe-to-toe with the elite of the British army and had held their own. Two days later, he called for an assembly of the entire army to give thanks. "The men are to wash themselves this afternoon and appear as clean and decent as possible," he ordered. "Seven o'Clock this evening is appointed that We may publickly unite in thanksgiving to the supreme Disposer of human Events for the Victory which was obtained on Sunday over the Flower of the British Troops."[42]

A few weeks later, Washington moved his army to posts outside New York City, and General Clinton's New York garrison was forced to take up defensive positions against a possible joint American-French attack. It was an extraordinary reversal of events. Two years earlier, General Howe had arrived in New York with more than thirty thousand troops. Forced to evacuate, Washington's army had been driven in retreat across New Jersey. Despite heartening victories at Trenton and Princeton, it had been unable to defend the nation's capital from British capture, had been defeated in battle at Brandywine and Germantown, and had entered winter camp at Valley Forge on the edge of disintegration.[43]

But, remarkably, Washington's army had emerged from Valley Forge as a more formidable, capable opponent. Now Philadelphia was again in American hands, Washington's troops had proved themselves a match for the British at the battle of Monmouth, the mighty British army had been forced to retreat back to New York, and American forces were being reinforced by France's world-class army and navy. "It is not a little pleasing, nor less wonderful to contemplate," Washington marveled in August of 1778, "that after two years manoeuvring and undergoing the strangest vicissitudes that perhaps ever attended any one contest since the creation, both Armies are brought back to the very point they set out from and that which was the offending party in the beginning is now reduced to the use of the spade and pick axe for defence." Once again, the American cause had been rescued and reinforced, according to Washington, by "the hand of Providence."[44]

CHAPTER EIGHT

"Under the Smiles of Heaven"

On Wednesday, June 24, 1778—less than a week after the British evacuated Philadelphia—the Continental Congress voted to reconvene there. What the delegates found upon their return was a much different city than the one they had fled. The British army had left its mark—and it was ugly. "Some of the genteel Houses were used for Stables and Holes were cut in the Parlor floors & their Dung shoveled into the Cellars," reported New Hampshire delegate Josiah Bartlett. "The Country Northward of the City for several Miles is one common waste. The Houses burnt, the Fruit Trees & others cut down & carried off, fences carried away, Gardens and Orchards destroyed. . . ." The delegates found their former assembly site—Independence Hall—in "a most filthy & sordid situation." Until the facility was cleaned up, the Continental Congress had to meet in College Hall at the College of Philadelphia.[1]

Even so, Congress declared, the American people had abundant reason to rejoice "under the smiles of Heaven" and to give thanks to "the great Governor of the universe." No longer was the national capital occupied by the enemy; the British had re-

treated back to New York City; Washington's army had distinguished itself at the battle of Monmouth; and America had gained
a powerful ally with France. One of Congress's first acts upon
returning to Philadelphia was to schedule a thanksgiving service of "divine worship," as Congress officially described it. On
Sunday, July 5, 1778, the delegates assembled in a local church to
profess—in their words—"thanks for the divine mercy in supporting the independence of these states."[2]

Celebrating the British evacuation of Philadelphia with a worship service was typical of the Continental Congress. Influenced
by the Judeo-Christian covenant theology that was foundational
Colonial American law and culture, the Continental Congress repeatedly reminded Americans that God's blessings on them as a
people depended upon their faithfulness. "The goodness of the
Supreme Being to all his rational creatures, demands their acknowledgements of gratitude and love," the Continental Congress
advised Americans at one point, "[and] his absolute government of
this world dictates, that it is the interest of every nation and people
ardently to supplicate his favor and implore his protection."[3]

The overwhelming consensus of the Continental Congress—
a view shared by the American people—was, in the words of historian James H. Hutson, "that a partnership between religion
and government was necessary, not merely for national happiness
and prosperity, but for the survival of the nation itself." It was the
viewpoint that had justified Congress's earlier vote to routinely
begin Congressional deliberations with prayer. Likewise, it was
the justification for the Congressional decisions to appoint chaplains for Congress and the nation's military; to encourage American troops to conduct themselves with Christian morality; to set
aside public lands for the purpose of sharing Christianity with
American Indian tribes; to officially support the printing of a
congressionally endorsed Bible; to take repeated action designed
to reinforce the Judeo-Christian worldview among the American
people; and, on numerous occasions, to officially proclaim the na-

tional days of prayer that, by now, many Americans had grown to expect.[4]

The most famous statement of faith created by the Continental Congress was the Declaration of Independence. In his twentieth-century work *The Biblical Heritage of American Democracy*, Jewish historian Abraham I. Katsh would summarize the Judeo-Christian foundation of the Declaration: "It affirms that the duty of the government is to uphold the rights of man as ordained by divine law, and that the duty of the citizen is to defend the same against any encroachment—even by his own government." That Bible-based faith was also expressed in the Articles of Confederation, the United States' first constitution, which the Continental Congress adopted on November 15, 1777, to govern the newborn nation. The Articles established a national government that was largely subordinate to the will of the states, and specifically acknowledged the supreme authority of "the Great Governor of the world."[5]

The Continental Congress would continue to officially issue public calls for national days of prayer, fasting, and thanksgiving throughout the Revolution. The congressional practice followed a tradition established long before by America's colonial legislatures, which had often called on American colonists to confess personal and community sins, fast, and pray for forgiveness, and prayerfully observe days of thanksgiving. The Continental Congress followed that precedent to the point that official "fast days" became known as "Continental fasts" or "Congressional fast days." Typically, a Congressional committee would be appointed to select the date for a prayer day and draft language for a public resolution—both of which had to be approved by Congress. Public days of prayer were based on biblical passages such as 2 Chronicles 7:14: "If my people, who are called according to my name, shall humble themselves, and pray, and seek my face, and turn from their wicked ways; then I will hear from heaven, and will forgive their sin, and heal their land."[6]

Colonial Americans took such biblical admonition seriously. So did the Continental Congress. Even so, while the American people were asked to pray at times by Congress, they were never ordered to do so, following the biblical principle that faith should be modeled rather than forced. Fast days were scheduled far in advance, so the American people could be notified by their legislatures, through newspapers, and by their ministers. On Congressional fast days, which were usually set on weekdays or Saturdays, countless Americans altered their daily routines to worship and pray. Congress routinely set the example by assembling in a church for prayer and a fast day sermon. Americans likewise thronged to their churches, sometimes attending both morning and evening worship services.[7]

The Continental fast day of 1775, for instance, was "observed with the utmost solemnity, by fasting, abstinence, and devotion," reported a New York City newspaper. "In all the churches in New York were large congregations, and excellent discourses, delivered from the several pulpits. . . ." A Delaware newspaper commented on the public's response to the same fast day, noting the large crowd that attended double services in one city. "Both of the services were attended by all the militia," the paper reported, "with their proper officers in their uniforms, and a numerous concourse of the other inhabitants."[8]

"This day is what was appointed for the Fast to be kept throughout this Continent," noted a Philadelphia journal keeper in 1776. "Our neighborhood [was] extremely quiet, observant and composed, in compliance with the resolve of the Honourable Congress. . . ." Serious observances were generally the norm on Congressional prayer days except in the wildest parts of the American frontier, in notorious big-city neighborhoods and in regions occupied by British forces. There, where occupation British forces ruled, proclamations by the Continental Congress were ignored or suppressed—even before the Congress declared independence. In Boston in 1775, for instance, British troops tried to disrupt a public worship service on a fast day. "When the people were assembling . . . ," a Bostonian reported, "[a British officer] sent for three drums and three fifes, and kept them beating and playing till the service was over."[9]

The national days of prayer called by Congress during the Revolution all followed the pattern established by the Continental Congress in the summer of 1775, prior to the nation's founding. That observance—a day of "public humiliation, fasting and prayer"—which was set for Tuesday, July 25, 1775, served as a model for the annual fast days and thanksgiving days recommended by Congress through the war. The original Congressional resolution of 1775 urged all Americans to unite and "confess and deplore our many sins; and offer up our joint supplications to the all-wise, omnipotent, and merciful Disposer of all events. . . ." Congress's intention in proclaiming days for fasting, prayer, and thanksgiving was concisely summarized by Massachusetts delegate John Adams in a letter to his wife, Abigail, in June of 1775. "Millions will be upon their knees at once before their great Creator," he wrote, "imploring his forgiveness and blessings; his smiles on American councils and arms."[10]

The Congressional calls for prayer in turn inspired various Colonial assemblies to do likewise. In the summer of 1775, for instance, the provincial congress of Massachusetts urged the citizens of that embattled colony to remember their "absolute dependence upon the Lord of Hosts, and God of Armies, for success in this important war, into which we are driven by our enemies." The legislators set an additional day of prayer for Massachusetts, so that "we may all, at one time, sincerely humble ourselves before the searcher of hearts for all our many sins, as a people, and as individuals, and humbly and earnestly beseech his forgiveness, and his blessing on us: that he would graciously afford his divine direction and assistance in our military operations, and speedily cause our enemies to be at peace with us upon a just and permanent foundation."[11]

The Presbyterian Synod of New York and Philadelphia called on their church members not only to observe Continental fast days, but also to set aside the last Thursday of every month as a day of fasting, repentance, and prayer. They quoted from the Old Testament book of Job: "If thou prepare thine heart, and stretch out thine hand towards him, if iniquity be in thine hand, put it far away, and let not wickedness dwell in thy tabernacles." American families should follow Congress's recommendation seriously, the Presbyterian leaders advised their church members. "If, in the present day of distress, we expect that God will hear our supplications, and interpose for our protection or deliverance," they announced, "let us remember, what he himself requires of us is, that our prayers should be attended with a sincere purpose, and thorough endeavour after personal and family reformation." [12]

When Congress declared a fast day in 1776—shortly before passage of the Declaration of Independence—the delegates officially urged "Christians of all denominations, to assemble for public worship and abstain from servile labour" while appealing to the "mediation of Jesus Christ [and] humbly imploring his assistance to frustrate the cruel purposes of our unnatural enemies." In December of that year, Congress authorized a committee to draft a call to the states, asking that each state establish a day of "solemn fasting and humiliation." It was important, the committee concluded, for the American people "to implore of Almighty God the forgiveness of the many sins prevailing among all ranks, and to beg the countenance and assistance of his Providence in the prosecution of the present just and necessary war." Congress published and distributed the committee report, noting that "it becomes all public bodies, as well as private persons, to reverence the Providence of God, and look up to him as the supreme disposer of all events, and the arbiter of the fate of nations." [13]

In the same Congressional action, the newly formed United States military was called to set a standard of Bible-based conduct in warfare—in word as well as in deed. "The Congress do also, in the most earnest manner, recommend to all the members of the United States, and particularly the officers civil and military under them, the exercise of repentance and reformation; and further, require of them the strict observation of the articles of war, and particularly, that part of the said articles, which forbids profane swearing, and all immorality, of which all such officers are desired to take notice." [14]

The first official national day of thanksgiving was arguably the observance called by the Continental Congress in late 1777 as George Washington's army marched toward winter camp at Valley Forge. The day of thanksgiving was set for December 18 of that year, and the proclamation—which was drafted by Samuel Adams, Richard Henry Lee, and Daniel Roberdeau—declared that it was the "indispensable duty of all men to adore the superintending providence of Almighty God" and to "acknowledge with gratitude their obligation to him for benefits received." Congress noted that God had chosen "to smile upon us in the prosecution of a just and necessary war, for the defence and establishment of our unalienable rights and liberties." [15]

Americans were officially encouraged to "consecrate themselves to the service of their divine benefactor; and . . . join the penitent confession of their manifold sins . . . that it may please God, through the merits of Jesus Christ, mercifully to forgive and blot them out of remembrance. . . ." Such a national outpouring of humble thanksgiving, the Continental Congress suggested, would hopefully honor God, and "please him graciously to afford his blessing on the governments of these states respectively, and . . . to secure for these United States the greatest of all human blessings, independence and peace . . . true liberty, virtue and piety, under his nurturing hand, and to prosper the means of religion for the promotion and enlargement of that kingdom which consisteth in righteousness, peace and joy in the Holy Ghost." [16]

Three months later, amid the sinking morale that afflicted

the American people in early 1778, the Continental Congress issued a public proclamation setting April 22, 1778, as a day of national fasting and prayer. Americans everywhere were asked to "abstain, on that day, from labour and recreations," and to recognize the defeats and hardships of war as "evident tokens of [God's] displeasure." It was the duty of the American people, Congress admonished, "to acknowledge God in all his ways, and more especially to humble themselves before him" and to "forsake their evil ways, and implore his mercy" on America in its dark time of peril.[17]

The 1778 Congressional fast day proclamation officially recommended:

> . . . *that at one time, and with one voice, the inhabitants may acknowledge the righteous dispensations of Divine Providence, and confess their iniquities and transgressions, for which the land mourneth; that they may implore the mercy and forgiveness of God; and beseech him that vice, prophaneness, extortion, and every evil, may be done away; and that we may be a reformed and happy people; that they may unite in humble and earnest supplication, that it may please Almighty God, to guard and defend us against our enemies, and give vigour and success to our military operations by sea and land; that it may please him to bless the civil rulers and people, strengthen and perpetuate our union, and, in his own good time, establish us in the peaceable enjoyment of our rights and liberties; that it may please him to bless our schools and seminaries of learning, and make them nurseries of true piety, virtue and useful knowledge; that it may please him to cause the earth to yield its increase, and to crown the year with his goodness.*[18]

The Continental Congress showed no reluctance to publicly and officially express a biblical faith, or to recommend that Americans pray in the name of Jesus Christ. On one occasion,

Congress asked the nation to pray that "God would grant to his Church the plentiful effusions of divine grace." Congress also solicited the prayers of its citizens for the expansion of biblically based education—schools and seminaries that would "bless and prosper the means of education and spread the light of Christian knowledge through the remotest corners of the earth." One prayer day resolution asked Americans to pray that God would "pour out his holy spirit on all ministers of the gospel. . . ." In another, along with prayer and fasting, the Continental Congress also recommended "the exercise of repentance and reformation" to all members of government.[19]

In May of 1778, the Continental Congress issued a nation-wide address "to the inhabitants of the United States." To ensure widespread distribution of the proclamation, Congress called on "ministers of the gospel of all denominations" to read the address "immediately after divine service . . . in their respective churches and chapels, and other places of religious worship." It was a faith-based state-of-the-union address that described the Revolution as meeting the biblical just war criteria—a contest between British "fraud and violence laboring in the service of despotism" and American "virtue and fortitude supporting and establishing the rights of human nature." It condemned British forces as unnecessarily brutal and thus violators of the just war requirements. "Thousands, without distinction of age or sex, have been driven from their peaceful abodes," Congress asserted, "to encounter the rigors of inclement seasons; and the face of Heaven hath been insulted by the wanton conflagration of defenceless towns."[20]

The address reminded Patriot Americans that despite sufferings and setbacks, the American cause had miraculously prevailed. "And what can be more wonderful than the manner of our deliverances," Congress declared. "How often have we been reduced to distress, and yet been raised up? When the means to prosecute the war have been wanting to us, have not our foes themselves been rendered instrumental in providing them?

This hath been done in such a variety of instances, so peculiarly marked, almost by the direct interposition of Providence, that not to feel and acknowledge his protection would be the height of impious ingratitude."[21]

Now aided by the alliance with France, the American cause seemed poised for victory, but only, Congress cautioned, if the American people continued to depend on "that Almighty Ruler of Princes, whose kingdom is over all." Americans would also have to avoid pride and self-congratulation. "Yet do not believe that you have been, or can be saved merely by your own strength," the address warned. "No! it is by the assistance of Heaven. . . . Thus shall the power and the happiness of these sovereign, free and independent states, founded on the virtue of their citizens, increase, extend and endure, until the Almighty shall blot out all the empires of the earth." Someday soon, the address concluded—using a biblical allusion from the Old Testament book of Micah—a day would come when "every man shall sit under his own vine and under his own fig-tree, and there shall be none to make him afraid."[22]

Such biblically based expressions of faith were not reserved solely for public encouragement—many members of Congress expressed the same perspective in private communications. "Put your Trust in the most High whose Providence in the late Event of the Enemy's leaving Philadelphia has been most signal," Connecticut delegate Oliver Wolcott wrote his wife. "God will establish us in Peace and safety." New Hampshire's Josiah Bartlett concurred. Americans "must Leave our affairs to the Government of the Great Supreme Disposer of all Events," he wrote in the summer of 1778, "humbly Hoping that He will order all things so as shall be for the Best." New Jersey delegate Abraham Clark shared similar sentiments in his correspondence. "I doubt not," he wrote, "but by the Providence of God we shall be enabled to withstand our Foes." Connecticut delegate Roger Sherman agreed. "I think in every encounter," he wrote a colleague, "through the merciful interposition of divine Providence the advantage has been much in our favor."[23]

Like most Americans, delegates to the Continental Congress were cheered by France's entry into the war—and many saw it as an act of God. "Thanks to the God of Heaven for the great Things he has done for America," wrote Massachusetts delegate Samuel Adams upon returning to Philadelphia, "and fervently pray that she may be virtuous, without which she cannot long enjoy the Blessings of Freedom." The American-French partnership was "a striking fresh call to praise our God for his Goodness," concluded delegate Elias Boudinot of New Jersey. "God grant them success & take the Glory to himself." Fellow New Jersey delegate Nathaniel Scudder believed French support would ensure an American victory, which in turn would lead to a "mighty, rising American Empire, the Glory of the Western world." It was an ideal time, he advised, for all to seek "through the Merits of your Redeemer, the inestimable Blessings of true Godliness & undefiled Religion."[24]

The delegates to the Continental Congress were not sunshine patriots or mountaintop believers. When defeat befell the American cause, many viewed it as God's call to national repentance—and they did not hesitate to share that unpleasant conviction with the American people. "It is God who has blunted the Weapons of our warfare, that has turned the Counsels of wise Men into Foolishness, that has thus far blasted & disappointed our Hopes, & made Us flee before our Enemies," wrote Connecticut delegate William Williams following an American defeat. "This is black & dark," he wrote, "but God's mercy is boundless . . . & I hope and trust He will not forsake us." The survival of the United States depended on the will of God, delegate John Witherspoon observed, reminding a correspondent that "the fear of God is the beginning of wisdom." It would be solely "by the Blessing of God that We shall by & by have Peace thro' all this Country," Rhode Island's Henry Marchant predicted, and only God could provide victory over "the King of England and his wicked people."[25]

Marchant was not the only American leader who came to view the London government as wicked. Many perceived the Revolution as a biblically justified struggle between good and evil. "These are instances of, I would say, an almost astonishing Providence in our favor . . . ," Samuel Adams observed at one point, "so that we may truly say, it is not our own arm which has saved us. We have fled from the political Sodom, let us not look back, lest we perish. . . ." The general perception among Americans that the king and Parliament were attempting to suppress God-given inalienable rights was the foundation for American resistance from the beginning—and in the fall of 1777, the heavy-handed tactics of the British peace commission reinforced that Bible-based resolve.[26]

Alarmed by the French-American alliance, the British government authorized the commission of British officials to negotiate a peace settlement with the Continental Congress. Headed by a British nobleman, the Earl of Carlisle, and sanctioned by Parliament, the Carlisle Peace Commission proposed a settlement of little interest to most Americans. It neither recognized American independence nor granted Americans representation in the British Parliament, and stipulated that the United States would have to break with France and revert to the status of colonies. In exchange, London would end the war and give its word that Parliament would place no taxes on the American colonies.[27]

It was a vain and unrealistic offer. After all that Americans had suffered for the cause of liberty and nationhood, few were willing to surrender it all and return to rule by a government they considered to be unjust and even wicked. The offer revealed a critical truth of the Revolution: Britain's leaders seemed unable to grasp the real and fundamental reasons behind American resistance. The king and most members of Parliament simply did not comprehend the theology behind "no taxation without representation"—the biblical principle of God-given, inalienable rights of life and liberty. Instead they continued to view Americans as simply rebellious tax resistors.[28]

The Continental Congress officially rejected the proposal. One of the British commissioners then tried to bribe several congressional delegates, who publicly exposed the attempt, provoking widespread indignation throughout America. When negotiations with Congress failed, the Carlisle Commission attempted to appeal directly to the state governments and the American people with a sensational "Manifesto" that encouraged Americans to switch sides. The offer came with a warning: if Americans rejected the proposal, Great Britain would wage war "by every means in her power." Already British agents were working to kindle Indian warfare against American civilians on the frontier. The threat, therefore, was taken to mean an escalation of the war to what a critic in Parliament called "a new system of barbarity."[29]

The Continental Congress and the American people were outraged. To Congress, it was yet another example of the British government violating God's Higher Law. Would one God-fearing people stir up savagery against another? "God forbid!" proclaimed delegate Oliver Wolcott. "No—he who sitteth in the Heavens, who holds Empires in his hands . . . will Crush the Power of the Oppressor, he will Vindicate the Cause of the righteous, he will preserve his People like a Flock, and by the Army of his Power make them to know their Almighty Deliverer, while the Malice of the Oppressor shall cease and he who fears not the Justice of God shall perish forever." With the same sentiment, Congress officially issued its own manifesto, denouncing London on grounds of biblical morality. "Foiled in their vain attempt to subjugate the unconquerable spirit of freedom," Congress charged, the Carlisle Commission—composed of professing Christians—had "made a mockery of religion by impious appeals to God, whilst in the violation of his sacred commandments."[30]

The congressional manifesto was published in newspapers and read from church pulpits throughout America in the autumn of 1778. It reassured the American people that Congress would continue "confiding in him who disposes human events." Said Congress: "We appeal to that God who searcheth the hearts of men, for the rectitude of our intentions, and in his holy presence we declare, that as we are not moved by any light and hasty suggestions of anger or revenge, so, through every possible change of fortune, we will adhere to this our determination." A public rebuke of the Carlisle Commission written by Samuel Adams was also published and widely read at the time. It too invoked the Higher Law of Scripture to condemn the commission's actions:

> *You know that the cause of America is just. You know that she contends for that freedom to which all men are entitled— that she contends against oppression, rapine, and more than savage barbarity. The blood of the innocent is upon your hands, and all the waters of the ocean will not wash it away. We again make our solemn appeal to the God of heaven to decide between you and us. And we pray that, in the doubtful scale of battle, we may be successful as we have justice on our side, and that the merciful Saviour of the world may forgive our oppressors. I am, my Lords and Gentlemen, the friend of human nature, and one who glories in the title of AN AMERICAN.*[31]

The Continental Congress followed its autumn manifesto with another call for "public thanksgiving and prayer," which was set for December 30, 1778. "It [had] pleased Almighty God, through the course of the present year, to bestow great and manifold mercies on the people of these United States," the resolution proclaimed, noting that it was "the indispensable duty of all men gratefully to acknowledge their obligations to Him for benefits received." Congress asked each of the thirteen state governments to declare the day of "thanksgiving and prayer" in each state—

and recommended that on the selected day, the American people set aside all "recreations unsuitable to the purpose of such a solemnity."[32]

It was fitting for the nation to thank God for the victories of the year, including the alliance with France, Congress announced, asking that "all the people may, with united hearts, on that day, express a just sense of his unmerited favours." The resolution then listed what the Continental Congress viewed as acts of God's grace, observing that "it hath pleased him, by his overruling providence, to support us in a just and necessary war, for the defence of our rights and liberties, by affording us seasonable supplies for our armies, by disposing the heart of a powerful monarch to enter into alliance with us, and aid our cause; by defeating the councils and evil designs of our enemies, and giving us victory over their troops; and, by the continuance of that union among these states, which, by his blessing, will be their future strength and glory."[33]

Along with thanksgiving, the Continental Congress urged the American people to humble themselves before the Lord, confessing their sins and seeking God's forgiveness in the face of his blessings. "And it is further recommended," urged the resolution, "that, together with devout thanksgiving, may be joined a penitent confession of our sins, and humble supplication for pardon, through the merits of our Saviour; so that, under the smiles of Heaven, our public councils may be directed, our arms by land and sea prospered, our liberty and independence secured, our schools and seminaries of learning flourish, our trade be revived, our husbandry and manufactures encreased, and the hearts of all impressed with undissembled piety, with benevolence and zeal for the public good."[34]

Like others proclaimed by the Continental Congress, the 1778 thanksgiving day resolution was a recommendation—not an order—and Congress imposed no rewards or penalties for observing it or ignoring it. Nor did the delegates who issued it ever proclaim themselves to be models of virtue. While it included in its ranks "the greatest men upon this continent"—in John Adams's words—the Congress also included, in the opinion of another contemporary, "open dissensions . . . parties who hate one another [and] stupid men." Despite such human frailties, the delegates to the Continental Congress consistently sought to exercise Bible-based leadership throughout the Revolution, and continuously called on the American people to keep the "sacred cause of liberty" a God-centered quest. Americans would soon need such encouragement. Neither King George III nor Parliament had given up *their* quest—the destruction of the newborn United States of America.[35]

CHAPTER NINE

"Grace to Repent of Our Sins"

F our days before Christmas in 1778, George Washington and a select few of his staff officers left army headquarters outside New York City and rode south to Philadelphia to brief the Continental Congress on military operations planned for the coming year. In Philadelphia, he was honored on the floor of Congress and treated by Philadelphians as "the glory and admiration of the city." He and his staff were the guests of honor at a parade of lavish receptions, dinners, and balls that were flattering, but also wearying and distracting. Washington was grateful for the many honors, but the festive atmosphere of wartime Philadelphia left him deeply troubled. Such "a scene of luxury and profusion," observed one of his officers, "gave him more pain than pleasure." Was Philadelphia typical of all America? Was the nation drifting from commitment to the cause of liberty into overconfidence and apathy? Did the people think that the alliance with France meant victory was at hand?[1]

Washington penned his concerns to his longtime friend Benjamin Harrison, with whom he had served in the House of Burgesses and the Continental Congress. Harrison was now back in

Williamsburg, serving as speaker in Virginia's legislature. "Many persons," Washington confided, "removed far distant from the scene of action . . . conceive that the contest is at an end. . . ." The General knew better. The British army remained present and powerful, and the much-heralded French alliance had yet to produce a decisive battlefield victory. Meanwhile, the new nation had sunk into an economic depression. Undermined by inflation, the Continental currency issued by Congress was plunging in value almost daily. Congress was still unable to adequately pay its soldiers, leaving officers and troops alike to worry that their families back home might become destitute.[2]

At the same time, unscrupulous speculators were pursuing self-enriching schemes that harmed the American War effort—which incensed Washington. Shysters and speculators who preyed on wartime sufferers ought to be "hung in gibbets upon a gallows five times as high as the one prepared by Haman," Washington told Harrison, using a reference from the Old Testament book of Esther. "No punishment, in my opinion," he wrote, "is too great for the man who can build his greatness upon his country's ruin." In contrast to the lean, disciplined, and committed atmosphere within his army, the frivolity of Philadelphia distressed him.[3]

"I have seen nothing since I came here," he grimly observed, "but abundant reason to be convinced, that our affairs are in a more distressed, ruinous and deplorable condition, than they have been since the commencement of the war." He hoped the unwarlike atmosphere he encountered in Philadelphia was not typical of all America. "I should in a word say," he lamented, "that idleness, dissipation, and extravagance seem to have laid fast hold of most of them." If most Americans believed that the war was won, Washington knew, the nation was in grave peril. "I am alarmed," he admitted to Harrison, "and wish to see my countrymen roused."[4]

Even as he wrote, however, Washington seemed to summon

the personal faith that had borne him through numerous other shadowed valleys. "But, alas, we are not to expect that the path will be strowed with flowers," he admitted. "That great and good Being, who rules the Universe, has disposed matters otherwise," he wrote, "and for wise purposes I am persuaded." Washington would persevere as he had before, despite new and looming threats, and, privately and publicly, he consistently restated his confidence that Almighty God in his sovereignty favored "the sacred cause of freedom." Despite his troubling concerns, he concluded his frank letter to Benjamin Harrison with a typical statement of faith and optimism. "Providence has heretofore taken us up," he declared, "when all other means and hope seemed to be departing from us. In this I will confide."[5]

Unknown to Washington, as he mused about potential challenges to the American cause, British forces were executing a new military strategy—with immediate success. The French alliance had undermined one of Britain's main strengths in the war, naval superiority, which had previously allowed British forces to move up and down the Atlantic coast with no serious American naval opposition. Now, however, the British navy might be confronted at any moment by a mighty French armada—as well as troop transports filled with French soldiers. Initial operations by the French navy in America, however, were deeply disappointing. In the summer of 1778, a powerful French fleet commanded by Admiral Comte d'Estaing had arrived in America, but missed an opportunity to trap the British fleet in Chesapeake Bay. Estaing sailed for New York, but declined to battle British ships in the city's harbor because he feared his heavy draught vessels would run aground. Instead, he suggested a joint army-navy attack at Newport, Rhode Island, which had been occupied by the British since 1776. Washington sent troops, but coordination was poor, the plan of attack failed—and Admiral d'Estaing and his French fleet sailed away to the West Indies. Despite its initial lack of success, the French navy was a new and serious threat to British operations in America, and the British high command developed a new strategy to win the war quickly.[6]

While the bulk of British forces would remain posted to New York City, ready to deploy as needed in the North, British army and naval forces would be dispatched to attack and capture a major seaport in the South. From that new base, British troops would move inland and conquer the South one state at a time. Loyalist support was stronger in the South than in the North, the British believed, and once a state was conquered, Loyalist forces could maintain order while the British army moved on to its next target. To launch this new Southern strategy, General Clinton dispatched an army-navy expedition from New York City in late 1778. Its target was Savannah, Georgia.[7]

On December 29, 1778, more than 3,500 British troops commanded by Colonel Archibald Campbell overwhelmed the small force of American defenders at Savannah, easily capturing the port city and establishing a Southern base of operations. British forces promptly moved inland across lightly inhabited Georgia. Soon the entire state was under British control. One of Washington's ablest officers, General Benjamin Lincoln, had recently been named by Congress as commander of the Department of the South, but Lincoln could do nothing to prevent Georgia from being overrun by the British. Meanwhile, on the New York and Pennsylvania frontier, Loyalist troops and their Iroquois allies launched savage attacks on several wilderness settlements, massacring their inhabitants. From recently established headquarters in New Jersey, Washington ordered an expedition to the frontier to drive back the Iroquois. He had few troops he could send to the South as reinforcements, but he dispatched those he could spare to South Carolina, where Lincoln was plotting to retake Savannah with French assistance.[8]

As had happened throughout the Revolution, the fortunes of

war initially seemed to favor Great Britain. When news of Savannah's fall reached Philadelphia, the delegates to the Continental Congress did more than simply weigh military options or wring their hands—they attempted to provide spiritual leadership for their young, war-torn nation. Was this major new battlefield setback a sign of God's disfavor? The British conquest of Georgia, Congress feared, might actually be God's discipline of America: "For whom the Lord loveth, he chasteneth," according to Scripture. In a remarkable public proclamation, Congress boldly announced that recent battlefield defeats might really be "the scourge of Omnipotence," and called on the American people to once again "set aside a day of fasting, humiliation and prayer."[9]

The proclamation was passed by Congress on March 20, 1779, setting the Continental fast for May 6. The war itself, the proclamation admitted, could be viewed as "just punishment of our manifold transgressions." Even though "the Supreme Disposer of all events" through "His divine Providence" had at times in the past intervened on behalf of America in "a wonderful manner," it appeared to the Continental Congress that too few Americans had been "sufficiently awakened to a sense of their guilt, or warmed with gratitude, or taught to amend their lives and turn from their sins, so that He might turn from His wrath."[10]

It was an exceptional public profession—members of Congress proclaiming themselves and the American people to be sinners—and it urged Americans everywhere to observe the national day of prayer. The nation was asked to:

> *repent of our sins, and amend our lives, according to his holy word: that he will continue that wonderful protection which hath led us through the paths of danger and distress: that he will be a husband to the widow and a father to the fatherless children, who weep over the barbarities of a savage enemy: that he will grant us patience in suffering, and fortitude in*

adversity: that he will inspire us with humility and modera-
tion, and gratitude in prosperous circumstances: that he will
give wisdom to our councils, firmness to our resolutions, and
victory to our arms.[11]

The proclamation also urged Americans to pray for France, asking the Lord to "bestow on our great ally all those blessings which may enable him to be gloriously instrumental in protecting the rights of mankind." Singled out for special attention were General George Washington and the Continental Army. Congress asked the people to pray for God's "paternal care to the commander-in-chief, and the officers and soldiers of the United States," and for peace and freedom. Finally, the proclamation recommended that Americans beseech the Lord to "extend the influence of true religion, and give us that peace of mind which the world cannot give"—that he would "be our shield in the day of battle, our comforter in the hour of death, and our kind parent and merciful judge through time and through eternity."[12]

Like other Congressional fast day proclamations, this one ordered nothing and carried no penalty if neglected. Instead it "recommended" action. Even so, it was reinforced by the authority eighteenth-century Americans respected above all others—the authority of Scripture—and it was replete with biblical precepts. From the book of Proverbs: "Righteousness exalteth a nation: but sin is a reproach to any people." From the Psalms: "LORD, thou hast heard the desire of the humble: thou wilt prepare their heart, thou wilt cause thine ear to hear." From the New Testament book of Hebrews: "For whom the Lord loveth he chasteneth . . . nevertheless afterward it yieldeth the peaceable fruit of righteousness. . . ." The proclamation's poignant plea in the midst of war for God to "be a husband to the widow and a father to the fatherless" was an obvious reference to numerous biblical passages, such as Psalms 146:9: "The Lord . . . relieveth the fatherless and widow: but the way of the wicked he turneth upside down."[13]

When Congress expressed its desire for "patience in suffering . . . fortitude in adversity" and "wisdom to our councils," its words echoed the New Testament book of James: "Knowing this, that the trying of your faith worketh patience. But let patience have her perfect work, that ye may be perfect and entire, wanting nothing. If any of you lacks wisdom, let him ask of God . . . and it shall be given him." Finally, the concluding expression of hope that God would grant "peace of mind, which the world cannot give" was a clear allusion to the biblical epistle to the Philippians: "Be [anxious] for nothing; but in everything by prayer and supplication with thanksgiving let your requests be made known unto God. And the peace of God, which passeth all understanding, shall keep your hearts and minds through Christ Jesus." [14]

On Thursday, May 6, the Congressional fast day was observed throughout the United States, except in the areas occupied by British forces. At his headquarters in Middlebrook, New Jersey, General Washington ordered the army to assemble for fast day worship services. The orders encouraged officers and soldiers alike to confess "our Sins and Ingratitude [and] implore the Protection of Heaven; Success to our Arms and the Arms of our Ally." Washington had issued orders "strictly forbidding all recreations and unnecessary labor" on the fast day, and army chaplains were ordered to "prepare discourses suitable for the occasion." At army headquarters, Washington and his officers set an example for the troops by attending a worship service that included a sermon by the Reverend James Francis Armstrong, a Presbyterian minister who was chaplain to a brigade of Maryland troops. [15]

As Americans observed the 1779 fast day that May, Washington was still deeply concerned about America's national attitude. Even so, he continued to proclaim his faith in the sovereignty of God. To the leaders of a Dutch Reformed church in New York, he wrote, "I trust the goodness of the cause and the exertions of the people, under Divine protection, will give us that honorable peace for which we are contending." While helping negotiate an alliance with Native Americans of the Delaware tribe on the western frontier that spring, he encouraged tribal leaders to "learn our arts and ways of life and above all—the religion of Jesus Christ." To a close colleague, he expressed his trust in God in an obvious reference to Romans 8:28: "I look upon every dispensation of Providence as designed to answer some valuable purpose," he wrote, "and bear without murmuring any stroke which may happen. . . ." [16]

New strokes were indeed about to be unleashed against the American cause, and the "Divine protection" Washington so desired would be desperately needed. Despite all the celebration over the French alliance, it had produced nothing yet of substance on the battlefield, and the heralded French navy had come and gone, doing little more than threaten British strongholds in New York and Rhode Island. What was Washington to do now? Should he move his army, try to recapture Georgia, and battle the British for control of the South? Perhaps it could be done, but would General Clinton and his British Redcoats then suddenly emerge from their New York City fortifications and mount a major new offensive on the unprotected North? [17]

Or should Washington lead a full-scale invasion of Canada? Such a campaign would surely draw the support of the French army and navy, and would likely enlist substantial support from disgruntled French-Canadians. If Canada were wrested from Britain and returned to France, would it not likely end the war? Some in Congress advocated such action, but Washington felt his army was not equipped for such a giant offensive task. Finally, Washington decided to remain in place in the North, try to preserve his army for future use, wait for an opportunity to mount a major joint campaign with the French army and navy, and hope to wear down British resolve by prolonging the war. [18]

While Washington waited for the next British move in the

North, and General Lincoln plotted to retake Georgia in the South, the Continental Congress continued to try to set an example of faith-centered leadership. On May 26, 1779, Congress issued a public address "to the inhabitants of the United States of America." In language laced with biblical allusions, Congress encouraged Americans to remain steadfast in their defense of American liberty and independence, and compared the struggle between America and Great Britain to the biblical battle between David and Goliath:

America, without arms, ammunition, discipline, revenue, government or ally, almost totally stript of commerce, and in the weakness of youth, as it were with a "staff and a sling" only, dared "in the name of the Lord of Hosts," to engage a gigantic adversary, prepared at all points, boasting of his strength, and of whom even mighty warriors "were greatly afraid." [19]

Great Britain was waging war against America with "remorseless fury," Congress admitted, but the "audacious defiances of his holy laws" by the British could only result in God's condemnation of the enemy. "Rouse yourselves," Congress urged the American people, and "finish the great work you have so nobly carried on for several years past." The "lives, liberties and estates" of future generations now depended on American perseverance. "Persevere, and you ensure peace, safety, freedom, glory, sovereignty, and felicity, to yourselves, your children, and your children's children." Remain grateful for God's "infinite goodness" and obedient to "the divine will," Congress admonished, and "vigorously employ the means placed by Providence in your hands . . . and may you be approved before Almighty God worthy of those blessings we devoutly wish you to enjoy." [20]

On the third anniversary of American independence— Sunday, July 4, 1779—the delegates to Congress observed the occasion by attending three public worship services in Philadelphia, and by publishing "sermons suitable to the occasion" by the Congressional chaplains. In the morning they attended a worship service at Christ Church, the Anglican church formerly pastored by their first Congressional chaplain, the Reverend Jacob Duché, who had fled to Britain after urging Washington to surrender. Now filling the pulpit in the prestigious church was thirty-one-year-old William White, Duché's former associate.[21]

The Reverend White was also the chaplain of the Continental Congress, a duty he shared with its associate chaplain, the Reverend George Duffield, who was pastor of Philadelphia's Pine Street Presbyterian Church. Both men had been appointed Congressional chaplains in 1777, following the capture of Philadelphia by the British and the defection of Chaplain Duché. White learned of his appointment as chaplain while fleeing the British with his family and other Patriot refugees. A courier overtook him in a Maryland village, notified him of his appointment, and summoned him to join Congress as it reconvened in a new location.[22]

Unlike Duché, William White had not been outspoken in his support for American liberties, but once he committed to the American cause, he never turned away from it. His appointment came in America's darkest hour of the war when the British were marching into the capital and Congress had fled. Accepting the post placed White and his family in serious peril—but he promptly assumed his duties anyway. His style of leadership was quiet but confident. In that same style, after the Revolution—when the Anglican Church was no longer America's official state church—White would be instrumental in helping transform the Anglican Church in America into the Protestant Episcopal Church. Now, on July 4, 1779, he delivered an Independence Day sermon to the Continental Congress assembled at Christ Church.[23]

He preached on the superiority of God's Higher Law over the whims of man, taking his text from chapter 13 of the New

Testament book of Romans. "Let every soul be subject unto the higher powers," instructed the passage. "For there is no power but of God; the powers that be are ordained of God. Whosoever therefore resisteth the power, resisteth the ordinance of God; and they that resist shall receive to themselves damnation." It was "an excellent sermon, suitable to the occasion," reported the *Pennsylvania Packet*. When the service at Christ Church concluded late that morning, the delegates promptly reassembled at St. Mary's Chapel—the newest of Philadelphia's two Catholic churches.[24]

Two days earlier, the first French minister to the United States, Conrad-Alexandre Gérard, had invited the Congress to St. Mary's on the Fourth of July "pour célébrer l'Anniversaire de l'Indépendance des États Unis de l'Amérique"—to commemorate the anniversary of the United States of America. The service included the "Te Deum Laudamus," the traditional Catholic thanksgiving praise to God, sung in Latin, and a sermon by the Reverend Seraphin Bandol, chaplain of the new French embassy. "That Being whose almighty hand holds all existence beneath its dominion undoubtedly produces in the depths of His wisdom those great events which astonish the universe," Bandol declared. "It is that God, that all powerful God, who hath directed your steps, when you knew not where to apply for counsel; who, when you were without arms, fought for you with the sword of justice; who, when you were in adversity, poured into your hearts the spirit of courage, of wisdom, and fortitude. . . ."[25]

The American Revolution, Bandol proclaimed, had produced "tranquility and happiness" for "a great part of the human race," and France was pleased to recognize the new United States among the nations of the earth. The struggle ahead, however, would not be determined by America and France, the priest reminded Congress, but by Almighty God. "Let us then," he declared, "prostrate ourselves at the feet of the immortal God, who holds the fate of Empires in His hands, and raises them up at His pleasure, or breaks them down to dust. . . . God will not regret our joy, for He is the author of it; nor will he forget our prayers, for they ask but the fulfillment of the decrees He has manifested. Filled with this spirit, let us, in concert with each other, raise our hearts to the Eternal; let us implore His infinite mercy."[26]

That afternoon, Congress attended its third Independence Day worship service—this one at Pine Street Presbyterian Church. During their occupation of Philadelphia, British troops had chopped the church pews into firewood, defaced the sanctuary, and transformed it into a hospital. Seated in a sanctuary once filled with enemies, but now restored, the delegates were addressed by the other Congressional chaplain—the Reverend George Duffield. A former frontier preacher who had come to Pine Street Presbyterian on the eve of the Revolution, Duffield divided his time between his pastorate, his duties as Congressional chaplain, and his service in the field as a military chaplain. A descendant of persecuted French Huguenots, he was an outspoken advocate of American liberty and had called for American nationhood even before Congress passed the Declaration of Independence. He was devoted to the soldiers in the field, and was considered so influential with the troops that the British had posted a reward for his capture. He was a gifted pulpit speaker— John Adams praised his eloquence—and, as did many Americans, he publicly likened the American people to the biblical Israelites fleeing Egyptian repression.[27]

"Can it be supposed that God, who made man free, and engraved the love of liberty in his mind, should forbid . . . freedom to erect her banner *here*, and constrain her to abandon the earth?" he declared in a typical sermon. He had been a classmate to a half-dozen members of Congress, and knew many more. He apparently felt no intimidation in preaching to them, for his sermon this day was bold and frank. He envisioned a bright future for America, but he did not hesitate to predict destruction if the nation ever abandoned God. "America shall remain a city of refuge for the whole earth," he proclaimed, "[unless] she herself shall play the tyrant, forget her destiny, disgrace her freedom and provoke her God." Thus fortified by three worship services, Congress concluded its Independence Day observances, having set an example of devotion for the nation.[28]

In the fall of 1779, a French fleet of thirty-eight warships mounting more than two thousand guns arrived off the coast of South Carolina, accompanied by transports bearing approximately four thousand French troops. The fleet was commanded by Admiral Charles d'Estaing. Washington had hoped that the returning French naval force would aid his army in operations in the North, but Admiral d'Estaing intended to lead a French-American attack on Savannah instead. Joined by General Lincoln's 1,500-man American army, d'Estaing opened a bombardment on Savannah's British defenses, which were manned by a force of approximately three thousand British troops.[29]

On October 9, 1779, after six days of artillery bombardment, d'Estaing and Lincoln launched an infantry assault on the British defenses. It was a disaster. Although their combined force outnumbered the British defenders, the French-American attack was poorly coordinated and executed in confusion. It was turned back with heavy French losses—a casualty rate of more than 20 percent—and Admiral d'Estaing and his fleet again left American waters. Admiral d'Estaing and the famed French navy had declined to attack the British navy at Chesapeake Bay and New York City, had been unsuccessful at Newport, and had now failed disastrously at Savannah. The one-sided British victory cheered British and Loyalist troops in New York and Georgia, left Americans disillusioned with their ally, and again sent morale plummeting throughout the United States.[30]

One who was not dismayed, however, was George Washington. From his New Jersey headquarters, the commander-in-chief confidently predicted that Admiral d'Estaing and the French fleet would eventually return. Americans would again take the battle to the British—and by God's grace the American cause would prevail. "To Count d'Estaing, then," he wrote a friend, "and that good Providence, which has so remarkably aided us in all our difficulties, the rest is committed." Despite American defeats, he counted his blessings. In the North, for example, General Anthony Wayne blunted a British advance north of New York City at Stony Point. At Paulus Hook, other American troops drove the British from their only major outpost in New Jersey. On the frontier of New York and Pennsylvania, the expedition Washington had earlier dispatched had dramatically reduced the threat from Loyalists and Indians there. New "difficulties" surely lay ahead— a "new scene," he wrote, "is opening to our view"—but he persisted in professing faith that "the supreme Disposer of human Events" would preserve America.[31]

So did the Continental Congress. Although the delegates came and went, and the composition of the Congress changed with each session, among the constants that marked the Congress throughout the American Revolution was its consistent, outspoken profession of a biblical faith. On October 20, 1779, less than two weeks after America's failed attempt to retake Savannah, the Continental Congress proclaimed another nationwide year-end "day of general thanksgiving." The proclamation was produced by a Congressional committee and approved by the full Congress, but it was penned by Connecticut delegate Jesse Root, who was also an army officer, adjutant general of Connecticut troops, a practicing attorney, and an ordained minister. Despite setbacks on the battlefield and a continuous, inflation-driven economic crisis, the Congress publicly urged the American people to give thanks to God for a host of reasons.[32]

"[It] becomes us humbly to approach the throne of Almighty God," the proclamation stated, "with gratitude and praise for the wonders which his goodness has wrought in conducting our forefathers to this western world, for his protection to them and to their posterity amid difficulties and dangers; for raising us, their children, from deep distress to be numbered among the nations of the earth. . . ." It praised God for the nation's abundant natural resources—for "spreading plenty throughout the land"; for the intercession of France—"our ally"; for being a "shield to our troops in the hour of danger"; for preserving the American cause; "and above all, that he hath diffused the glorious light of the gospel, whereby, through the merits of our gracious Redeemer, we may become the heirs of his eternal glory. . . ."[33]

A day of national thanksgiving was thus in order, Congress declared, and it "recommended to the several states" that Thursday, December 9, 1779, be observed as "a day of public and solemn thanksgiving to Almighty God for his mercies, and of prayer for the continuance of his favor and protection to these United States." Americans were asked to beseech the Lord to "influence our public councils, and bless them with wisdom from on high, with unanimity, firmness and success; that he would go forth with our hosts and crown our arms with victory; that he would grant to his church the plentiful effusions of divine grace, and pour out his holy spirit on ministers of the gospel . . . and spread the light of Christian knowledge through the remotest corners of the earth. . . ." Congress ended the proclamation by urging Americans to pray that God "would dispense the blessings of peace to the contending nations; that he would in mercy look down upon us, pardon our sins and receive us into his favor, and finally, that he would establish the independence of these United States upon the bases of religion and virtue. . . ."[34]

In this way, the year 1779 ended with a renewed Congressional plea for God's pardon and favor—even as the British high command prepared to unleash the full fury of its new strategy on the American South. Washington, meanwhile, waited and watched for the next British action and continued to profess his trust in "that Being, who controls all things, to bring about his own determination." To his friend and fellow Virginian Benjamin Harrison, he wrote again, saying: "We are now in appearance, launching into a wide and boundless field—puzzled with mazes and o'er-spread with difficulties. A glorious object is in view, and God send we may attain it. . . ."[35]

"Fight Against Them That Fight Against Me"

Militarily, it was the worst American calamity of the Revolution, and George Washington learned about it from an enemy newspaper. On May 30, 1780, a late-night courier arrived at army headquarters with a special edition of the *Royal Gazette*. Published in New York City, the *Gazette* was a Loyalist newspaper notorious for its inaccuracy. After reading the paper's lead story, however, General Washington concluded that it contained too many specific details to be false: Charleston, South Carolina—the largest seaport and most important city in the South—had been captured by British forces.[1]

The report was true. The day after Christmas, 1779, General Henry Clinton, the British commander in America, led an expedition of almost nine thousand troops from New York to attack Charleston. By February, the expedition was off the South Carolina coast. General Benjamin Lincoln, the officer Congress had put in charge of the Southern Department, had earlier withdrawn to Charleston with his army following the failed French-American attempt to retake Savannah. Unwilling to abandon such a strategically important city, Lincoln fortified Charleston, which lay on a peninsula, and called for reinforcements to defend it. Washington sent what few troops he could spare from the North, and a few militia forces joined him, but Lincoln's three-thousand-man garrison was no match for the formidable army-navy task force that Clinton led against Charleston. By mid-April, the British had the city surrounded and under a military siege.[2]

Low on rations, ceaselessly bombarded by British artillery and pressured by fearful local politicians, Lincoln surrendered on May 12, 1780. An entire American army was captured, along with a huge store of critically needed arms and equipment, and the most important seaport in the South now belonged to the enemy. In many ways, it was a greater disaster than the British occupation of New York, and some historians would rank it as the worst Continental defeat of the war. Now that it was controlled by the British, Charleston and its superb seaport would provide an efficient enemy supply line and open South Carolina to invasion, just as the British intended. In Britain, King George III was enjoying a royal horseback ride when the news of Charleston's capture reached him. In response, he ordered four thousand British troops assembled in London's Hyde Park, where the victory was celebrated with a military parade and a massive artillery salute— answered by a corresponding barrage by troops assembled near Parliament.[3]

Americans received the news of Charleston's fall with shock and despair. "The fall of Charleston seems the most disagreeable affair we have ever met with," observed John Adams. Washington, however, showed no emotion when he read the *Royal Gazette*'s account at army headquarters. With little official comment, he calmly ordered the news forwarded to Congress in Philadelphia. Privately, however, even Washington was discouraged. Just days earlier, he had managed to quell a potential mutiny by troops who had not been adequately paid or fed for months. In order to cover any British advance from New York City, he had bivouacked the army in two camps—one at Morristown, New Jersey, where he now had his headquarters, and the other at West Point, New York. At both posts, camp conditions had become almost as desperate as in the days of Valley Forge.[4]

"Since the date of my last [letter]," Washington wrote a friend in Congress, "we have had the virtue and patience of the army put to the severest trial; sometimes it has been five or six days without bread, at other times as many days without meat, and once or twice two or three days without either." With America's Continental currency ravaged by inflation and almost worthless, the Continental Congress had been unable to adequately pay the troops, leaving soldiers desperate to provide for their families back home. Meanwhile, attempts by Congress to induce the states to assist the army with money, rations, and supplies had bogged down in a bureaucratic quagmire.[5]

Congress had not ignored the crisis facing the country and the army—the delegates had repeatedly attempted to deal with the sinking Continental currency, the lack of pay for troops, and the desperate shortage of rations for Washington's army. They had beseeched the states to produce new recruits for the army, rations for the troops, and tax monies for the national treasury—but little had been forthcoming. The state governments also suffered from wartime conditions, as did the American people, and under the Articles of Confederation, Congress had little authority to enforce its requests. The national treasury was empty, credit was gone, and Continental currency was not worth printing. Again, the Continental Congress had turned to prayer—even before the capture of Charleston. Another day of "fasting, humiliation and prayer" was set for April 28, 1780 and Congress urged the American people to seriously observe it.[6]

"It having pleased the righteous Governor of the World, for the punishment of our manifold offenses, to permit the sword of war still to harass our country," Congress announced, "it becomes us to endeavour, by humbling ourselves before him, and turning from every evil way, to avert his anger and obtain his favour and blessing. . . ." On the designated fast day, Congress entreated Americans "with one heart and one voice" to

implore the sovereign Lord of Heaven and Earth to remember mercy in his judgments; to make us sincerely penitent for our transgressions; to prepare us for deliverance, and to remove the evils with which he hath been pleased to visit us; to banish vice and irreligion from among us, and establish virtue and piety by his divine grace; to bless all public councils throughout the United States, giving them wisdom, firmness and unanimity, and directing them to the best measures for the public good; to bless the magistrates and people of every rank, and animate and unite the hearts of all to promote the interests of their country; to bless the public defence, inspiring all commanders and soldiers with magnanimity and perseverance, and giving vigor and success to the military operations by sea and land; to bless the illustrious Sovereign and the nation in alliance with these states, and all who interest themselves in the support of our rights and liberties; to make that alliance of perpetual and extensive usefulness to those immediately concerned, and mankind in general; to grant fruitful seasons, and to bless our industry, trade and manufactures; to bless all schools and seminaries of learning, and every means of instruction and education; to cause wars to cease, and to establish peace among the nations.[7]

The plea for "success to the military operations by land and sea" that prayful Americans made through the 1780 fast day did not materialize any time soon. Washington's troops continued to be beset by empty bellies and empty pockets—and after the capture of Charleston, British forces promptly moved into inland South Carolina. It seemed that "the sovereign Lord of Heaven and Earth" apparently intended—for a season at least—to allow the country to remain under "the sword of war." Even for a leader of faith and optimism like Washington, it was a dark time. Would the British follow their conquest of Georgia and Charleston with a successful invasion of both Carolinas? Then, would that lead to an enemy occupation of Virginia? If the British Union Jack again flew over the American South, would the border of the United States become the Potomac River?[8]

With the fall of Charleston added to the American woes of 1780, losing the war again seemed possible. Washington's concern was evident in a letter to a Virginia friend written immediately upon receipt of the news from South Carolina. "Certain I am," the general admitted, "unless Congress speaks in a more decisive tone, unless they are vested with powers by the several States competent to the great purposes of war, or assume them as matter of right, and they and the States respectively act with more energy than they hitherto have done, that our cause is lost." To improve communications with the commander-in-chief, Congress appointed a three-man committee and parked it at Washington's headquarters. While Washington's gloom soon passed, erased by his characteristic faith and optimism, the calamities that befell the American cause in 1780 did not—instead, they worsened.[9]

After the capture of Charleston, General Clinton returned to New York, leaving operations in South Carolina in the hands of his capable, aggressive forty-two-year-old second in command— General Charles Cornwallis. Under his command, British forces systematically occupied the state, establishing outposts at key locations and recruiting a significant number of Loyalist troops. Almost immediately, however, Patriot support began to swell in South Carolina due to the brutality of British tactics. In late May of 1780, for instance, a force of seven hundred British dragoons and infantry overtook four hundred retreating Virginia troops at a place called Waxhaws on the South Carolina–North Carolina border. The Virginians tried to surrender, but they were massacred by the British, who were commanded by a ruthless officer—Lieutenant Colonel Banastre Tarleton. "For fifteen minutes after every man was prostrate," an eyewitness would recall, "they went over the ground plunging their bayonets into everyone that exhibited any signs of life. . . ." The Waxhaw Massacre and other acts of British brutality fueled Patriot support in the Carolinas.[10]

Congress, meanwhile, named General Horatio Gates as commander of the Department of the South. Acclaimed as the victor of Saratoga, Gates hurried to the Carolinas to mount an offensive against the invading British army. On August 16, 1780, near Camden, South Carolina, he led an army of about four thousand regulars and militia against Cornwallis's army of 2,400, which consisted mainly of well-trained British regulars. Although Gates's army was larger, about half its numbers were inexperienced militia, and many of the troops were ill and weakened from a diet of green peaches, green corn, and local molasses.[11]

Gates ineptly executed a clumsy battlefield strategy, which opened the American front-line troops to a devastating British artillery barrage, while Banastre Tarleton's British dragoons struck the American rear with a shock-force attack. The militia troops panicked, threw down their weapons, and ran. A small force of Continental troops from Maryland and Delaware made a courageous defense but were overwhelmed, and their commander—the volunteer French general Baron de Kalb—was mortally wounded. The American army was almost annihilated. General Gates abandoned his army and fled, racing away from the battlefield, and not stopping until he was far away in North Carolina. The dramatic, one-sided triumph at Camden strengthened the British hold on South Carolina and Georgia, and General Cornwallis now began preparations for invading North Carolina.[12]

In London, Lord George Germain, the British Secretary of

State for North America, learned of Cornwallis's one-sided victory at Camden and led the ambitious general to believe that he now exercised an independent command in the Carolinas. Germain meddled in British military operations reportedly because he favored Cornwallis's aggressive tactics over Clinton's. Cornwallis initiated a harsh campaign designed to suppress all resistance in South Carolina. British policy there dictated that anyone who supported the American cause, he ordered, "should be punished with the greatest rigour," and men who refused to join the Loyalist militia should "be imprisoned and their whole property taken from them or destroyed." In rural Patriot strongholds, countless homes were routinely torched. Churches were burned. Elderly men whose sons or grandsons were serving in the American army were imprisoned, and untold numbers of young men were hanged for refusing to join the Loyalist militia. At one point Tarleton's fearsome Green Dragoons raided the home of a deceased American officer, set the house ablaze, then burned the farm's barns—with the livestock penned inside. Adding a brutal insult to his terror tactics, Tarleton reportedly ordered the dead American officer's body hauled from its grave.[13]

As he received the disheartening news from South Carolina, Washington also had to deal with grim events in the North. While the rumblings of mutiny in his army passed, the army continued to suffer from lack of food and pay. In the summer of 1780, a 5,500-man French army commanded by the Comte de Rochambeau landed in Rhode Island, but without full naval support—which again kept the American-French alliance from accomplishing anything of significance. In the North, the American people seemed on the verge of losing hope of an American victory, while in the South they were being terrorized by their British conquerors. It was in this dark era of the war that Washington suffered a shocking act of betrayal.[14]

One of his most trusted senior commanders, Major General Benedict Arnold, secretly switched sides and attempted to hand over the important American fortress at West Point to the British. A hero for his actions at the battle of Saratoga, Arnold was a gifted battlefield commander and a leading officer in the Continental Army. He was an experienced combat officer, had served as military commander of Philadelphia, and in 1780, he commanded the West Point defenses. Unknown to Washington, however, Arnold had agreed to betray his country in exchange for payment and privileges in the British army. For more than a year, he had used his high-level position to sell critical American military secrets to the British. In the autumn of 1789, his plan to turn over West Point to British forces was nearly complete when the plot was exposed. Arnold fled his post and escaped to the British army.[15]

To Washington, the timing and circumstances that foiled Arnold's conspiracy were not coincidental. "That overruling Providence, which has so often and so remarkably interposed in our favor," Washington told a fellow officer, "never manifested itself more conspicuously than in the timely discovery of [Arnold's] horrid design of surrendering the post and garrison of West Point into the hands of the enemy." To another officer, he wrote, "In no instance since the commencement of the war, has the interposition of Providence appeared more remarkably conspicuous than in the rescue of the post and garrison of West Point from Arnold's villainous perfidy."[16]

Members of the Continental Congress also saw the hand of God in the failure of Benedict Arnold's plot. On October 17, 1780, the Congress proclaimed another national day of prayer and thanksgiving. The resolution entreated the American people to give thanks to "Almighty God, the Father of all mercies" for the "remarkable interposition of his watchful providence, in rescuing the person of our Commander in Chief and the army from imminent dangers, at the moment when treason was ripened for execution . . . and, above all, in continuing to us the enjoyment of the gospel of peace." Congress recommended that the fast day be scheduled for December 7, 1780, and that

all the people may assemble on that day to celebrate the praises
of our Divine Benefactor; to confess our unworthiness of the
least of his favours, and to offer our fervent supplications to the
God of all grace; that it may please him to pardon our heinous
transgressions and incline our hearts for the future to keep all
his laws; to comfort and relieve our brethren who are any wise
afflicted or distressed; to smile upon our husbandry and trade;
to direct our publick councils, and lead our forces by land and
sea, to victory; to take our illustrious ally under his special pro-
tection, and favor our joint councils and exertions for the estab-
lishment of speedy and permanent peace; to cherish all schools
and seminaries of education, and to cause the knowledge of
Christianity to spread all over the earth.[17]

It was a humble statement by chastened American leaders at a low point in the American Revolution. The British Southern strategy seemed on the verge of complete success. With Georgia and South Carolina apparently subdued and occupied, General Cornwallis marched his victorious army into North Carolina as planned in September of 1780, encamping near the crossroads village of Charlotte. From there he planned to conquer North Carolina, then push on into Virginia. Not only might he subdue the entire American South and restore those states to the Crown, he believed, but from Virginia he might be able to mount a joint offensive with General Clinton against Washington's army.[18]

If Cornwallis and Clinton could pin Washington's army between their two forces, they might deliver a deathblow to both the army and American independence. From Windsor Castle, King George III exulted, "America is distressed to the greatest degree." Then, just when British victory seemed most likely, events in the South took an extraordinary turn. Less than a week after the October prayer day proclamation was issued by Congress, Washington—and the American people—received just cause for thanksgiving. The turnaround began in embattled South Carolina.[19]

The British strategy of terrorizing South Carolinians into submission stood in stark contrast to Washington's biblically based policy of treating civilians with respect. The brutal tactics often employed by British forces in South Carolina prompted most South Carolinians to abandon any loyalty to the Mother Country and drove scores to join the ranks of guerrilla leaders Thomas Sumter, Andrew Pickens, and Francis Marion. Known as the "Swamp Fox of the Revolution," Marion was the descendant of Huguenots who had fled persecution in France, and he recruited many of his troops from local church congregations—including a sizable number from Scots-Irish Presbyterian Congregations. "The men of South Carolina [were not] the sort of folk with whom it was safe to trifle," a nineteenth-century British historian would write. "Carolinian farmers and planters were said to eat more venison than beef.... There were few among them who could not use a rifle." Bolstered by such men, Marion's daring guerrilla band continuously raided British outposts and supply lines, forcing Cornwallis to leave behind much-needed troops when he launched his invasion of North Carolina.[20]

Instead of drawing more British regulars from South Carolina's occupation forces, Cornwallis used eleven hundred Loyalist militia troops to cover his army's left flank as he advanced into North Carolina. They were commanded by Major Patrick Ferguson, a bold, experienced British officer. As he moved his Loyalist force through the South Carolina piedmont in support of Cornwallis, Ferguson sent a public warning to the distant frontier settlements in western North Carolina and eastern Tennessee. If he learned of any opposition to British rule in the mountain country, Ferguson warned, he would "march my army over the mountains, hang your leaders, and lay your country to waste with fire and sword."[21]

The mountaineers took the threat seriously and decided not

to wait for Ferguson to attack their homes and families. They organized a thousand-man force of experienced hunters and Indian fighters, commanded by frontier leaders Isaac Shelby and John Sevier, and set out to destroy the threatening Loyalists. En route, the "Over Mountain Men"—as they came to be known—were reinforced by nine hundred Patriot militia troops from South Carolina and Virginia. The Virginians were led by Colonel William Campbell, who was elected commander of the makeshift Patriot army. Ferguson and his Loyalist militia, meanwhile, had halted southwest of Charlotte just inside the South Carolina border, and had dug in on a forested, boulder-cluttered knoll known as Kings Mountain. There they planned to do battle with the Patriot frontiersmen, who they learned were marching toward a confrontation. Ferguson was close enough to easily have joined Cornwallis's formidable army in Charlotte; why he chose to stay and fight on Kings Mountain remains a mystery. He reportedly vowed to his troops that he was "king of that mountain" and even God Almighty could not remove him. The Patriot frontiersmen and backcountry warriors heading for Kings Mountain were determined to prove him wrong.[22]

Many of them were also Scots-Irish Presbyterians, with "no small infusion of religious enthusiasm," according to a knowledgeable Englishman. "Their favourite end of the Bible was the Old Testament, and . . . they bore some likeness to Cromwell's soldiers." The Over Mountain Men had mustered at a wilderness settlement on the Watauga River in east Tennessee—a place known as Sycamore Shoals—and before leaving the mountains they had been primed by a pioneer clergyman named Samuel Doak. A Presbyterian preacher in the mountain country, Doak fired up the frontiersmen with the biblical account of the Old Testament warrior Gideon, who routed the enemy despite his smaller numbers. The battle cry against Ferguson and his invaders should be the same as Gideon's, Doak is said to have proclaimed: "The sword of the Lord and of Gideon!"[23]

In reality, their battle cry was more Indian-like than bibli-cal, but they fell on the enemy with the full fury of Israelite war-riors. They overtook Ferguson and his troops at Kings Mountain on October 7, 1780, and in a one-hour battle they shattered Fer-guson's Loyalist army and shot the major dead from the saddle. Ferguson's poor choice of a wooded, rocky battlefield allowed the Patriot frontiersmen to fight with a familiar advantage—firing frontier-style from the cover of trees and boulders—and they quickly thinned the ranks of Loyalists. Still incensed at Tarle-ton's massacre of the Virginians at Waxhaws earlier in the year, the Patriot troops, especially the Virginians, had to be restrained by their officers from executing prisoners. Almost all the Loyal-ists were killed or captured—more than nine hundred casualties compared to twenty-eight Patriots—which annihilated the entire left wing of General Cornwallis's invasion force.[24]

Kings Mountain was not a large battle, but it provided a mighty morale boost to the discouraged American people, fired Patriot resistance in the Carolinas—and decisively halted the momentum of the British Southern strategy. It would become known as the turning point of the Revolution in the South. Cornwallis was forced to abandon his North Carolina inva-sion for the moment and return to South Carolina to secure his base of operations. "This advantage," observed Washing-ton in his typically reserved manner, "will in all probability have a very happy influence. . . ." General Henry Clinton, the Brit-ish commander-in-chief, was much more outspoken, eventu-ally viewing the battle as a disastrous reversal of British strategy. Kings Mountain, he later admitted, "though in itself confessedly trifling, overset in a moment all the happy effects of his Lord-ship's glorious victory at Camden, and so encouraged that spirit of rebellion in both Carolinas that it never could be afterward humbled."[25]

The victory at Kings Mountain was the first in a series of remarkable events that would change the direction of the war in America's favor. Another was the appointment of Major General Nathanael Greene as the new American commander in the South. Previously, the department's commanders—Generals Lincoln and Gates—had been picked by the Continental Congress. Both had lost—Lincoln at Charleston and Gates at Camden—and on the eve of Kings Mountain, the Congress had asked Washington to pick the next Southern commander. Washington chose Greene. It was a carefully considered decision, and it would have tremendous consequences for the American cause.[26]

It was to Greene that Washington had turned for help at Valley Forge, entrusting him as his new quartermaster general to resupply the ragged, starving Continental Army that winter. Despite the enormity of the task, Greene had prevailed, and had reformed Washington's supply system with superb skill. He had also been at Washington's side in the worst of war—as a battlefield commander at Trenton, Brandywine, Germantown, and Monmouth. Now, a week after Kings Mountain, Washington dispatched Greene to the Carolinas to do battle with Cornwallis's British army. "Amidst the complicated dangers with which you are surrounded," Washington told his new commander, "a confidence in your abilities is my only consolation." It was a monumental challenge, even for the gifted Nathanael Greene, but Washington had made a wise choice. Greene would emerge from a year's fighting in the Carolinas as a military commander second in stature only to Washington. He would play a key role in the ultimate British defeat—forcing the British from the Carolinas—yet he would do so without winning a single battle.[27]

Nathanael Greene was an unlikely military leader. Although robust and intelligent, he was initially turned down by the army due to a chronically stiff knee—and perhaps because of his pacifist Quaker childhood in Rhode Island. In fact, while Greene would always consider himself a Quaker, his local congregation had suspended him as a young man because of his interest in the military. His transformation from pacifist to Patriot warrior was nothing short of a "dispensation of . . . Providence," according to an early biographer. Quickly proving his natural command ability, Greene rose from private to brigadier by age thirty-four. Like Washington, he believed that God had a plan for America, and that "the arm of providence" would provide an American victory against the British. "Heaven has decreed that tottering empire to irretrievable ruin," Greene declared early in the war, "and, thanks to God, since providence has so determined it, America must raise an empire of permanent duration, supported upon the grand pillars of truth, freedom, and religion. . . ."[28]

By early December of 1780, Greene was in North Carolina at the head of a small army of about twenty-five hundred troops. He brought with him some of Washington's ablest officers, and as a former quartermaster general, he had taken care to equip his army well. The troops he took command of in North Carolina were ragged and demoralized, but Greene quickly rebuilt their morale and appeared confident of eventual victory. "Our army will appear like Gideon and his pitchers," he had predicted at one point. "God grant us the same success; the cause is equally righteous, and claims his heavenly protection." In the Carolinas, his skillful leadership in time made the British army resemble the hapless Midianites of old as they faced Gideon's army.[29]

Although outnumbered, Greene divided his small army. With part of it, he distracted General Cornwallis's main force, while his subordinate, Brigadier General Daniel Morgan, was pursued by Banastre Tarleton and eleven hundred British troops deep into the South Carolina backcountry. On January 17, 1781, Morgan suddenly turned and made a stand on a well-selected field of battle at a broad meadowland called Cowpens. At six feet, two hundred pounds, the middle-aged Morgan was a combat-savvy former frontier teamster and Indian fighter, and had played a decisive role at the battle of Saratoga. Once a rough-and-tumble frontiersman, Morgan at the time of Cowpens was on his way to becoming the devout Presbyterian layman of his later years. Like the Welsh Presbyterians of his ancestral home, "the Old Wagoner," as he liked to call himself, was willing to sacrifice for what he believed. As a young teamster in the French and Indian War, he had reportedly received more than a hundred lashes for striking a British officer. At Cowpens, he settled that score: using unorthodox tactics, Morgan and his eight-hundred-man force drew Tarleton's rash and overconfident troops into a deadly ambush.[30]

It was a humiliating British defeat: Tarleton's dead and wounded outnumbered the Americans' four to one. Most of the British survivors were taken prisoner; and Tarleton barely escaped death or capture—ingloriously fleeing the battlefield at a gallop. At battle's end, General Morgan reportedly rode victoriously across the field praising God aloud from the saddle. "Such was the inferiority of our numbers," he reported to Greene, "that our success must be attributed, under God, to the justice of our cause and the bravery of our troops." The same sentiment was more colorfully expressed within the ranks by an Irish Presbyterian soldier from the Carolina backcountry. "Good Lord, our God that art in Heaven," he prayed in his native brogue, "we have great reason to thank Thee for the many battles we have won . . . the great and glorious battle of King's Mountain . . . and the iver glorious and memorable battle of the Cowpens, where we made the proud Gineral Tarleton run doon the road helter-skelter."[31]

Cowpens was a decisive American victory. Combined with Kings Mountain, it stunned the British high command, further undermined the British Southern strategy, and at a critical time brought cheer to Washington's headquarters in the faraway North. There, Washington had been forced to resolve yet another near-mutiny among some of his underpaid and underfed troops. Despite the continued grim conditions in the North, however, Washington remained resolute about the eventual outcome of the war. "I have no doubt," he wrote in early 1781, "that the same bountiful Providence which has relieved us in a variety of difficulties heretofore, will enable us to emerge from them ultimately, and crown our struggles with success."[32]

After Kings Mountain and Cowpens, the chain reaction of critical events that shaped the outcome of the Revolution continued in dramatic succession. The next occurred off the field of battle. At noon on March 1, 1781, the Articles of Confederation were finally ratified, officially giving the United States of America its first constitution, and causing the Continental Congress to become known as the United States Congress. The Articles declared that "it hath pleased the Great Governor of the world to incline the Legislatures . . . to approve of, and authorize . . . the said articles of confederation"—though it had taken three and a half years for all thirteen states to do it. Most states voted for ratification with reasonable deliberation, in the spirit of the New York legislature, which endorsed ratification in early 1780 by declaring that "nothing under Divine Providence, can more effectually contribute to the tranquility and safety of the United States of America, than a federal alliance." The long holdout was Maryland, where legislators were concerned over land claims. Maryland had finally voted for ratification in late February of 1781, and Congress promptly declared the American Confederation to be official.[33]

The national government established by the Articles of Confederation was intentionally weak: there was neither a president nor a supreme court, and the unicameral Congress was subject to the will of the states. Even so, ratification of the Articles was generally viewed by the American people as confirmation that the United States of America was indeed "perpetual," as the Articles pronounced. The ratification was "exceedingly pleasing to me," wrote George Washington, who hoped it would help "Obtain men for the War" and alleviate "the wretched State of our finances." Despite many grim challenges it still faced, the newborn nation was holding its own in a war with the greatest military power on earth, and now had officially ratified a national government. Great Britain remained a formidable "Goliath"—but, hopefully, as the Continental Congress had predicted back in 1779, America would surely prevail, as did David, with the help of "the Lord of Hosts."[34]

In March of 1781, America's "David" slung another mighty stone at the British "Goliath" in North Carolina. Humiliated by the British defeat at Cowpens, General Cornwallis was determined to invade North Carolina, restore the British Southern strategy, and crush the defiant American opposition. He put his army on a demanding forced march in pursuit of Greene and Morgan. To lighten his lumbering army and speed its march across North Carolina, he took the risky action of ordering his troops to burn their baggage wagons and tents. His seasoned British veterans dutifully obeyed, but it was a demoralizing order that left Cornwallis's troops poorly supplied while deep in enemy country.[35]

It was also just what Greene wanted. Reunited with Morgan's force and strengthened by reinforcements, he hoped to lure Cornwallis and his two thousand veterans far from their South Carolina base and deep into North Carolina—where they would be exposed and vulnerable to attack. Cornwallis took the bait, and pushed his army all the way to the Dan River in Virginia. Finally, he gave up and reversed course—and then Greene struck. He pursued Cornwallis's weary army, and drew it into battle at Guilford Courthouse in North Carolina on March 15, 1781.[36]

Guilford Courthouse was a bloody, hard-fought contest, and Cornwallis's army won a tactical victory—but at great cost. The British suffered 532 casualties, twice as many as the Americans and more than one-fourth of Cornwallis's army—which was precisely what Greene had intended. While he had lost the battle, he had badly damaged Cornwallis's army, forcing him to again abandon plans to conquer North Carolina. Instead of expanding the

British Southern strategy, Cornwallis's invasion of North Carolina turned out to be a costly strategic failure. Exhausted, short of rations, and riddled by illnesses, Cornwallis's army limped across North Carolina to the seaport of Wilmington, where his army could be resupplied by water from Charleston.[37]

While Cornwallis was withdrawing to Wilmington, Congress also took action: five days after Guilford Courthouse, Congress proclaimed another day of humiliation, fasting, and prayer set for May 3, 1781. "At all times it is our duty to acknowledge the over-ruling providence of the great Governor of the universe," Congress proclaimed, "and devoutly to implore his divine favour and protection. But in the hour of calamity and impending danger . . . we are peculiarly excited, with true penitence of heart, to prostrate ourselves before our great Creator, and fervently to supplicate his gracious interposition for our deliverance." For these reasons, the proclamation stated, Congress did "earnestly recommend" that on the designated fast day Americans everywhere "with united hearts, confess and bewail our manifold sins and transgressions, and by sincere repentance and amendment of life, appease his righteous displeasure, and through the merits of our blessed Savior, obtain pardon and forgiveness."[38]

Americans were asked to beseech God to "inspire our rulers with wisdom and uncorruptible integrity," to inspire the American people with "a fervent and disinterested love of their country," and to "strengthen their union." As for the American Patriots living under the occupation of British troops, their countrymen were urged to pray that God would "regard with divine compassion our friends in captivity, affliction and distress, to comfort and relieve them under their sufferings and to change their mourning into grateful songs of triumph." The people were encouraged to pray for the French, and that the French-American alliance would provide "a mutual and lasting benefit to both nations." Finally, Congress urged the American people to unite in asking the Lord to

animate our officers and forces by sea and land with invincible
fortitude, and to guard and protect them in the day of battle,
and to crown our joint endeavours for terminating the calam-
ities of war with victory and success: that the blessings of peace
and liberty may be established on an honourable and perma-
nent basis, and transmitted inviolate to the latest posterity: that
it may please him to prosper our husbandry and commerce,
and to bless us with health and plenty: that it may please him
to bless all schools and seminaries of learning, and to grant that
truth, justice and benevolence, and pure and undefiled religion,
may universally prevail.[39]

Again, the American people's prayerful request for "victory and success" on the battlefield initially seemed to be answered in the negative. When Cornwallis withdrew to Wilmington, Nathanael Greene led his army into South Carolina to take advantage of Cornwallis's absence. He engaged British troops at the battle of Hobkirk's Hill in April of 1781, and later in the fall at Eutaw Springs. In both actions, the British won—but their tactical victories became strategic defeats. They suffered so many casualties in victory, that they were compelled to give up their occupation of South Carolina's interior, and withdraw back to Charleston. Then, one by one, Greene captured other key British outposts, liberating South Carolina and leaving the British isolated in Charleston.[40]

General Cornwallis, meanwhile, could have moved his army back to South Carolina—which is what General Clinton expected him to do. Instead, believing he had independent command, he abandoned the Carolinas and marched his army northward to Virginia—a "mad advance," in the words of a modern British military historian. His actions surprised and dismayed Clinton, who had ordered Cornwallis to make South Carolina's occupation his priority. "I shall tremble for every post except Charleston, and even Georgia," Clinton privately confided. While Cornwallis marched his army around Virginia and debated his options, Clinton struggled to respond to Cornwallis's unexpected abandonment of the Carolinas. He initially ordered him to send part of his army to New York, but countermanded that order, pondered making an attack on Philadelphia, and then directed him to establish a base in coastal Virginia.[41]

To anyone who recalled events on the third day of the fledgling First Continental Congress—held so long before in 1774—the confusion of the British high command might have seemed like fulfillment of prophecy. On that remarkable day almost seven years earlier, Congress had officially begun its day with prayer, and Psalm 35 had been read aloud to the assembled delegates. Now, in 1781, those words of Scripture held a new meaning when applied to the shocking reversals suffered recently by British forces in America: "Plead my cause, O Lord, with them that strive with me; fight against them that fight against me. . . . Let them be confounded and put to shame. . . ." Lord Cornwallis had been shamed aplenty by his surprising setbacks in the Carolinas, where the British occupation was now disintegrating along with the British Southern strategy. From what had been a position of victory and strength a year earlier, the British war effort in the South appeared to have melted into one of shameful loss and confusion.[42]

Now both Cornwallis and Clinton had to regain lost ground—or develop an entirely new strategy to defeat the Americans. If Virginia could be brought under British control, perhaps the British occupation of South Carolina could be restored, and Washington's army might still be caught between two major British forces—Clinton's and Cornwallis's. Leaving his options open, Cornwallis consolidated his troops with other British forces in Virginia and moved the enlarged army to a coastal base where he could be reinforced and resupplied by the British navy. The location Cornwallis selected for a new base of operations was a riverside port on Virginia's York River upstream from Chesapeake Bay. Its name was Yorktown.[43]

CHAPTER ELEVEN

"Such Astonishing Interpositions of Providence"

While General Cornwallis attempted to reorganize British forces in Virginia and General Clinton fretted about conditions in South Carolina, George Washington was attending church. On Sunday morning, May 20, 1781, Washington was in Wethersfield, Connecticut, for a conference with General Rochambeau, whose French army was bivouacked in Rhode Island. Washington and his party had reached Wethersfield, near Hartford, a day ahead of the French commander, and joined Connecticut governor Jonathan Trumbull for a worship service at the town's stately First Congregational Church. Washington was reportedly "greatly impressed by the singing of the choir" and listened to the church's pastor, the Reverend John Marsh, preach about humility from the Sermon on the Mount—"Blessed are the poor in spirit, for theirs is the kingdom of heaven." [1]

It had surely been a season of humility for Washington. By now he was openly acknowledging God as the wellspring of his optimism concerning the eventual success of the American cause. Despite continued short rations and a lack of funds to pay his troops, Washington was encouraged by the way the war in the

South had shifted to favor the American cause. "We have . . . abundant reasons to thank Providence for its many favorable interpositions in our behalf," he had written in March. "It has at times been my only dependence, for all other resources seemed to have failed us."[2]

Washington's personal faith continued to be a foundational source of strength and encouragement, judging from the commander-in-chief's numerous references to God. Even in official correspondence with General Rochambeau, he did not draw back from making references to his faith. When an aide drafted a letter to the French general about an unconfirmed French victory, Washington personally penned, "I pray God [the victory] may be confirmed. . . ." A few weeks before scheduling the conference with Rochambeau, he had again expressed confidence that "the hand of Providence" would save America. "The many remarkable interpositions of the divine government in the hours of our deepest distress and darkness," he wrote a friend, "have been too luminous to suffer me to doubt the happy issue of the present contest."[3]

Now, having professed his belief that the "same bountiful Providence" who had guided America in the past would again "crown our struggles with success," Washington weighed the unexpected success in the South, and met with Rochambeau at Wethersfield. There on May 22, the two planned a joint offensive against British forces in New York City. Washington realized an offensive against heavily defended New York could not succeed without the full support of the French army, which was questionable—but, even so, the campaign might help the South by diverting British troops from there. The campaign began in early July, but it got off to a sluggish start, and little was accomplished. Even that problem, however, produced benefits for the American cause: the American and French armies were encamped beside each other, and the delay in the campaign enabled the men in the ranks to befriend each other despite the language barrier. The two armies became—in the words of British historian George Otto Trevelyan—"like sworn brothers in arms,— growing accustomed to each other's ways. . . ."[4]

Then Washington received good news "of very great importance"—forces under General Greene had driven the British troops in Georgia back to Savannah. Potentially even more important was the message he received on August 14, 1781—a powerful fleet of French warships under Admiral François de Grasse was sailing for America and the coast of Virginia. Washington and Rochambeau promptly changed strategy: instead of attacking the British at New York City, they would put their combined army on a rapid march to Virginia, where they would attempt to trap and defeat Cornwallis's army at Yorktown. The campaign would be backed by the French fleet. Rochambeau put his four-thousand French troops under Washington's command. "Vous pouvez faire avec moi quoi que vous faites," he told Washington—"You may do with me whatever you will."[5]

To camouflage the march to Virginia, Washington had ovens for baking bread constructed in New Jersey—as if he planned a prolonged siege against the British in New York City—and put part of his army in motion as if preparing for a major attack against Clinton's New York defenses. He also had word leaked into British lines that he was moving a large portion of his army around New York City to Staten Island. Meanwhile, he put half his army and all of Rochambeau's French troops on a forced 450-mile march from New York to Chesapeake Bay in Maryland, where they would board French troopships for coastal Virginia. Clinton was outfoxed. Washington's rapid maneuver took the British completely by surprise, and Clinton made no attempt to block Washington's march.[6]

It was a complicated, risky offensive. Cornwallis could have retreated to South Carolina while Clinton advanced from his New York defenses to attack the remnant of the army Washington left behind. Instead both Clinton and Cornwallis dallied indecisively as events overtook them. Washington, in contrast, was both decisive and confident. He led his combined army from New York, through New Jersey and into Philadelphia, which the troops reached on September 2, 1781. That day Admiral De Grasse and the French fleet reached Chesapeake Bay with thirty-four warships and three thousand more French troops. Three days later, De Grasse's French warships engaged a British fleet in an epic sea battle that would significantly help determine the outcome of Washington's bold offensive.[7]

Alerted to the arrival of the French fleet offshore Virginia, but unaware of its huge size, General Clinton had dispatched a fleet of nineteen British warships under Admiral Thomas Graves with orders to do battle if he encountered the French navy. On September 5, the British fleet arrived off the capes of Chesapeake Bay—Cape Charles and Cape Henry—and found the French navy there in force. The two fleets immediately engaged each other in battle in what would become known as the battle of the Chesapeake Capes. The opposing lines of warships battered each other for two and a half hours until darkness ended the contest. The engagement was a tactical draw, but the British fleet was so badly damaged that Admiral Graves ordered it back to New York City for repairs. The French navy was left in absolute control of Chesapeake Bay, and Cornwallis's army was left stranded at Yorktown.[8]

Now unopposed, the French fleet picked up Washington's and Rochambeau's troops at points on upper Chesapeake Bay and transported them to landing sites on the James River from which they could easily deploy against Cornwallis's army at Yorktown. Washington, Rochambeau, and a few staff officers rode ahead of the army and stopped to rest at Mount Vernon. It was the first time Washington had been home since 1775. Then it was on to Yorktown. The combined American and French forces at Yorktown gave Washington rare numerical superiority over Cornwallis—an army of about seventeen thousand to approximately ten thousand. By September 28, the combined French-

American army was in place at Yorktown, supported by the French navy. On October 10, Washington opened a siege of the British defenses. The allied artillery—including French heavy artillery—pounded the British lines as allied infantry steadily advanced through extended entrenchments. A few days into the siege, a courier got through to Cornwallis with news from General Clinton in New York City: the British navy and seven thousand reinforcements would soon sail for Yorktown.[9]

Cornwallis responded to the news by taking action that has baffled military experts ever since. Instead of holding on until reinforcements arrived, he inexplicably ordered his outer defensive lines abandoned and pulled his troops back toward his inner defenses. The move allowed Washington to advance his siege lines and increase the pressure on the encircled British. By October 11, the American and French artillery were only three hundred yards from the British lines, inflicting severe damage and serious casualties. Three days later, French and American troops assaulted and captured two key British redoubts, tightening the hold on Cornwallis's increasingly desperate army. Much of the British artillery had been wrecked, the numbers of dead and wounded were mounting, the harsh conditions inside Yorktown had spread illness among the besieged troops—and the British reinforcements had not arrived.[10]

In a desperate attempt to escape, Cornwallis tried to ferry his army across the broad York River on the night of October 16. It was a bold plan, daringly executed by well-trained troops—but a ferocious, gale-like storm unexpectedly struck that night and scuttled the British evacuation. "[At] this critical moment," Cornwallis would later report, "the weather, from being moderate and calm, changed to a violent storm of wind and rain, and drove all the boats, some of which had troops on board, down the river. It was soon evident that the intended passage was impracticable. . . ." The surprise storm sealed Cornwallis's last opportunity to escape: he and his army were trapped.[11]

The next morning, October 17, Washington directed a stunning allied artillery barrage against British lines. "One saw nothing but balls and bombs raining on our whole line," a British soldier would report. It was too much for the battered British defenders, but Cornwallis could not bear the indignity of surrender. Finally, he came to the front, surveyed the disastrous situation in person—and left stunned, hopeless, and humiliated. Soon afterward, at about ten o'clock, frontline American troops saw a British drummer appear on the distant enemy parapet, followed by an officer holding a white flag. The guns fell silent for the moment, and the British officer, blindfolded, was escorted into the American lines with a dispatch from General Cornwallis. It was a message he never expected to send: the British army would surrender.[12]

On a sunny autumn afternoon, October 19, 1781, Cornwallis's army surrendered—without Lord Cornwallis. The famous British general claimed to be ill, and sent his second-in-command, Brigadier General Charles O'Hara, to represent him. American troops lined one side of the road leading from Yorktown, with French troops lining the other. General Washington and his staff waited on horseback across the road from General Rochambeau and his staff. The defeated British and German soldiers—their battle flags rolled up in their cases—sullenly filed between the lines of victorious troops as a British regimental band reportedly played a tune called "The World Turned Upside Down." When opposite Rochambeau, General O'Hara paused and attempted to surrender to the French general—either as a slight to the Americans or simply from confusion.[13]

An American aide intercepted him, and General Rochambeau directed him across the road to Washington. Apparently embarrassed and flustered, the British general hurriedly turned and crossed the road to surrender to Washington. Mounted on horseback beside Washington was Brigadier General Benjamin Lincoln, who had been exchanged as a prisoner-of-war after surrendering to the British at Charleston. With characteristic grace, General Washington directed O'Hara, as Lord Cornwallis's subordinate, to make the ceremonial surrender to Lincoln, who was Washington's subordinate. "The General," an American officer would later recall, "feeling [O'Hara's] embarrassment, relieved it by referring him with much politeness to General Lincoln." And so the historic surrender was ceremoniously concluded by two subordinate officers.[14]

The surrender of Cornwallis's army did not officially end the war—occasional scattered skirmishing would continue for more than a year. Washington's great victory, however, was the unofficial end. Significant military operations ceased with Yorktown, and peace negotiations began. The news of the surrender upended the British government in London: "What are we to do after Lord Cornwallis's catastrophe, God only knows," bewailed one member of Parliament. "Oh, God! It is all over!" exclaimed British prime minister Frederick North. Sentiment in Parliament abruptly shifted against continuing the war. The prime minister soon announced an end to military operations in America and resigned his post. So did Lord George Germain. Eventually, begrudgingly, even King George III conceded that the Americans had won their independence.[15]

Long before, early in the war, George Washington had evaluated what lay ahead with a commander's wisdom and a believer's faith, and had made a telling observation. "Ours is a kind of struggle," he wrote, "designed by Providence, I dare say, to try the patience, fortitude and virtue of men. None, therefore, who is engaged in it, will suffer himself, I trust, to sink under difficulties, or be discouraged by hardships." He had not sunk under its difficulties, though he had borne far more than most Patriots. His discouragement in the face of harsh and repeated hardships had always been short-lived, and the "patience, fortitude and virtue" he had displayed throughout the conflict had honored both his country and the God whose providential ways he had so often praised.[16]

Washington did not presume the war was over—he would urge unrelenting vigilance until the last British soldier left America—but he realized the momentous victory at Yorktown would likely force an end to the fighting. From his Yorktown headquarters following the October 19 surrender, Washington composed an official dispatch to the president of Congress, using words that had been difficult to even imagine for six hard years: "Sir: I have the honor to inform Congress, that a Reduction of the British Army under the Command of Lord Cornwallis, is most happily effected." Then, how should he officially observe this unlikely, and long-awaited triumph? Bonfires? Formations of cheering troops? A festive celebration? Those would have to wait. First, he called the army to worship. After all the years of professing his faith that Almighty God would preserve the American cause—that the "interposition of Providence" would prevail—Washington would not neglect publicly professing thanks to God for the extraordinary victory. Accordingly, he ordered an army-wide thanksgiving service for the day after the British surrender.[17]

"Divine service is to be performed to-morrow in the several brigades and divisions," his official order read. "The Commander-in-Chief earnestly recommends, that the troops not on duty should universally attend, with that seriousness of deportment and gratitude of heart, which the recognition of such reiterated and astonishing interpositions of Providence demand of us." As he had done so often throughout the war, Washington now credited this latest victory—likely to be the decisive action of the war—not to himself but to God, whose intervention at Yorktown, in Washington's words, was "astonishing." American Patriots everywhere cheered the surrender of Cornwallis's army, understanding that it likely signaled the end of the war, and they too shared Washington's gratitude to God.[18]

Congress also reacted with a worship service. News of the

surrender reached Philadelphia just before three a.m. on October 22. Soon the city's neighborhoods were awakened by the night watchmen calling the hour and shouting, "Cornwallis is taken!" Philadelphia's streets were soon thronged by joyful crowds as church bells tolled thoughout the city. Some people cheered; others wept with relief. Throughout the thirteen states, Americans celebrated with bonfires, parades, and speeches. At Yale University, students raised a bonfire and sang a "triumphal hymn." Throughout the nation, people praised God for the victory. When Congress received Washington's official report of the surrender, which arrived on Wednesday, October 24, the delegates promptly voted to assemble in church that afternoon to "return thanks to Almighty God." [19]

Although its members had put their lives at risk during the Revolution by merely holding office, the Continental Congress had its critics—then and later—for how it had handled America's financial woes, dealt with the state governments, responded to the needs of the army, and deliberated on countless issues. However, in one area deemed of vital importance by eighteenth-century Americans—spiritual leadership—the delegates established a record that would be difficult for future Congresses to surpass. Throughout the long war, The Continental Congress had consistently reflected the biblical worldview of the American people, and had repeatedly attempted to provide spiritual leadership for the nation. Now, as it had done when it voted to open deliberations with prayer on the eve of the war, Congress reacted to the war's apparent end with another display of biblical faith. [20]

At two o'clock on the afternoon of October 24, the delegates left Independence Hall in a solemn procession and marched several blocks to Philadelphia's Zion Lutheran Church. A magnificent structure also known as the "Dutch Lutheran Church," it had been chosen as the site for the Congressional thanksgiving service. There, passing between towering Greek-style columns, the delegates entered Zion's spacious sanctuary, where they were joined by the members of the Pennsylvania legislature; the French minister to America, Conrad-Alexandre Gérard; and a crowd of joyous Philadelphians. Just four years earlier, British troops had commandeered the church and converted it into a military hospital. Now, where victorious enemy soldiers had once recuperated to again wage war on America, the delegates to Congress celebrated the American triumph over Great Britain with a "divine service suitable to the occasion." It was conducted by Congressional chaplain George Duffield.[21]

Congressional leaders also professed in private what the Congress proclaimed in public. "Thanks to almighty God for his special Favour in the capture of his Lordship & the British Army . . . ," New Jersey delegate Elias Boudinot wrote his family. Soon to be named president of the Congress, Boudinot had been baptized by evangelist George Whitefield and would become the first president of the American Bible Society. "May God of his infinite Mercy make us thankfull for his uncounted Favours to Us," he wrote following Cornwallis's surrender, "and enable us to stand with our Loins girt & Lamps trimmed always waiting for the Coming of the Bridegroom"—a reference to the second coming of Christ.[22]

Boudinot's God-centered elation was shared by Connecticut's Samuel Huntington, a recent president of Congress. "That the superintending power of Divine government over the affairs of men cannot be baffled by designing mortals is a consoling truth to the confident heart," Huntington observed. New York delegate Robert Livingston, who had been named U.S. secretary of foreign affairs, noted that "a feather would have turned the balance [of the war] last year, notwithstanding the powerful aid we received from abroad. Providence blinded our adversary. . . ."[23]

American citizens agreed, and from the same church pulpits that had denounced the British government for suppressing God-given inalienable rights came proclamations of "praise and thanksgiving to the Lord of Hosts." The president of Yale University, Dr. Ezra Stiles, spoke for many when he attributed the surrender of Cornwallis and the independence of America to the sovereignty of God. "May we all be led to discern the hand of the Most High in controlling & bringing about events & revolutions in the political world," Stiles declared, "and particularly to see & acknowledge & give glory to God for the great favorable events of the last campaign."[24]

On October 26, 1781, the Congress issued an official reaction to the victory at Yorktown by scheduling a day of "public thanksgiving and prayer" for December 13, 1781. "Whereas," the proclamation announced, "it hath pleased Almighty God, father of mercies, remarkably to assist and support the United States of America in their important struggle for liberty against the long continued efforts of a powerful nation; it is the duty of all ranks to observe and thankfully acknowledge the interpositions of his Providence in their behalf. Through the whole of this contest, from its first rise to this time, the influence of divine Providence may be clearly perceived in many signal instances. . . ."[25]

The Congressional proclamation listed a parade of events that Congress considered to be acts of God in support of the American cause, such as "revealing the councils of our enemies" in the timely exposure of Benedict Arnold's treason, the unbroken unity of the thirteen states, the vitally important assistance of France, numerous "remarkable deliverances" such as the ordeal of Valley Forge, and God's "blessing us with the most signal success, when affairs seemed to have the most discouraging appearance." Congress marveled over "the many instances of prowess and success in our armies, particularly in the southern states, where . . . they have recovered the whole country which the enemy had overrun . . . and which, after the success of our allies by sea, a General of the first Rank, with his whole army, has been captured by the allied forces under the direction of our Commander in Chief."[26]

In the face of such evidence of divine intervention, Congress explained, "we cannot help leading the good people of these states to a retrospect on the events which have taken place since the beginning of the war, so we recommend in a particular manner to their observation, the goodness of God. . . ." The proclamation concluded by calling on all Americans to "religiously observe" the designated "Day of Thanksgiving and Prayer" by assembling

> *with grateful hearts, to celebrate the praises of our gracious Benefactor; to confess our manifold sins; to offer up our most fervent supplications to the God of all grace, that it may please Him to pardon our offences, and incline our hearts for the future to keep all his laws; to comfort and relieve all our brethren who are in distress or captivity; to prosper our husbandmen, and give success to all engaged in lawful commerce; to impart wisdom and integrity to our counsellors, judgment and fortitude to our officers and soldiers; to protect and prosper our illustrious ally, and favor our united exertions for the speedy establishment of a safe, honorable and lasting peace; to bless all seminaries of learning; and cause the knowledge of God to cover the earth, as the waters cover the seas.*[27]

On Saturday, November 3, 1781, Congress went back to church for another thanksgiving service—this time in response to an invitation by the French minister, Monsieur Gérard. It was a thanksgiving mass, held at Saint Mary's Catholic Church in Philadelphia, where the Congress had assembled for an Independence Day observance in 1779. Reverend Bandol, chaplain of the French embassy, again conducted the service, and delivered a sermon praising God for the victory at Yorktown. "Those miracles, which he once wrought for his chosen people," Bandol proclaimed, "are renewed in our favour; and it would be equally ungrateful and impious not to acknowledge, that the event which lately confounded our enemies, and frustrated their designs, was the wonderful work of that God who guards your liberties. . . .

It is he, whose voice commands the winds, the seas and seasons, who formed a junction on the same day, in the same hour, between a formidable fleet from the south and an army rushing from the north, like an impetuous torrent." [28]

Regardless of what any secular-minded observer might conclude, the priest declared, the victory at Yorktown was far more than the work of mere men:

> *Worldlings would say it is the wisdom, the virtue, and moderation of their chiefs; it is a great national interest which has performed this prodigy. They will say, that to the skill of the generals, to the courage of the troops, to the activity of the whole army, we must attribute this splendid success. Ah! they are ignorant, that the combining of so many fortunate circumstances, is an emanation from the all perfect mind; that courage, that skill, that activity, bear the sacred impression of him who is divine. . . . Let us offer him pure hearts, unsoiled by private hatred or public dissention; and let us with one will and one voice, pour forth to the Lord that hymn of praise, by which Christians celebrate their gratitude and His glory.* [29]

After the thanksgiving mass at St. Mary's, Congress reconvened that Saturday for an event that could hardly have been imagined throughout the six years of war: Lieutenant Colonel David Humphreys, one of Washington's chief aides, arrived from Yorktown with a report from the commander-in-chief on the number of British prisoners, artillery, and equipment captured at the surrender. Humphreys also presented the Congress with two dozen British battle flags surrendered by Cornwallis's army. The captured standards had been paraded through Philadelphia— each battle flag carried by an American cavalryman—then dramatically "laid at the Feet of Congress." Instead of exulting in triumph, however, many members of Congress found the presentation sad and sobering. "Members tell me that instead of Viewing this transaction as a mere matter of Joyful Ceremony, which they expected to do," reported former Pennsylvania delegate Robert Morris, "they instantly felt themselves impressed with Ideas of the most Solemn and Awful nature. It brought to their Minds the distresses our Country has been exposed to [and] the Calamities we have repeatedly suffered. . . . But Glory be unto thee, Oh Lord God, who hath Vouchsafed to rescue from Slavery and Death these thy servants."[30]

On the national day of thanksgiving proclaimed by Congress—December 13, 1781—Americans again packed their churches to praise God for the victory at Yorktown. This year's Congressional call to thanksgiving "produced such strong emotions, both of ministers and people, that they could not await the arrival of the day," noted New England clergyman William Gordon. In fact, in some places Americans did not wait, but held thanksgiving services earlier. When the official day of thanksgiving finally arrived, one pastor would later recall, America's churches "resounded with grateful praises to the Lord of Hosts, the God of battles."[31]

In Pennsylvania, the Reverend Robert Smith, a Presbyterian, preached a thanksgiving day sermon that framed the Revolution as a biblically justified defense of God-given inalienable rights. His text—"Let the people praise thee, O God; let all the people praise thee"—came from Psalm 67. "The great object in contest is," Smith pronounced, "whether our essential and unalienable rights and privileges, as well civil as sacred, shall be in our own power, or at the sovereign will of tyrants. Take these from the people, and commit them to any absolute lord, or lords, and no man has security for the rights of conscience, for life, or for property and the means of procuring it. . . . America betook herself to arms in opposition to the most unlawful exercise of power, and in defence of privileges which the inalienable rights of mankind absolutely forbid her to yield!"[32]

The victory sermon that perhaps best reflected the heart and faith of America's Revolutionary generation was preached that thanksgiving day by an Anglican pastor, the Reverend William Smith of Maryland. "In every city, in every village, nay in every private house and family," Smith soberly noted, "long hath the voice of sorrow been heard for heroes slain in battle, fathers deprived of sons, sons of fathers, wives of husbands, brothers of brothers and friends of friends. . . ." American freedom had come at great sacrifice, he reminded his audience, and thus victory should be celebrated appropriately—with a reverent joy:

> *The joy of this day, therefore, brethren, must not be that noisy and tumultuous joy, which consists in outward actions; the glare and pomp of victory, the display of the spoils of war and enemies, shouts of triumph, illuminations, feastings and carnal mirth. It must be a Religious joy; the joy of the heart before the Lord, mixt with a holy and reverential fear. But let us act the part of good citizens, good men and good Christians, and then we may safely trust the direction of that Almighty Being—who is supremely just, wise and holy.*[33]

CHAPTER TWELVE

"He Has Approved Our Beginnings"

In the weeks that followed the American victory at York-town, George Washington repeatedly expressed his gratitude to God. He praised his army, and he valued the French assistance—but he gave God the credit for the victory. He did so publicly. He did so privately. He did so officially. Congress summoned him from Yorktown to Philadelphia for consultation, and en route he spent a week at his Mount Vernon plantation. Other than his quick stop there on the march to Yorktown, he had not been home for more than six years. While there, he wrote to his old friend Jonathan Trumbull, the governor of Connecticut, who had supported his army more than had any other state executive. It was "the smiles of Heaven," he told Trumbull, that would "lead us to the end of this long and tedious war." To the Maryland state legislature, which he visited en route to Philadelphia, he gave credit to "the favor of Divine Providence" for "the freedom, independence, and happiness of America."[1]

He was equally grateful in a statement to Congress, which bestowed its official thanks upon him in a letter he received while at Mount Vernon. The delegates commended the commander-in-chief for the "vigor, attention and military skill" he displayed in his strategy at Yorktown and the "wisdom and prudence" that led to the British surrender. "I consider myself to have done only my duty," Washington responded, "and in the execution of that I ever feel myself happy." Then he shifted the focus from himself to God. "I take a particular pleasure in acknowledging," he explained, "that the interposing hand of Heaven, in the various instances of our extensive preparations for this operation, has been most conspicuous and remarkable."[2]

In Philadelphia, Washington made a brief appearance before Congress. John Hanson of Maryland, the president of Congress, assured Washington that the members of Congress "feel particular pleasure in your presence at this time, after the glorious success of the allied arms in Virginia." Washington accepted the Congressional praise graciously, and assured the delegates of his continued submission to their authority. "I shall yield a ready obedience to the expectation of Congress," he told them, and explained that he was prepared to serve at "whatever place my duty calls." He continued to hope that Congress and the state governments would remain vigilant until peace was formally secured. One more military campaign against the British might be necessary, he believed, and if conducted "under the smiles of Heaven," he predicted, it would surely produce "the establishment of peace, liberty, and independence."[3]

Washington remained in Philadelphia through much of the following winter. He established a command post of sorts in a rented home on Philadelphia's South Third Street. From this house, which he occupied with Martha, he consulted with Congress and conducted army business. While staying in the city, he worshipped at nearby St. Peter's Church, an Anglican church that was the sister congregation to the landmark Christ Church. The pastor of St. Peter's was the Reverend William White, who also still served as chaplain of Congress. White would later recall Washington as a frequent worshiper—"he attended regularly

St. Peter's," he would report, noting that Washington's attitude in church "was always serious and attentive."[4]

Another military campaign to end the war would not be needed. The British surrender at Yorktown did indeed prove to be the end of serious military operations in America. In early 1782, despite the disapproval of King George III, the British Parliament voted to oppose all efforts aimed at "reducing the revolted colonies to obedience by force." Congress directed John Adams, Benjamin Franklin, and John Jay to open peace talks with Britain in Paris, beginning in April. From Paris, Franklin penned an observation that reflected the view of many Americans, especially those in Congress: "Tyranny is so generally established in the rest of the world, that the prospect of an asylum in America for those who love liberty gives a general joy, and our cause is esteemed the cause of all mankind. . . . Glorious it is for Americans to be called by Providence to this post of honor." British forces meanwhile evacuated Wilmington and Savannah at midyear—and at year's end, hundreds of sails filled Charleston Harbor as the British army left South Carolina aboard a fleet of troopships. General Nathanael Greene paraded his victorious troops down Charleston's brick streets as crowds of rejoicing Charlestonians shouted, "God bless you! God bless you!"[5]

As peace negotiations slowly went forward in Paris, Washington tried to keep supplies flowing to his army, which he had moved from Yorktown back to New York, with headquarters at Newburgh. Thousands of British troops were still garrisoned nearby in New York City, and Washington had to keep his army in fighting condition in the unlikely event that peace negotiations suddenly failed. Confident peace was at hand, however, weary Americans began to relax their wartime mind-set, while Washington's troops still had to endure lack of pay and meager rations. Then, in 1782, an American army officer, Colonel Lewis

Nicola, proposed mobilizing the army to make Washington king of America.[6]

Washington reacted with "astonishment" and "abhorrence" and promptly quashed the notion. "If I am not deceived in the knowledge of myself, you could not have found a person to whom your schemes are more disagreeable," Washington wrote Nicola. "Let me conjure you, then, if you have any regard for your Country, concern for yourself or posterity, or respect for me, to banish these thoughts from your mind. . . ." Washington was convinced that the "interposition of Providence" throughout the Revolution was designed to establish American liberty and independence free of any monarch—including himself.[7]

At war's end, he was as quick as ever to attribute the American victory to the grace of God—perhaps even more so. "I join in adoring that Supreme being to whom alone can be attributed the signal successes of our Arms," he wrote New York church leaders in 1782. "May the same providence that has hitherto in so remarkable a manner Evinced the Justice of our Cause, lead us to a speedy and honorable peace. . . ." To a group of city officials, he observed: "In a cause so just and righteous as ours, we have every reason to hope the divine Providence will still continue to crown our Arms with success, and finally compel our Enemies to grant us that Peace upon equitable terms, which we so ardently desire." To another church, he wrote, "May the preservation of your civil and religious Liberties still be the care of an indulgent Providence; and may the rapid increase and universal extension of knowledge, virtue and true Religion be the consequence of a speedy and honorable Peace."[8]

Congress, meanwhile, continued to take public, faith-centered actions even as it struggled under its limited power to correct severe economic problems and meet the needs of the army's increasingly frustrated troops. In June of 1782, Congress adopted a design for the Great Seal of the United States, and the image prominently reflected America's foundational Judeo-Christian worldview. Six years earlier, in 1776, Congress had appointed a three-man committee—composed of Thomas Jefferson, John Adams, and Benjamin Franklin—to develop a national seal. Eventually the committee had come back with a biblical image for the design: it depicted the Israelites being led by God from slavery in Egypt—an image that many Americans equated with their quest for independence and freedom.[9]

In their official committee report, Franklin, Adams, and Jefferson had described the proposed image for the seal in detail:

> *On the other side of the said Great Seal should be the following Device. Pharaoh sitting in an open Chariot, a Crown on his head and a Sword in his hand passing through the divided Waters of the Red Sea in pursuit of the Israelites: Rays from a Pillow of Fire in the Cloud, expressive of the divine Presence and Command, beaming on Moses who stands on the Shore, and extending his hand over the Sea causes it to overwhelm Pharaoh.*

The proposed seal also featured a pyramid towering over all other symbols, topped by the "Eye of Providence in a radiant Triangle whose Glory extends over the Shield and beyond the Figures." On the seal was a proposed national motto that generations of Americans had heard preached from their church pulpits: "Resistance to Tyrants Is Obedience to God."[10]

The committee's proposal had been put aside amid the wartime demands on Congress, but another committee was named to develop a seal in 1779. Its members had recommended an elaborate design, introduced the image of an eagle, dropped the Exodus imagery, kept the "Eye of Providence," and added the phrase *Deo Favente*—"with the favor of God." Congress had not taken action on the revised design, either, but in the summer of 1782, the need for a national seal was again raised by Congress. This time, Charles Thomson, the longtime and widely respected secretary of Congress, took charge of efforts—and achieved success. A Presbyterian elder as well as a Greek and Latin scholar, Thomson would later produce an American translation of the Old Testament directly from the Greek Septuagint. The design for the national seal that he brought before Congress that summer preserved the Judeo-Christian focus originally proposed by Adams, Franklin, and Jefferson, but with Thomson's adjustments.[11]

Congress approved this latest design on June 20, 1782. It would become the official national seal of the United States—the Great Seal—and among what would become familiar features to generations of Americans were distinctive, dominant biblical elements. Among the most striking was the pyramid originally proposed by Adams, Jefferson, and Franklin. It was adorned with the year 1776 rendered in Roman numerals, and the underlying Latin words *novus ordo seclorum*—"a new order for the ages"—which Thomson said "signify the beginning of the new American Era." The image of the pyramid was crowned by the all-seeing eye of God—"an eye in a triangle, surrounded by a glory." In large letters above it was the Latin phrase *annuit coeptis*—"He [God] has approved our beginnings." As secretary of the Congress, Thomson entered an explanation of the symbols into the *Journals of Congress*. "The Pyramid signifies strength and duration," he wrote. "The eye over it and the motto allude to the many signal interpositions of Providence in favour of the American cause."[12]

Three months later, in September of 1782, the Continental Congress made another significant expression of faith when it endorsed the first English-language Bible published in America. Known eventually as the Aitken Bible, it was published by Philadelphia printer Robert Aitken, and was also known as the Congressional Bible. Its publication at war's end was the conclusion of a five-year effort by Congress to commission, fund, and publish the first English-language Bible printed in America.

The project had begun in the summer of 1777, when three Presbyterian ministers from Philadelphia appeared before the Continental Congress to express their concern about a spiritual emergency in America—a shortage of Bibles. The American colonies had always imported Bibles from British publishers—no English-language Bible had ever been printed in America—but the Revolution had halted the flow of Bibles. Unless Congress did something to alleviate the problem, the ministers explained, "we shall not have bibles for our Schools, & families, & for the publick Worship of God in our Churches."[13]

To the Continental Congress, a shortage of Bibles was a major national dilemma, and they gave serious attention to the plea of the pastor-petitioners. One was Dr. Francis Alison, a Scots-Irish emigrant who had helped establish what would one day become known as the University of Pennsylvania and the University of Delaware. A minister and educator, he was known in his day as "the greatest classical scholar in America" and had mentored several members of the Continental Congress. In 1777, he was also assistant pastor of First Presbyterian Church in Philadelphia. The church's senior pastor, the Reverend John Ewing, joined Alison in his petition to Congress. Ewing was also Scots-Irish and a renowned scholar, and was said to have hiked forty miles in his youth to borrow a book on mathematics. A Princeton graduate, he was a multilingual scholar and would later become provost of the University of Pennsylvania. The third pastor, the Reverend William Marshall, had immigrated to America from Scotland as a youth, had held a pastorate in rural Pennsylvania, and was pastor of Philadelphia's Pine Street Presbyterian Church.[14]

The war had interrupted the importation of Bibles into America, the clergymen told Congress. "We therefore, think it our Duty to our Country & to the Churches of Christ to lay this design before this honourable house," they petitioned, "humbly requesting that under your care, & by your encouragement, a Copy of the holy Bible may be printed, so as to be sold nearly as cheap as the Common Bibles, formerly imported from Britain & Ireland, were sold." Congress reacted promptly. A Congressional committee was established to study the issue, and three delegates were appointed to it—John Adams, Daniel Roberdeau, and Jonathan Bayard Smith.[15]

A regular churchgoer and a lifelong student of the Scriptures, John Adams was devout, and had considered the ministry as a young man. "Suppose a nation in some distant region should take the Bible for their only law-book," he once mused. "What a Utopia; what a Paradise would this region be!" Daniel Roberdeau was a successful Philadelphia merchant whose father had fled France in the mass exodus of persecuted French Huguenots. A Presbyterian elder, he too was devout and was married to a minister's daughter. Jonathan Bayard Smith—a friend of Roberdeau's and a fellow Presbyterian—was a leading Philadelphia Patriot, an officer in the Pennsylvania militia, and a prominent Philadelphia businessman who undoubtedly knew the city's printers.[16]

The committee members contacted five Philadelphia printers to determine what would be necessary for the Continental Congress to print thirty thousand American-made Bibles for public distribution. While the printers developed specifications for the job and researched its feasibility, the three-man committee went to work devising plans for a Congressional edition of the Bible that would duplicate the revered King James Version—but without an endorsement by the British king. Instead, as they envisioned it, the American Bible would be endorsed by the American Congress. The committee even provided the official Congressional endorsement for the Bible's title page: "That instead of the Words, 'newly translated out of the original Tongues, & by his Majesty's special Command,' in the title page of our Bibles, it be said, 'translated from the original Tongues and Printed by Order of Congress.' "[17]

"As the Price of Bibles for the Use of Families and Schools is greatly advanced beyond what was formerly given for them, thro their Scarcity and Difficulty in importing them from Europe," the committee advised, "it is highly expedient for Congress to order a common Bible to be printed under their Inspection for Use of the United States of America." The committee estimated that there were approximately a half-million families in the United States and observed that each one was "standing in Need of one or more Bibles." Therefore, the committee members calculated, "many Thousand copies of the holy Scriptures are immediately wanted. . . ."[18]

To spearhead production of the Congressional Bible, Adams, Roberdeau, and Smith presented a lengthy list of recommendations titled "Regulations proposed for the Printing of a Bible for common Use under the Direction & by the Authority of Congress." It suggested printer's specifications for the job, and recommended that the government hire a skilled proofreader "at a proper salary" because "the greatest Precaution is necessary to preserve the sacred Text uncorrupted & free from Errors." To further ensure an accurate version, Congress was advised to provide the printer with "the most correct Copy of the Bible that can be found," and to require the printer to be "bound by solemn Oath not to vary from it knowingly in his Edition, even in a single Iota."[19]

Despite so much time-consuming research and such careful recommendations, production of the Congressional version of the Bible was stymied: the Philadelphia printers reported that adequate paper and type for the job could not be found in wartime America. Importing the necessary tools and materials from Europe was cost-prohibitive and impractical. Even so, Adams, Roberdeau, and Smith did not want to give up on the idea, so they offered Congress an alternative. The committee's official recommendation to Congress noted that "use of the Bible is so universal, and its importance so great," that Congress should take action to "import 20,000 Bibles from Holland, Scotland, or elsewhere, into the different ports of the states in the Union." Upon receiving the committee's report, Congress immediately moved to vote on the recommendation.[20]

The quick vote was partly due to a looming emergency—the measure came before Congress at the time the British army was advancing on Philadelphia. On the day of the vote—September 11, 1777—Congress learned that Washington's army had been defeated at the battle of Brandywine, leaving the capital open to occupation by the British army. Amid the crisis, five of the thirteen states had but a single delegate present to vote on the Bible measure, but Congress did so anyway. The bill instructed "the Committee of Commerce to import twenty thousand copies of the Bible." Some thinly manned delegations declined to vote, and others voted no for unstated reasons—but the measure passed "in the affirmative" anyway.[21]

Further action on the details of the measure was postponed for two days while Congress dealt with the existing emergency. On the day the measure was scheduled to be taken up—Saturday, September 13—Congress found itself facing the imminent capture of Philadelphia by British forces. As the delegates hurriedly made decisions necessary for the evacuation of Congress, follow-up action on the measure to import Bibles was again postponed. Soon armed British soldiers occupied the Congressional chamber in the Pennsylvania State House.[22]

Four years later, in early 1781, the issue of the Congressional Bible was again brought before Congress. This time action was requested by Philadelphia printer Robert Aitken—one of the printers who had provided Congress with specifications for printing the Bible back in 1777. Aitken petitioned Congress to take up where it had left off when interrupted by the British occupation of Philadelphia four years earlier, and sponsor publication of an American edition of the King James Bible. Congressional chaplains William White and George Duffield were asked to evaluate Aitken's printing job, and they gave it an enthusiastic endorsement. "Having selected and examined a variety of passages throughout the work," they reported, "we are of opinion, that it is executed with great accuracy as to the sense, and with a few grammatical and typographical errors as could be expected in an undertaking of such magnitude."[23]

Even so, Congress still had no money to fund the Bible project. The American economy was in shambles, the national government was near bankruptcy, and Congress owed months of back pay to American troops. Aitken decided to publish the Bible anyway, and pay for it himself—and Congress voted to endorse it. On September 12, 1782, Congress passed a resolution officially recommending the Aitken Bible "to the inhabitants of the United States." When the Bible came off the press, the Congressional resolution was printed within its opening pages:

Whereupon, Resolved, That the United States in Congress assembled, highly approve the pious and laudable undertaking of Mr. Aitken, as subservient to the interest of religion as well as an instance of the progress of arts in this country, and being satisfied from the above report, of his care and accuracy in the execution of the work, they recommend this edition of the Bible to the inhabitants of the United States, and hereby authorise him to publish this recommendation in the manner he shall think proper.[24]

Peace negotiations had still not begun on March 19, 1782, when Congress called for another day of humiliation, fasting, and prayer, setting the fast day for April 25. A fast day proclamation was drafted by a committee composed of Joseph Montgomery, Oliver Wolcott, and John Morin Scott. Typically, Congress selected men known for their faith to draft the Congressional prayer day proclamations. A veteran member of Congress from Pennsylvania, Joseph Montgomery was a Presbyterian pastor who had seen combat during the war as a chaplain the Continental

Army. Oliver Wolcott of Connecticut, a signer of the Declaration of Independence, was a devout Christian, described as a man of "deep Puritan faith" and known to his fellow delegates as "a man of integrity." New York delegate John Morin Scott, a prominent attorney and early leader of New York's independence movement, had served as a brigadier general in the war, and was a Scots-American Presbyterian known for his gift with words.[25]

"The goodness of the Supreme Being to all his rational creatures, demands their acknowledgements of gratitude and love," stated the proclamation as approved by Congress. It noted that God's "absolute government of this world dictates, that it is the interest of every nation and people ardently to supplicate his favor and implore his protection." Peace was not yet officially established, the proclamation reminded Americans, and Great Britain might still attempt to suppress America's "sacred and invaluable privileges." Therefore, Congress advised, it was appropriate for the American people to "fly unto that God for protection, who hears the cries of the distressed, and will not turn a deaf ear to the supplications of the oppressed." The resolution continued:

> *The United States in Congress assembled, therefore, taking into consideration our present situation, our multiplied transgressions of the holy laws of our God, and his past acts of kindness and goodness toward us, which we ought to record with the liveliest gratitude, think it their indispensable duty to call upon the several states, to set apart the last Thursday in April next, as a day of fasting, humiliation and prayer, that our joint supplications may then ascend to the throne of the Ruler of the Universe, beseeching Him to diffuse a spirit of universal reformation among all ranks and degrees of our citizens; and make us holy, so we may be an happy people. . . .*[26]

Congress asked Americans to beseech the Lord to "impart wisdom, integrity and unanimity to our counselors," to protect

American troops and prisoners of war, to "protect the health and life of our Commander in Chief," and to "establish peace in all our borders, and give happiness to all our inhabitants. . . ." The proclamation concluded by urging the American people to unite in asking God to "take under his guardianship all schools and seminaries of learning, and make them nurseries of virtue and piety; that He would incline the hearts of all men to peace, and fill them with universal charity and benevolence and that the religion of our Divine Redeemer, with all its benign influences, may cover the earth as the waters cover the seas." [27]

In October of 1782, as peace negotiators in Paris neared agreement, Congress recommended another national day of thanksgiving and prayer. This time Congress ordered the proclamation drafted by a trio of Presbyterian congressmen. Joining Joseph Montgomery for the task were the Reverend John Witherspoon of New Jersey and North Carolina congressman Hugh Williamson. The president of Princeton University and a signer of the Declaration of Independence, Witherspoon was a current leader in Congress. Hugh Williamson was an internationally renowned scientist, a former American army surgeon credited with improving military medicine, and was a devout Presbyterian layman. Their proclamation, which was approved and publicly disseminated by Congress, recognized "Almighty God, the giver of all good, for his gracious assistance in a time of distress," and called on Americans to praise God "for his goodness in general, and especially for great and signal interpositions of his Providence in their behalf." [28]

Congress set November 28, 1782, as "a day of solemn thanksgiving to God for all his mercies." The Congressional proclamation acknowledged "the many instances of divine goodness" to America in the course of the Revolution, and celebrated "the present happy and promising state of public affairs." As it had so many times in the course of the Revolution, Congress recommended that the American people humbly go to their knees. In an obvious allusion to scriptures such as Exodus 19:5 and

John 14:23, Congress also openly urged Americans everywhere to "testify their gratitude to God for his goodness, by a cheerful obedience to his laws, and by promoting, each in his station, and by his influence, the practice of true and undefiled religion, which is the great foundation of public prosperity and national happiness."[29]

Setting the day of thanksgiving for late November proved appropriate—early that month British and American commissioners meeting in Paris agreed to peace terms. Two months later, in January of 1783, representatives from Great Britain and France also agreed to peace terms, and on February 4, 1783, the British government declared warfare with the United States to be at an end. The official end to the American Revolution came some months later, due to the time required for communications to pass back and forth across the Atlantic by ship. Congress received the text of the provisional peace treaty on March 13, 1783, and on April 11, it too ordered an end to hostilities. Four days later, Congress ratified the provisional peace treaty. The finalized treaty would not be signed by the American and British peace commissioners in Paris until September 3, 1783.[30]

Known hereafter as the Treaty of Paris or the Peace of Paris, the long-awaited peace accord acknowledged the end of the war, recognized the independence of the United States of America, and established its national borders. As with so many key Congressional acts, the Treaty of Paris—as approved by Congress—clearly expressed the Judeo-Christian worldview. It began with an official statement of biblical faith—"In the name of the most holy and undivided Trinity"—and stated its intent with a preamble that acknowledged the sovereignty of God:

> *It having pleased the Divine Providence to dispose the hearts of the most serene and most potent Prince George the Third, by the Grace of God, king of Britain . . . and of the United States of America, to forget all past misunderstandings and differ-*

ences that have unhappily interrupted the good correspondence and friendship which they mutually wish to restore, and to establish such a beneficial and satisfactory intercourse, between the two countries upon the ground of reciprocal advantages and mutual convenience as may promote and secure to both perpetual peace and harmony. . . .[31]

Washington was at his headquarters in Newburgh, New York, on April 18 when he learned that Congress had officially declared an end to hostilities and ratified the peace treaty. He followed the Congressional direction with a military order that officially ended all fighting on April 19, 1783—the eighth anniversary of the war's opening shots at Lexington and Concord. "The Commander in Chief orders the cessation of Hostilities between the United States of America and the King of Great Britain . . . ," Washington announced in a general order. To commemorate the long-awaited end of the war Washington ordered an army-wide prayer service for his officers and troops. Army commanders were ordered to read the cease-fire proclamation to the assembled troops, and afterward, Washington ordered, "the Chaplains with the several Brigades will render thanks to almighty God for all his mercies, particularly for his over ruling the wrath of man to his own glory, and causing the rage of war to cease amongst the nations."[32]

As peace was celebrated throughout America, giving God the credit for America's victory became a principal theme of Washington's public and private remarks. Repeatedly, he had publicly implored God's help for the American cause throughout eight years of war, and now that it had ended, he just as consistently acknowledged "the hand of Providence for the American triumph." "I have ever turned my Eye, with a fixed Confidence on that superintending Providence which governs all Events," he told the Massachusetts legislature, "and the lively Gratitude I now feel, at the happy termination of our Contest, is beyond my Expression." To well-wishers in Albany, New York, he wrote: "I accept with heart-felt satisfaction your affectionate congratulations on the restoration of Peace, and the formal recognition of the Independence of the United States. We may indeed ascribe these most happy and glorious Events to the Smiles of Providence. . . ." To an old army colleague, he wrote: "I commend . . . the Interests and Happiness of our Dear Country, to the keeping and protection of Almighty God." To the members of Congress, where he appeared that summer to discuss end-of-war operations, he stated: "No occasion may offer more suitable than the present to express my humble thanks to God, and my grateful acknowledgements to my country. . . ."[33]

It was a theme he reiterated in a farewell letter he wrote on June 8, 1783, to the chief executives of the thirteen states, and thus to the American people. In it, Washington went beyond the normal role of commander-in-chief to urge the states and the American people to always support "an indissoluble Union of the States," to make national unity a priority, and to pursue what he called a "Sacred regard to Public Justice." Washington made it clear that he believed the future of the nation depended upon the American people's faithfulness toward God:

> *I think it a duty incumbent upon me, to make this my last official communication, to congratulate you on the glorious events which Heaven has been pleased to produce in our favor. . . .*
> *The Citizens of America . . . are, from this period, to be considered as the Actors on a most conspicuous Theatre, which seems to be peculiarly designated by Providence for the display of human greatness and felicity. . . . I now make it my earnest prayer, that God would have you . . . in his holy protection, that he would incline the hearts of the Citizens to cultivate a spirit of subordination and obedience to Government, to entertain a brotherly affection and love for one another, for their fellow citizens of the United States at large, and particularly for their*

brethren who have served in the Field, and finally, that he
would most graciously be pleased to dispose us all, to do Justice,
to love mercy and to demean ourselves with that Charity, hu-
mility and pacific temper of mind, which were the characteris-
ticks of the Divine Author of our Blessed Religion, and without
an humble imitation of whose example in these things, we can
never hope to be a happy Nation.[34]

On November 1, 1783, Congress received the news that the British and American commissioners had signed the peace treaty in Paris. A day later, Washington issued a formal farewell to the soldiers of the Continental Army. Already, by an act of Congress, troops were being furloughed and finally sent home. As the army disbanded, Washington issued an "order" to the troops "for the last time." In it, he bade them "an affectionate, a long farewell." He referred to them as "those he holds most dear," praised them for their "spirited and able assistance" to the American cause, noted their sacrifices—"hardships" and "extremes of hunger and nakedness"—and reveled with them in "the astonishing events" that they had witnessed as "a patriotic band of brothers." And, as always, he returned to his familiar theme. Victory against "so formidable a power cannot but inspire us with astonishment and gratitude," he reminded them. "The singular interpositions of Providence in our feeble condition were such, as could scarcely escape the attention of the most unobserving, while the unparalleled perseverance of the Armies of the [United] States, through almost every possible suffering and discouragement for the space of eight long years, was little short of a standing miracle."[35]

The ultimate proof that the war was over and the United States was an independent nation occurred on November 25, 1783. At noon on that date—a sunny, windy winter's day— General Clinton's British army evacuated New York City, the British chief base of operations in America. For seven years the city had been occupied by enemy forces, and when the British left, some seven thousand Loyalist collaborators left with them. Despite the reduction of forces that had begun back in June, Washington still had enough troops left to lead a military parade into New York City.[36]

As Washington and his troops entered the liberated city, which he and his defeated army had been forced to flee so long ago in 1776, their route of march was lined by crowds of ecstatic Patriots. It was an extraordinary, unforgettable experience for Washington and his men. It had required the lives of more than thirty thousand Patriot troops, but the war was truly over, the British were gone, America was free and independent, and peace was at hand. Ten days later on December 4, Washington and his remaining officers and staff met at New York's Fraunces Tavern to bid one another a final goodbye.[37]

Assembled in that liberated New York City eatery, what events did those warriors quietly recall to one another? Perhaps they remembered the unlikely arrival of the artillery that forced the British to evacuate Boston so long ago . . . the gloom and frustration of retreating from New York with a relentless enemy pursuing them across New Jersey . . . and the elation of the snowy victory at Trenton. Maybe they recalled the joyful news of the unlikely triumph at Saratoga . . . how hardship turned to hope at Valley Forge . . . the loss and recapture of Philadelphia . . . and the heady report of an alliance with France. Did they relive the disastrous fall of Charleston and how it was followed by unexpected victories at Kings Mountain and Cowpens? Surely they reveled in memories of the Yorktown campaign with their French allies, and recalled the jubilation of final victory at Cornwallis's surrender. Did they speak of begrimed and ragged troops, and remember the sounds of starving soldiers chanting, "No meat! No meat!?" And did they also recall the heartrending moans of the wounded and the grim, silent rows of American dead awaiting burial in mass graves?[38]

It was a tearful farewell. Men who had routinely risked death in war now fought to control their deepest emotions as they parted company. "With a heart full of love and gratitude, I now take leave of you," Washington told them. "I most devoutly wish that your later days may be as prosperous and happy as your former ones have been glorious and honorable." With a breaking voice, he beckoned to them. "I cannot come to each of you," he said, "but shall feel obliged if each of you will come and take me by the hand." Then, after grasping each man's hand in his, the commander-in-chief was gone, headed for a final appearance before Congress.[39]

Congress was meeting in Annapolis, Maryland, at the time, and Washington traveled there to personally resign his commission as commander-in-chief before the body that had appointed him to the post long ago, in 1775. All along his route, he was saluted by official assemblies and grateful citizens. By December 11, 1783, he was in Philadelphia, where he joined Americans everywhere in observing a "National day of Thanksgiving for Independence and Peace" set by Congress. As it had done throughout the Revolution, Congress recommended the observance with a faith-centered proclamation. "Whereas," the Congressional resolution read, "it hath pleased the Supreme Ruler of all human events" to end the war and grant the American people "their freedom, sovereignty and independence . . . "[40]

The Revolution had been a contest, the proclamation noted, "on which the most essential rights of human nature depended"— and "the interposition of Divine Providence in our favour hath been most abundantly and most graciously manifested." Therefore, Congress advised the American people, "the citizens of these United States have every reason for praise and gratitude to the God of their salvation" for his intervention on their behalf:

Impressed, therefore, with an exalted sense of the blessings by which we are surrounded, and of our entire dependence on that Almighty Being, from whose goodness and bounty they are derived, the United States in Congress assembled do recommend it to the several States . . . that all the people may then assemble to celebrate with grateful hearts and united voices, the praises of their Supreme and all bountiful Benefactor, for his numberless favors and mercies.

That he hath been pleased to conduct us in safety through all the perils and vicissitudes of the war; that he hath given us unanimity and resolution to adhere to our just rights; that he hath raised up a powerful ally to assist us in supporting them, and hath so far crowned our united efforts with success, that in the course of the present year, hostilities have ceased, and we are left in the undisputed possession of our liberties and independence, and of the fruits of our own land, and in the free participation of the treasures of the sea; that he hath prospered the labour of our husbandmen with plentiful harvests; and above all, that he hath been pleased to continue to us the light of the blessed gospel, and secured to us in the fullest extent the rights of conscience in faith and worship.

And while our hearts overflow with gratitude, and our lips set forth the praises of our great Creator, that we also offer up fervent supplications, that it may please him to pardon all our offences, to give wisdom and unanimity to our public councils, to cement all our citizens in the bonds of affection, and to inspire them with an earnest regard for the national honor and interest, to enable them to improve the days of prosperity by every good work, and to be lovers of peace and tranquility; that he may be pleased to bless us in our husbandry, our commerce and navigation; to smile upon our seminaries and means of education, to cause pure religion and virtue to flourish, to give peace to all nations, and to fill the world with his glory.[41]

As Congress had recommended, throughout the newborn nation Americans assembled in their churches to praise God for delivering them from war and oppression—and for the establishment of American liberty and nationhood. In Portsmouth, New Hampshire, the Reverend Joseph Buckminster, pastor of the First Church of Christ, delivered a sermon based on Psalm 98—*O sing unto the Lord a new song; for he hath done marvellous things: his right hand, and his holy arm, hath gotten him the victory.* "Could we comprehend the divine plan—could we look through the scheme of heaven," preached Connecticut pastor Nathan Strong, "we should doubtless see that all natural events, all political events, and all the wisdom of this world, are permitted and designed by the Most High. . . ." In newly liberated New York City, where many of the city's churches had been vandalized by British troops, New Yorkers filled one of the few serviceable churches—St. George's Chapel. There, in a service marked by joyful tears, the congregation was cheered by Presbyterian pastor John Rodgers's sermon from Psalm 116—*What shall I render unto the Lord, for all His benefits toward me?* [42]

In Philadelphia, where Washington observed the day of thanksgiving en route to Annapolis, a large congregation assembled at Philadelphia's Third Presbyterian Church to hear a sermon by Congressional chaplain George Duffield. Like many Americans, Duffield believed that God had delivered the American people from British rule much as the Israelites had been repeatedly rescued in the Old Testament. "'T'is He, the Sovereign Disposer of all events, hath Wrought for us, and brought the whole to pass," he declared on the national day of thanksgiving. "It was He who led his Israel of old, by the pillar of fire and the cloud, through their wilderness journey, wherein they also had their wanderings. 'Twas He who raised a Joshua to lead the tribes of Israel in the field of battle—[and who] raised and formed a Washington to lead on the troops of his chosen States . . . and inspired thy inhabitants, O America!" Washington agreed—and consistently gave God, not himself, the credit for America's victory and independence. "At best," he would write, "I have only been an instrument in the hands of Providence."[43]

Finally, on Tuesday, December 23, 1783, George Washington, the American commander-in-chief, stood before the Continental Congress to resign his command. Congress was temporarily meeting in the Maryland State House. In recent days he had been the guest of honor at celebrations in Annapolis, including a ceremonial banquet sponsored by Congress that had drawn two hundred guests, and an elaborate grand ball. Now it was time to stand down—to officially give up the command he had exercised so faithfully. He had promised Martha that he would be home at Mount Vernon on Christmas, and he intended to keep his word. The war was done. Americans had their freedom, and the United States was an independent nation. He had done his duty and it was finally time to go home.[44]

Eight years earlier, on June 15, 1775, the Continental Congress had unanimously appointed him to lead an army of American amateurs against the greatest military power on earth. So much had passed in those eight years. Most of those delegates of 1775 who placed their faith in God and their approval on Washington were gone now. Many had left Congress to return to homes and livelihoods. Some had gone to serve their states, some to serve in uniform, some to retire. Others were dead, including some who had apparently succumbed to the strain of wartime service. Many had lost homes, health, property, and family in the struggle for American independence. Yet, despite repeated crises, interruptions, controversies, squabbles, and mistakes, the Continental Congress had been unflinching in its defense of American liberty and consistent in its demonstration of a biblical faith. And now it was over, and America had won an astonishing victory.[45]

"We hold these truths to be self-evident," the Continental Congress had boldly proclaimed in the Declaration of Independence, "that all men are created equal, that they are endowed by their Creator with certain unalienable Rights, that among these, are Life, Liberty and the pursuit of Happiness." Now those God-given "unalienable" rights had been secured on the field of battle. Like Washington, Congress publicly credited American victory and independence to "the Supreme Ruler of all human events." Many delegates also believed that God had used George Washington as a key architect of America's extraordinary triumph. Earlier that year, Congress had so advised Washington, stating: "It has been the singular happiness of the United States, that, during a war so long, so dangerous and so important, Providence has been graciously pleased to preserve the life of a general, who had merited and possessed the uninterrupted confidence and affection of his fellow citizens." Now that general stood before them with his duty done.[46]

At noon on December 23, 1783, before a gallery packed with visitors, the new president of Congress—Pennsylvania delegate Thomas Mifflin—addressed Washington: "Sir, the United States in Congress assembled are prepared to receive your communications." For those present, it was an unforgettable event. "The spectators all wept," an observer reported, "and there was hardly a member of Congress who did not drop tears." Standing at attention, attired in his Continental Army dress uniform, Washington delivered his final communication to Congress as commander-in-chief. "I have now the honor of offering my sincere congratulations to Congress," Washington began, "and of presenting myself before them, to surrender into their hands the trust committed to me, and to claim the indulgence of retiring from the service of my country."[47]

In the hushed silence of the chamber, he continued. "Happy in the confirmation of our independence and sovereignty," he said, "and pleased with the opportunity afforded the United States of becoming a respectable nation, I resign with satisfaction the appointment I accepted with diffidence. . . ." His words recalled the feelings he had shared with his wife upon receiving

Congress's unanimous vote to be commander-in-chief so long before in 1775—his acknowledgment that his great task could succeed only through "that Providence which has heretofore preserved and been bountiful to me." His "diffidence" or lack of confidence in taking up his command, he now told Congress, had been "superseded by a confidence in the rectitude of our cause, the support of the supreme power of the Union, and the patronage of Heaven."[48]

Now, standing before the assembled delegates with his duty done and the war won, he again professed his faith in the overruling sovereignty of God. "The successful termination of the War has verified the most sanguine expectations," he said, "and my gratitude for the interpositions of Providence. . . ." At this point—as he spoke of God and his providential protection of America—Washington paused, obviously struggling to maintain his legendary composure. His voice "faltered and sunk," Maryland delegate James McHenry would later recall, and "the whole house felt his agitations." Then the famous Washington self-control asserted itself, and the general resumed his speech, officially resigning his command with a final expression of faith. "I consider it an indispensable duty to close this last solemn act of my official life," he stated, "by commending the interests of our dearest country to the protection of Almighty God, and those who have the superintendence of them to his holy keeping."[49]

Despite Washington's deep longing for his home, his wife, the much-earned peace of a planter's life at Mount Vernon, his resignation would not be the last act of his official life. Congress would be unable to adequately govern the new nation with the limited powers afforded by the Articles of Confederation. In 1787, Congress voted to adopt a proposal to hold a convention for "the express purpose of revising the Articles of Confederation." The states named delegates to the convention, which convened in Philadelphia—at Independence Hall—and the assembly became known as the Constitutional Convention. George Washington was unanimously elected by the delegates as president of the Constitutional Convention, which eventually produced the United States Constitution.[50]

According to the new Constitution, Congress would no longer serve as the sole arm of the national government. Instead, the new federal government would be a democratic republic, composed of three branches: a bicameral Congress with a House of Representatives and a Senate, a federal court system, and an executive branch headed by the President of the United States. Even as the new national government was being formed, Americans favored George Washington to be president. In February of 1789, state-appointed presidential electors unanimously elected him as the nation's first president.[51]

At first he resisted. At age fifty-six, he professed to have no ambition beyond the planter's life at Mount Vernon. "For the great Searcher of human hearts knows there is no wish in mine," he wrote a friend, "beyond that of living and dying an honest man, on my own farm." As always, however, duty came first, and he accepted his country's call. On April 30, 1789, George Washington was inaugurated President of the United States at Federal Hall in New York City, which was the nation's capital at the time. Assembled before him was a giant and jubilant crowd of his fellow Americans. When the moment arrived for him to take the first presidential oath of office, he raised his right hand, and placed his left hand—the hand closest to his heart—upon an open Bible. As he prepared to repeat the oath of office that would make him the first president of the United States, what memories may have flashed through his mind?[52]

Did he remember the narrow escapes he had experienced as a traveler, surveyor, soldier, and commander—the many personal rescues that he considered to be "interpositions of Providence"? Did he recall his countless close calls in combat—so numerous that Congress had declared, "Providence has been graciously pleased to preserve" his life? Did he dwell again for a fleeting moment on his deep belief that the new American nation existed by "the hand of providence"—and that it was by the grace of God that "Life, Liberty and the pursuit of Happiness" would be available to generations yet unborn?[53]

America had been rescued and raised up, he believed, as a place of refuge "for the oppressed and needy of the earth"—and as a model for "the general liberties of mankind." The new nation offered a unique, God-given opportunity for all Americans and others of the world, he predicted—if the American people remained "wise enough to pursue the paths which lead to virtue and happiness" in the future. "I am sure," he would later declare as president, "there never was a people who had more reason to acknowledge a divine interposition in their affairs, than those of the United States; and I should be pained to believe that they have forgotten that agency, which was so often manifested during our Revolution, or that they failed to consider the omnipotence of that God who is alone able to protect them."[54]

As he stood there at that first inauguration with his left hand on the Bible, surely his words and deeds revealed his heart. The oath of office was administered by a Robert Livingston, a former delegate to the Continental Congress and now New York's ranking judge, and the Bible was held by Samuel Otis, the secretary of the new United States Senate. "Do you solemnly swear," Livingston asked, "that you will faithfully execute the office of the President of the United States and will, to the best of your ability, preserve, protect, and defend the Constitution of the United States?" Washington answered in the affirmative. Then, setting a precedent that would be followed by all American presidents to come, he deliberately added the phrase, "So help me God." With his oath of office thus officially affirmed, George Washington then took his first action as President of the United States: he leaned forward over the open Bible and reverently kissed the Scriptures.[55]

ACKNOWLEDGMENTS

In 1848, thirty-five-year-old Benson J. Lossing, an American journalist and historian, set out on a tour of Revolutionary War battle sites in the South as he researched one of the earliest histories of the American Revolution. "I purchased a strong, good-natured horse," he later recalled, "harnessed him to a light dearborn wagon, stowed my luggage under the seat, and, taking the reins, on a bright and balmy afternoon departed on a *drive* of nearly fourteen hundred miles." Lossing's history, *Pictorial Field-Book of the Revolution*, would prove to be immensely popular with nineteenth-century Americans, but his research trip was a daunting challenge. "It was a lonely journey," he admitted, "sometimes among mountains, sometimes through swamps, sometimes through vast pine forests and over sandy plains. . . ." Despite the difficulties and demands of his self-imposed ordeal, Lossing came to view his history-seeking adventure as "a journey of great interest." The hardships of the task, he proclaimed, "were all forgotten when sitting down, pencil in hand, in the midst of some arena consecrated by patriotism and love of country. Then glorious associations would crowd thickly upon the memory, weariness and privations would be forgotten, and the truthful heart would chant, 'Great God! We thank thee for this home—the bounteous birth-land of the free.'"

After researching and writing *By the Hand of Providence*, I can identify with Benson Lossing's observations. I didn't have the pleasure of putting a "strong, good-natured horse" to work or the challenge of bumping along atop a Dearborn wagon, but the unique demands of this long-overlooked topic did at times feel like "a lonely journey," and by the grace of God, I was able to overcome a trail of obstacles that seemed comparable to mountains, swamps, forests, and sandy plains. Thankfully, like Lossing, I frequently found myself "in the midst of some arena consecrated by patriotism and love of country." The historical evidence that records how the Judeo-Christian worldview shaped the American

Revolution is both extensive and extraordinary. It is a story that deserves to be preserved, retold, and remembered. It is uniquely American, and it remains capable of causing one to reverently exclaim, in Lossing's words, "Great God! We thank thee for this home—the bounteous birth-land of the free."

I'm grateful to many people who provided direction and a helping hand on the journey that produced this work. My thanks to the talented teams of professionals in Nashville and New York who contributed to this book, especially Jonathan Merkh, Becky Nesbitt, Susan Wilson, Libby Reed, Bruce Gore, Jaime Putorti, and Kevin McCahill. I'm sure Benson Lossing never met a trail guide who provided better direction and encouragement than my literary agent, Lee Hough of Alive Communications. His contribution was invaluable.

I greatly appreciate the support of the administration of Coastal Carolina University for my work and for the Center for Military and Veterans Studies. I'm also thankful for the assistance I received from the Mount Vernon Library and Archives at George Washington's Mount Vernon, the Library and Archives at Independence National Historic Park in Philadelphia, the Library of Congress, the National Archives, the American Philosophical Society, the Historical Society of Pennsylvania, William R. Perkins Library at Duke University, Kimbel Library at Coastal Carolina University, my fellow historian Max Russell, and Christ Church of Alexandria, Virginia.

As I researched this work, I was frequently reminded of happy, fascinating boyhood visits to the Cornwallis House, Saratoga battlefield, Independence Hall, Yorktown, and other Revolutionary War sites on trips with my parents, Skip and Elizabeth Gragg. Our vacation routes were always laden with historical treasures, and their patience and encouragement fueled my lifelong love of history. I'm equally thankful to my brother Ted, and my cousins Bob and Charles, who kept the fires of history well lit—and for Connie, Sandra, and Martha for endless tolerance. Tony Lunsford and "Aunty" Delores also stoked those fires. I continue to value my always-encouraging Outlaw in-laws: Mama-O, Newt, Deborah, Jimmy, Gail, John, Tina, Doug, Jackie, Joe, and Margaret, and younger generations of potential history hunters—Wendy, John, Eddie, Vaughn, Holly, Shelley, Meagan, Chris, Caroline, William, Mary Catherine, Clayte, Will, Christie, Tommy, Abbey, Shannon, Joseph, Margaret, Sam, and Caleb.

I'm sure Benson Lossing's 1848 jaunt through the backwoods of the antebellum South was no more adventurous than some of the countless treks to far-flung historical sites that I've enjoyed with my family. If not always enthusiastic, they were at least long-suffering—usually. Cheerful thanks to my children—Faith, Rachel, Elizabeth, Joni, Penny, Matt, and Skip—and to my great blessings, Jon, Jay, and Troy. Ahead, I pray, are equally memorable adventures with Kylah, Sophia, Jaxon, and Gracie. Finally, my deepest love and gratitude to my wife, Cindy, who remains the love of my life.

Rod Gragg

NOTES

ABBREVIATIONS

DAB   *Dictionary of American Biography.* Allen Johnson and Dumas Malone, editors. New York: Charles Scribner's Sons, 1928–36.

DNB   *Dictionary of National Biography.* Leslie Stephens and Sidney Lee, editors. London: Oxford University Press, 1921.

GWP   George Washington Papers, 1741–99. Washington, DC: Manuscript Division, Library of Congress.

JCC   *Journals of the Continental Congress, 1774–1789.* Worthington C. Ford, editor. Washington, DC: U.S. Government Printing Office, 1906.

LDC   *Letters of Delegates to Congress, 1774–1789.* Paul H. Smith, editor. Washington, DC: Library of Congress, 1976–2000.

PCC   Papers of the Continental Congress, 1774–89. Washington, DC: National Archives and Records Administration.

WGW   Washington, George. *Writings of George Washington from the Original Manuscript Sources, 1745–1799.* John Clement Fitzpatrick, editor. Washington, DC: U.S. Government Printing Office, 1944.

WJA   Adams, John. *The Works of John Adams: Second President of the United States.* Charles Francis Adams, editor. Boston: Little, Brown, 1850–56.

WTJ   Jefferson, Thomas. *The Writings of Thomas Jefferson.* Paul Leicester Ford, editor. New York: G. P. Putnam's Sons, 1904.

INTRODUCTION

1. George Washington to John Armstrong, 11 March 1792, GWP; George Washington to Gay Fisher, 4 September 1776, GWP; George Washington to Thomas Nelson, Jr., 20 August 1778, GWP.

2. Patricia U. Bonomi, *Under the Cope of Heaven: Religion, Society, and Politics in Colonial America*, New York: Oxford University Press, 1986: 188, 209–11; JCC 21: 1071, 1074–75.

3. JCC 2:81; JCC 22:137; JCC 21:1074–75; James H. Hutson, "Religion and the Founding of the American Republic," official exhibition website of the Library of Congress, 1988; Bonomi, *Under the Cope of Heaven* 3–4.

4. Edward W. Richardson, *Standards and Colors of the American Revolution*, Philadelphia: University of Pennsylvania Press, 1982: 17; Bonomi, *Under the Cope of Heaven* 215; *The Oxford Companion to American Military History*, edited by John Whiteclay Chambers II, New York: Oxford University Press, 1999: 600.

5. Edmund Burke, *Edmund Burke's Speech in the House of Commons, May 22, 1775, on Moving His Resolutions for Conciliation with the Colonies*, edited by Frances R. Lange, New York: Silver, Burdett, 1897: 9, 33; *Perspectives on Church Government: Five Views of Church Polity*, edited by Chad Owen Brand and R. Stanton Norman, Nashville: Broadman & Holman, 2004: 312.

6. Mellen Chamberlain, *John Adams, The Statesman of the Revolution: With Other Essays and Addresses, Historical and Literary*, Boston: Houghton Mifflin, 1898: 249; Henry Williamson Haynes, *Memoir of Mellen Chamberlain*, Cambridge: John Wilson, 1906: 3.

7. JCC 14:649; George Washington to Lucretia Van Winter, 30 March 1785, GWP.

8. Judith Dobrsynki, "Don't Know Much About History: Americans' Knowledge of the Revolutionary War Is Surprisingly Scant," 7 December 2009, Forbes.com; George Washington to Thomas Nelson, Jr., 20 August 1778, GWP.

I. "BY THE PROVIDENCE OF ALMIGHTY GOD"

1. George Otto Trevelyan, *The American Revolution*, New York: Longmans and Green, 1922: 4: 235–36; John Montresor, "Journal of Captain John Montresor, July 1, 1777 to July 1, 1778," edited by G. D. Scull, *Pennsylvania Magazine of History and Biography*, Philadelphia: Pennsylvania Historical Society, 1882: 6: 41–42; Benjamin Lossing, *Field Book of the American Revolution*, New York: Harper's, 1860: 2: 164; Richard McCall Cadwalader, *Observance of the 123rd Anniversary of the Evacuation of Philadelphia by the British Army*, Lancaster: New Era Printing, 1901: 16; Henry Melchior Muhlenberg, "Extracts from the Rev. Dr. Muhlenberg's Journals of 1776 and 1777,"

Collections of the Historical Society of Pennsylvania, Philadelphia: John Pennington, 1853: 1: 164.

2. Trevelyan, *American Revolution* 4: 235–36, 350; Edmund Cody Burnett, *The Continental Congress: A Definitive History of the Continental Congress from Its Inception in 1774 to March, 1789*, New York: W. W. Norton, 1941: 269; Lossing, *Field Book of the Revolution* 2: 164.

3. Trevelyan, *American Revolution* 4: 226–34; David G. Martin, *The Philadelphia Campaign, June 1777—July 1778*, Cambridge: Da Capo Press, 1993: 96–98; Burnett, *Continental Congress* 269; Lossing, *Field Book of the Revolution* 2: 154.

4. "Journal of Captain Montresor" 6: 41–42; Trevelyan, *American Revolution* 4: 235–36, 249; Trevelyan, *American Revolution* 4: 242–49.

5. John E. Ferling, *Almost a Miracle: The American Victory in the War of Independence*, New York: Oxford University Press, 2007: 567; Robert Middlekauff, *The Glorious Cause: The American Revolution, 1763–1789*, New York: Oxford University Press, 1982: 391–95; Trevelyan, *American Revolution* 4: 242–49.

6. J. W. Fortescue, *History of the British Army*, London: Macmillan, 1902: 3: 413; George Otto Trevelyan, *George the Third and Charles Fox: The Concluding Part of the American Revolution*, London: Longmans & Green, 1916: 2: 387; Michael and Jane Novak, *Washington's God: Religion, Liberty and the Father of Our Country*, New York: Basic Books, 2006: 64; George Washington to Benjamin Harrison, 18 December 1778, GWP; George Washington, *The Writings of George Washington*, edited by Jared Sparks, Boston: Russell, Odiorne & Metcalf, 1834: 5: 402; 6: 154; George Washington to Jonathan Williams, 2 March 1795, GWP.

7. Thomas J. Fleming, *Affectionately Yours, George Washington: A Self-Portrait in Letters of Friendship*, New York: W. W. Norton, 1967: 227; George Washington to Marquis de Lafayette, 28 July 1781, GWP; *Writings of George Washington* 10: 179; Novak, *Washington's God* 163–64; Peter A. Lillback, *George Washington's Sacred Fire*, Bryn Mawr: Providence Forum Press, 2006: 612–15.

8. Bonomi, *Under the Cope of Heaven* 3; Abraham Isaac Katsh, *The Biblical Heritage of American Democracy*, New York: KTAV, 1977: 116; Merle Curti, *The Growth of American Thought*, New York: Harper & Row, 1943: 24, 3.

9. Clarence L. Ver Steeg, *The Formative Years 1607–1763*, New York: Hill & Wang, 1965: 21–24; First Charter of Virginia, April 10, 1606, Avalon Project, Lillian Goldman Law Library, Yale University; Samuel Eliot Morison, *Oxford History of the American People*, New York: Oxford University Press, 1965: 1: 86–87; George Percy, "A Trewe Relacyon: Virginia from 1609–1612," *Tyler's Historical and Genealogical Magazine*, edited by Leon G. Tyler, 1922: 3: 267; John Smith, *Travels and Works of Captain John Smith, President of Virginia and Admiral of New England, 1580–1631*, edited by Edward Arber, Edinburgh: John Grant, 1910: 2: 474, 498–99, 502, 537; 2 Thessalonians 3:10.

10. Gary Amos and Richard Gardiner, *Never Before in History: America's Inspired Birth*, Dallas: Haughton, 1998: 128–29; Bonomi, *Under the Cope of Heaven* 16; Winton U. Solberg, *Redeem the Time: The Puritan Sabbath in Early America*, Cambridge: Harvard University Press, 1977: 89; Ver Steeg, *Formative Years* 24; Alexander Brown, *Genesis of the United States*, Boston: Houghton Mifflin, 1890: 2: 835; Records of the Virginia Company, 1606–26, Thomas Jefferson Papers, Manuscript Division, Library of Congress 8: 3: 153; William Smith, *History of the First Discovery and Settlement of Virginia*, New York: Joseph Sabin, 1865: 33.

11. Roland G. Usher, *The Pilgrims and Their History*, New York: Macmillan, 1918: 75; William Bradford, *Bradford's History "Of Plimoth Plantation,"* Boston: Wright & Potter, 1899: 92, 94; Morison, *Oxford History of the American People* 94–95; Richard B. Morris, *Encyclopedia of American History*, New York: Harper & Row, 1961: 36.

12. Usher, *Pilgrims and Their History* 17–53; Morison, *Oxford History of the American People* 94–95; Alexis de Tocqueville, *Democracy in America*, New York: George Adlard, 1839: 28; *The Oxford Encyclopedia of the Reformation*, edited by Hans J. Hillerbrand, New York: Oxford University Press, 1996: 3: 31, 469–70; *The Oxford Dictionary of the Christian Church*, edited by F. L. Cross and E. A. Livingstone, Oxford: Oxford University Press, 1953: 135, 859–60.

13. Usher, *Pilgrims and Their History* 17–53; Morison, *Oxford History of the American People* 94–95; *Oxford Encyclopedia of the Reformation* 3: 31, 469–70; *Oxford Dictionary of the Christian Church* 135, 859–60; Bradford, *Bradford's History* 94–95; Usher, *Pilgrims and Their History* 75, 83–89; "Mayflower Compact, 1620," Avalon Project, Lillian Goldman Law Library, Yale University.

14. John Richard Green, *History of the English People*, London: Macmillan, 1885: 2: 124–30; "Henry VIII," *Oxford Dictionary of the Christian Church* 752–54; Crane Brinton, John B. Christopher, and Robert Lee Wolff, *A History of Western Civilization*, Saddle River: Prentice Hall, 1976: 1: 203–9.

15. Bill R. Austin, *Austin's Topical History of Christianity*, Wheaton: Tyndale House, 1983: 1: 426–40; *Oxford Dictionary of the Christian Church* 1007–9; Thomas Lindsey, *A History of the Reformation*, New York: Charles Scribner's Sons, 1906: 207; *Eerdmans' Handbook to the History of Christianity*, edited by Tim Dowley, Grand Rapids: Eerdmans, 1977: 362–63; Martin Luther, *The Works of Martin Luther*, edited by Adolph Spaeth, L. D. Reed, and Henry Jacobs, Philadelphia: J. Holman, 1915: 29–38; George Fisher, *The Reformation*, New York: Scribner & Armstrong, 1873: 324.

16. Green, *History of the English People* 2: 124–30, 244–49, 257–59, 292–93; Ira M. Price, *The Ancestry of the English Bible: An Account of Manuscripts, Texts and Versions of the Bible*, Philadelphia: The Times, 1906: 260–67; F. F. Bruce, *The Books and the Parchment*, Westwood: Fleming H. Revell, 1963: 222–26; *Eerdmans' History of Christianity* 390–91; Christopher Hib-

bert, *Tower of London*, New York: Newsweek Books, 1981: 65–74; Brinton, Christopher, and Wolff, *A History of Civilization* 1: 470–72; 520–22; Anderson, *Annals of the English Bible*, London: Jackson, Walford & Hodder, 1862: 2: 160, 510–20, 585–96; *Oxford Dictionary of the Christian Church* 752–54, 1051, 1511.

17. Green, *History of the English People* 5: 68–69; *Eerdmans' History of Christianity* 388–89; Daniel J. Ford, *In the Name of God, Amen: Rediscovering Biblical and Historical Covenants*, St. Louis: Lex Rex, 2003: 13–33; Tocqueville, *Democracy in America*, 17.

18. "The Pilgrim Fathers," *The Westminster and Foreign Quarterly Review*, London: Trubner, 1871: 40: 319; *Austin's History of Christianity* 280–83; *Oxford Dictionary of the Christian Church* 135; Jacob Abbott, *Makers of History: Charles I*, New York: Harper & Brothers, 1876: 113, 145; William Henry Stowell, *History of the Puritans in England*, London: Thomas Nelson, 1878: 255–56; Green, *History of the English People* 5: 68–69.

19. Francis Newton Thorpe, *The Federal and State Constitutions, Colonial Charters, and Other Organic Laws of the States, Territories and Colonies Now or Heretofore Forming the United States of America*, Washington, DC: U.S. Government Printing Office, 1877: 1: 77, 1841, 1677, 523, 249–52, 523, 529, 557, 765, 2548, 2753, 3047–70; Peter G. Mode, *Sourcebook and Bibliographical Guide for American Church History*, Menasha: Collegiate Press, 1921: 192.

20. George Bancroft, *History of the Colonization of America*, New York: Julius Hart, 1886: 79; Green, *History of the English People* 4: 1664; Bonomi, *Under the Cope of Heaven* 15–17; Katsh, *Biblical Heritage of American Democracy* 135–38; Amos and Gardiner, *Never Before in History* 173.

21. Bancroft, *History of the Colonization of America*, 79; Green, *History of the English People* 4: 1664; Bonomi, *Under the Cope of Heaven* 15–17, 46–52; Evarts B. Green, *The American Nation: A History*, New York: Harper Brothers, 1905: 6: 100–04; G. W. Acton, A. W. Ward, and Stanley Prothero, *Cambridge Modern History of the United States*, Cambridge: Cambridge University Press, 1970: 7: 59.

22. Joseph Tracy, *The Great Awakening: A History of the Revival of Religion in the Time of Edwards and Whitefield*, Boston: Charles Tappan, 1845: 2–5; Alexander Allen, *Jonathan Edwards*, Boston: Houghton Mifflin, 1890: 180–82; Carl Bridenbaugh, *Cities in Revolt: Urban Life in America 1743–1776*, New York: Capricorn Books, 1964: 150–51; John Findling and Frank Thackery, *Events That Changed America in the Eighteenth Century*, Westport: Greenwood, 1998: 7.

23. Tracy, *Great Awakening* 2–5; Allen, *Jonathan Edwards* 180–82; Bridenbaugh, *Cities in Revolt* 150–51; DAB 6:30–33; Mark A. Noll, *A History of Christianity in the United States and Canada*, Grand Rapids: William B. Eerdmans, 1992: 92; Findling and Thackery, *Events That Changed America* 7; Oliver William Means, *A Sketch of the Strict Congregational Church of Enfield, Connecticut*, Boston: Harvard Seminary Press, 1899: 19; Alan Heimert, *Religion*

and the American Mind: From the Great Awakening to the Revolution, Cambridge: Harvard University Press, 1966: 15; James P. Gledstone, *George Whitefield: Field Preacher*, Boston: American Tract Society, 1901: 91, 102, 149–50; DAB 20: 124–25.

24. Derek H. Davis, *Religion and the Continental Congress 1774–1789*, New York: Oxford University Press, 2000: 66; David W. Hall, *The Genevan Reformation and the American Founding*, Lanham: Lexington Books, 2003: 364–67; 392; Bonomi, *Under the Cope of Heaven* 87–95, 123–26; Heimert, *Religion and the American Mind* 253–55, 290, 346; Claude H. Van Tyne, "Influence of the Clergy and of Religious and Sectarian Forces on the American Revolution," *American Historical Review*, October 1913: 19: 1: 64; John Wingate Thornton, *The Pulpit of the American Revolution*, Boston: Gould & Lincoln, 1860: 86; Proverbs 14:34.

25. Harry S. Stout, *The New England Soul: Preaching and Religious Culture in Colonial New England*, New York: Oxford University Press, 1986: 240–41, 296; Hall, *Genevan Reformation and the American Founding* 388; Abigail and John Adams, *The Letters of John and Abigail Adams*, edited by Frank Shuffelton, New York: Penguin Books, 2004: 122; Abigail Adams to John Adams, 5 November 1775, *The Adams Papers Digital Edition*, edited by C. James Taylor, Charlottesville: University of Virginia Press, 2008; *Biographical Dictionary of the United States Congress 1774–2005*, edited by Andrew Dodge, Washington, DC: U.S. Government Printing Office, 2005: 1779.

26. David Ramsay, *The History of the American Revolution*, Trenton: James J. Wilson, 1811: 1: 47.

2. "FOR SUCH A TIME AS THIS"

1. George Washington, *The Daily Journal of Major George Washington 1751–1752*, edited by J. M. Toner, Albany: Joel Munsell's Sons, 1892: 51–53; DAB 19: 510; Donald R. Hopkins, *The Greatest Killer: Smallpox in History*, Chicago: University of Chicago Press, 2002: 5, 90, 258–60; John E. Ferling, *The First of Men: A Life of George Washington*, Knoxville: University of Tennessee Press, 1988: 15; George Washington to John Augustine Washington, 18 July 1755, GWP.

2. Ferling, *First of Men* 8–12; DAB 19: 509–10; James MacGregor Burns, Susan Dunn, and Arthur M. Schlesinger Jr., *George Washington*, New York: Macmillan, 2004: 4–6; Freeman, *George Washington: A Biography*, New York: Charles Scribner's Sons, 1948: 1: 64.

3. DAB 19: 509–10; Freeman, *George Washington* 1: 64; Marion Harland, *The Story of Mary Washington*, Boston: Houghton Mifflin, 1892: 50–51.

4. Burns, Dunn, and Schlesinger, *George Washington* 4–6; DAB 19: 509–510; Freeman, *George Washington* 1: 64; Washington, *Daily Journal of Major George Washington* 51; Harland, *Story of Mary Washington* 50–51; Esther 4:14.

5. DAB 19: 509–10; Freeman, *George Washington* 1: 50–70; Ferling, *First of Men* 6; J. M. Toner, *Washington's Rules of Civility and Decent Behavior in Company and Conversation*, Washington, DC: W. H. Morrison, 1888: 25, 34.

6. Frank E. Grizzard, Jr., *The Ways of Providence: Religion and George Washington*, Charlottesville: Mariner, 2005: 34; Novak, *Washington's God* 15; Freeman, *George Washington* 3: 449; George Washington to Caleb Gibbs, 26 May 1789, GWP; Jared Sparks, *The Life of George Washington*, London: Henry Colburn, 1839: 2: 357.

7. Grizzard, *Ways of Providence* 34; Novak, *Washington's God* 15; Sparks, *Life of George Washington* 2: 357; Freeman, *George Washington* 3: 449.

8. George Washington Parke Custis, Mary Randolph Custis Lee, and Benson John Lossing, *Recollections and Private Memoirs of George Washington*, Philadelphia: J. W. Bradley, 1861: 152; George Washington, *The Diaries of George Washington, 1741–1799*, edited by Donald Jackson and Dorothy Twohig, Charlottesville: University of Virginia Press, 1986: 1: 4, 13, 17; Freeman, *George Washington* 2: 39–42; DAB 19: 510; Ferling, *First of Men* 12.

9. Freeman, *George Washington* 2: 39–42; DAB 19: 510–11; Ferling, *First of Men* 12; Washington, *Daily Journal of Major George Washington* 51–53.

10. DAB 19: 510–11.

11. Freeman, *George Washington* 2: 178–82; George Washington, *Diary of George Washington from 1789 to 1791*, Richmond: Historical Society Press, 1861: 242–43; DAB 19: 510–11; Sparks, *Life of Washington* 2: 147–48.

12. Ferling, *First of Men* 28–31; Freeman, *George Washington* 1: 371–75; DAB 19: 510–11.

13. Ferling, *First of Men* 28–31; Freeman, *George Washington* 1: 371–75; DAB 19: 511.

14. Freeman, *George Washington* 2: 37, 82; Mark Mayo Boatner, *Encyclopedia of the American Revolution*, New York: David MacKay, 1966: 103.

15. DAB 19: 511; Freeman, *George Washington* 2: 37; Boatner, *Encyclopedia of the American Revolution* 255.

16. DAB 19: 511.

17. Boatner, *Encyclopedia of the American Revolution* 1165–66; DAB 19: 511; Ferling, *First of Men* 40; George Washington to Robert Dinwiddie, 18 July 1755, GWP.

18. Ferling, *First of Men* 33–39; Boatner, *Encyclopedia of the American Revolution* 103, 1165–66; DAB 19: 511; David Humphreys, *Life of George Washington*, Athens: University of Georgia Press, 1991: 15–20; George Washington to John Augustine Washington, 18 July 1755, GWP.

19. DAB 19: 511–12; Boatner, *Encyclopedia of the American Revolution*, 1166–67; Ferling, *First of Men* 40; George Washington to Robert Dinwiddie, 18 July 1755, GWP.

20. DAB 19: 513; Ferling, *First of Men* 52, 62–67, 78–85, 101, 329–31; Boatner, *Encyclopedia of the American Revolution* 1148.

21. DAB 19: 513; "Miscellaneous Colonial Documents," *Virginia Magazine of History and Biography*, 1913: 18: 160–62; Washington, *Diaries of George Washington* 3: 254; Trevelyan, *American Revolution* 4: 17; Evening Orders, 2 July 1776, GWP; Ferling, *First of Men* 62.

22. DAB 19: 510–13; Washington, *Diaries of George Washington* 3: 254; Trevelyan, *American Revolution* 4: 17; Evening Orders, 2 July 1776, GWP; Ferling, *First of Men* 62.

23. Brinton, Christopher, and Wolfe, *History of Civilization* 2: 74–75; Fred Anderson, *Crucible of War: The Seven Years' War and the Face of Empire in British North America, 1754–1766*, New York: Alfred A. Knopf, 2000: 563, 648; Green, *History of the English People* 5: 218; Robert Rogers, *Diary of the Siege of Detroit in the War with Pontiac*, edited by Franklin B. Hough, Albany: Joel Munsell, 1860: 125–35.

24. Brinton, Christopher, and Wolfe, *History of Civilization* 2: 74–75; Green, *History of the English People* 5: 218.

25. Middlekauff, *Glorious Cause* 75–83; Claude H. Van Tyne, *The American Nation: A History*, New York: Harper & Brothers, 1905: 9: 10–15.

26. Van Tyne, *American Nation* 9: 9; Middlekauff, *Glorious Cause* 75–83, 159; Carl Becker, *Eve of Revolution*, New Haven: Yale University Press, 1920: 122–24.

27. Green, *History of the English People* 5: 218; Brinton, Christopher, and Wolfe, *History of Civilization* 2: 74–75; Benjamin Franklin, *Memoirs of Benjamin Franklin*, edited by William Templeton Franklin, New York: Derby & Jackson, 1859: 2: 79.

28. Green, *History of the English People* 5: 218; Brinton, Christopher, and Wolfe, *History of Civilization* 2: 74–75; Middlekauff, *Glorious Cause* 75–83; Trevelyan, *American Revolution* 3: 293.

29. Herman Wellenreuther, *The Revolution of the People: Thoughts and Documents on the Revolutionary Process in North America 1774–1776*, Gottingen: University of Gottingen, 2006: 91–96; Harry S. Stout, *The New England Soul: Preaching and Religious Culture in Colonial New England*, New York: Oxford University Press, 1986: 299; Thornton, *Pulpit of the American Revolution* 43; Alice Mary Baldwin, *The New England Clergy and the American Revolution*, New York: Ungar, 1928: 87; Heimert, *Religion and the American Mind* 244; 2 Corinthians 3:17.

30. *Journals of the House of Burgesses of Virginia, 1761–1765*, edited by John Pendleton Kennedy, Richmond: Virginia State Library, 1907: 359–60; Moses Coit Tyler, *Patrick Henry*, Boston: Houghton Mifflin, 1899: 66–74; Becker, *Eve of the Revolution* 70–77.

31. Bonomi, *Under the Cope of Heaven* 4, 186–88; Heimert, *Religion and the American Mind* 356–58; Becker, *Eve of the Revolution* 77–88.

32. John Fiske, *The American Revolution*, Boston: Houghton Mifflin, 1902: 1: 72; George Bancroft, *History of the United States*, New York: D. Appleton, 1884: 3: 323; Middlekauff, *Glorious Cause* 163–65.

33. Fiske, *American Revolution* 1: 65–68; Middlekauff, *Glorious Cause* 163–65.

34. William E. Leckey, *A History of England in the Eighteenth Century*, London: Longmans & Green, 1906: 4: 175; Becker, *Eve of the Revolution* 208.

35. Abiel Holmes, *The Annals of America*, Cambridge: Hilliard & Brown, 1929: 2:186; Heimert, *Religion and the American Mind* 157–58, 385–89; *The Patriot Preachers of the American Revolution*, edited by Frank Moore, New York: Charles T. Evans, 1862: 200.

36. Kevin J. Hayes, *The Road to Monticello: The Life and Mind of Thomas Jefferson*, New York: Oxford University Press, 2008: 152; William Wirt, *Sketches of the Life and Character of Patrick Henry*, Ithaca: Andrus & Gauntlett, 1850: 75; John Esten Cooke, *Virginia: A History of Its People*, Boston: Houghton Mifflin, 1903: 418.

37. Burnett, *The Continental Congress* 33–39; JCC 1: 27; Washington, *Diaries of George Washington*, 3: 254–55.

3. "A KIND OF DESTINY"

1. Washington, *Diaries of George Washington* 3: 252; A. R. Goodwin, *Bruton Parish Church Restored and Its Historic Environment*, Petersburg: Franklin Press, 1907: 45, 47, 109; Freeman, *George Washington* 3: 355–57; Washington, *Daily Journal of Major George Washington* 51, 54; William S. Baker, *Itinerary of General Washington from June 15, 1775 to December 23, 1783*, Philadelphia: J. B. Lippincott, 1892: 219–20.

2. Washington, *Daily Journal of Major George Washington* 51–53; Washington, *Diaries of George Washington* 3: 252, 254, 272–73; DAB 19: 512–15; WGW 2: 418–19; Freeman, *George Washington* 3: 355–60.

3. Washington, *Diaries of George Washington* 3: 254–55; Freeman, *George Washington* 3: 351; William James Van Schreeven, *Revolutionary Virginia: The Road to Independence*, edited by Robert Scribner, Charlottesville: University of Virginia Press, 1977: 3: 205; Genesis 18:23, 32.

4. Washington, *Diaries of George Washington* 3: 258–59; WGW 3: 344, 418–19; Exodus 8:19; Freeman, *George Washington* 3: 350.

5. Washington, *Diaries of George Washington*, 3: 272–73; Tyler, *Patrick Henry* 1: 213; Freeman, *George Washington* 3: 372–73.

6. JCC 1: 13–28; LDC 1: 34–36, 75; WJA 2: 368–73, 386.

7. JCC 1: 25–28; WJA 2: 368–73, 386; LDC 1: 31, 34–36, 45, 55; Psalms 35.

8. WJA 2: 368–373; JCC 1: 26–28; JCC 5: 530; LDC 1: 31, 35–36, 45, 55; Thomas Jefferson, *The Works of Thomas Jefferson*, edited by Paul L. Ford, New York: G. P. Putnam's Sons, 1905: 11: 420.

9. Boatner, *Encyclopedia of the American Revolution* 620–32; Middlekauff, *Glorious Cause* 268–72; *Spirit of Seventy-Six: The Story of the American Revolution as Told by Participants*, edited by Henry Steele Commager and Richard B. Morris, New York: Da Capo, 1979: 79–89; Trevelyan, *American Revolution* 89–91.

10. David McCullough, *John Adams*, New York: Simon & Schuster, 2001: 110–11; Freeman, *George Washington* 3: 420, 426: George Washington to John A. Washington, 25 March 1775, General Correspondence, GWP; DAB 19: 514.

11. JCC 2:91; Freeman, *George Washington* 3: 432–38; DAB 19: 514.

12. LDC 1: 498; Roger Atkinson, "Letters of Roger Atkinson, 1769–1776," edited by A. J. Morrison, *Virginia Magazine of History and Biography*, 1908: 15: 4: 356; George Washington, *The Papers of George Washington, Revolutionary War Series*, edited by Dorothy Twohig, Charlottesville: University of Virginia Press, 1985: 1: 3–6; Freeman, *George Washington* 3: 446, 449, 452–53; McCullough, *John Adams* 110–11.

13. Washington, *Papers of George Washington* 1: 3–6; LDC 1: 498; Freeman, *George Washington* 3: 446, 449, 452–53.

14. Usher, *The Pilgrims and Their History* 75, 83–89; Perry Miller and Thomas H. Johnson, *The Puritans: A Sourcebook of their Writings*, New York: Harper & Row, 1963: 181; *Calvinism and the Political Order*, edited by George L. Hunt, Philadelphia: Westminster Press, 1965: 185.

15. Christopher Hibbert, *George III: A Personal History*, New York: Basic Books, 1998: 3–8, 11, 14, 20; DNB 7: 1051–70; Neil Grant, *Kings & Queens*, Glasgow: HarperCollins, 1996: 188–205; Brinton, Christopher, and Wolff, *History of Civilization* 2: 11–12.

16. Hibbert, *George III*, 3–8, 11–14, 20; DNB 7: 1051–70; Brinton, Christopher, and Wolff, *History of Civilization* 2: 11–12.

17. DNB 7: 1051–59; William Makepeace Thackeray, *The Four Georges: Sketches of Manners, Morals, Court and Town Life*, London: John Long, 1905: 46, 55, 106, 109.

18. Frank Arthur Mumby, *George III and the American Revolution*, London: Constable, 1924: 17–21; Hibbert, *George III* 3–8, 11–14; DNB 7: 1051–70; Brinton, Christopher, and Wolff, *History of Civilization* 2: 11–12; *Book of Days: A Miscellany of Popular Antiquities*, edited by R. Chambers, Detroit: Gale Research, 1967: 1: 723.

19. Lewis Melville, *Farmer George*, London: Pittman & Sons, 1907, 1: x; DNB 7: 1051–57; Grant, *Kings & Queens* 200–201; *Book of Days* 1: 723; Thackeray, *Four Georges* 92, 96.

20. Hibbert, *George III* 33; DNB 7: 1054; *Book of Days* 1: 253–54; Mumby, *George III* 17–21.

21. *A Faithful Account of the Processions and Ceremonies Observed in the Coronations of the Kings and Queens of England*, edited by Richard Thomson, London: John Major, 1820: 58; Hibbert, *George III* 33–34; DNB 7: 1051–59; Mumby, *George III* 4; Melville, *Farmer George* 1: 223–24; Jerrilyn Green Marston, *King and Congress: The Transfer of Political Legitimacy, 1774–1776*, Princeton: Princeton University Press, 1987: 40–41; *Book of Days* 1: 723.

22. Grant, *Kings & Queens* 204–5; Hibbert, *George III* 79; Melville, *Farmer George* 75, 85; Marston, *King and Congress* 23–26; Thackeray, *Four Georges* 98; DNB 7: 1051–59.

23. Hibbert, *George III* 79; Melville, *Farmer George* 75, 85; Marston, *King and Congress* 23–26; Thackeray, *Four Georges* 98; DNB 7: 1051–59.

24. DNB 7: 1051–59; Mumby, *George III* 99; Melville, *Farmer George* 1: 278; Thackeray, *Four Georges* 106, 109; David Saul, "The Disorder Responsible for George III's 'Madness' Also Affected Many of His Descendants," London *Sunday Telegraph*, 19 July 1998; William R. Wineke, "Modern Medicine Studies the Madness of King George," *Wisconsin State Journal*, 15 April 1996; Dan Newling, "Did George III's Powdered Wig Send Him Mad?" London *Daily Mail*, 15 July 2004.

25. Hibbert, *George III* 91; DNB 7: 1051–54; Mumby, *George III* 4–13; Thackeray, *The Four Georges* 46; Marston, *King and Congress* 23–26.

26. JCC 2: 154–57.

27. JCC 5: 507, 510–15; WJA 2: 368–73.

28. WTJ 10: 268; Katsh, *Biblical Heritage of American Democracy* 116.

29. JCC 5: 510–15; WTJ 10: 268.

30. JCC 5: 510–15; Bonomi, *Under the Cope of Heaven* 213–16.

31. JCC 5: 510–15.

32. WGW 11: 216; JCC 5: 510–15.

4. "THE LORD FIGHTETH FOR THEM"

1. DAB 19: 414; George Washington to Thomas Gage, 11 August 1775, GWP.

2. Richard Frothingham, *History of the Siege of Boston*, Boston: Little & Brown, 1903: 193–94; Richard M. Ketchum, *The Battle for Bunker Hill*, New York: Doubleday, 1962: 190; Boatner, *Encyclopedia of the American Revolution* 406–7.

3. George Washington to Thomas Gage, 11 August 1775, GWP; Ferling, *First of Men* 33, 84–85, 126–27; DAB 19: 514; "Miscellaneous Colonial Documents" 18: 160–62.

4. George Washington to Thomas Gage, 20 August 1775, GWP.

5. William B. Reed, *Life and Correspondence of Joseph Reed*, Philadelphia: Lindsay & Blakeston, 1847: 1: 112–14; John Hall, *History of the Presbyterian Church in Trenton, New Jersey*, New York: Anson Randolph, 1859: 199–200; DAB 9: 375, 15: 451–52, and 19: 18; Samuel A. Harrison and Oswald Tilghman, *Memoir of Lieut. Col. Tench Tilghman*, Albany: Joel Munsell, 1876: 61, 75; Peter Kumpa, "Robert Hanson Harrison: Lost Hero of the Revolutionary Era," *Baltimore Sun*, 31 December 1990; George Washington to the Schenectady Reform Church, 30 June 1782, GWP.

6. Freeman, *George Washington* 3: 460, 489–92; Ferling, *First of Men* 126–35; Boatner, *Encyclopedia of the American Revolution* 96–98; DAB 19: 514; George Washington, *The Orderly Book of General George Washington, Commander in Chief of the American Armies, Kept at Valley Forge 18 May— 11 June 1778*, New York: Lamson & Wolf, 1898: 13–14, 16, 47.

7. Freeman, *George Washington* 3: 489–92; Ferling, *First of Men* 126–35.

8. Freeman, *George Washington* 3: 489–92; General Orders, 21 January 1777, GWP; Ferling, *First of Men* 126–35; General Orders, 28 November 1775, GWP.

9. Bonomi, *Under the Cope of Heaven* 3–8; Samuel Johnson, *A Dictionary of the English Language*, Dublin: Thomas Ewing, 1768; Romans 8:28.

10. General Orders, 5 October, 1777, GWP; General Orders, 2 May 1778, GWP; George Washington to Meshech Weare et al. 8 June 1783, GWP; George Washington to Benedict Arnold, 14 September 1775, GWP; General Orders, 9 July 1776, GWP; General Orders, 28 November 1775, GWP; General Orders, 15 May 1776, GWP; General Orders, 5 May 1778, GWP; George Washington to John Armstrong, 11 March 1792, GWP.

11. General Orders, 5 May 1778 and 30 June 1778, GWP; George Washington to Jonathan Trumbull, 20 July 1788, GWP; George Washington to Congress, 30 April 1789, GWP; Presidential Thanksgiving Proclamation, 3 October 1789, GWP; George Washington to the Portsmouth Safety Committee, 5 October 1775, GWP; George Washington to Harrisburg Citizens, 4 October 1794, GWP; George Washington to Jonathan Williams, 2 March 1795, GWP; George Washington to the Hebrew Congregation of Newport, 17 August 1790, GWP; George Washington to Pierre Charles L'Enfant, 28 April 1788, GWP; George Washington to the Massachusetts Senate and House of Representatives, 10 August 1783, GWP; George Washington to the Albany Reformed Dutch Church, 28 June 1782; George Washington to Alexander Hamilton, 26 August 1792, GWP; George Washington to John Armstrong, 26 March 1781, GWP; George Washington to John Armstrong, 20 August 1778, GWP.

12. General Orders, 9 July and 16 July 1775, GWP; Ferling, *First of Men* 126–27; Freeman, *George Washington* 3: 490–92; General Orders, 22 March 1783, GWP.

13. General Orders, 9 July 1776, GWP; General Orders, 16 July 1775, GWP; Ferling, *First of Men* 126–27; Freeman, *George Washington* 3: 490–92; General Orders, 22 March 1783, GWP.

14. DAB 19: 514; Ferling, *First of Men* 126–27; General Orders, 3 August 1776, GWP.

15. George Washington to Benedict Arnold, 14 September 1775, GWP; DAB 19: 514; George Washington to Fisher Gay, 4 September 1776, GWP; General Orders, 9 July 1776, GWP.

16. General Orders, 28 November 1775, GWP; George Washington to John Armstrong, 26 March 1781, GWP; George Washington to Portsmouth Safety Committee, 5 October 1775, GWP; General Orders, 30 November 1777, GWP; General Orders, 17 December 1777, GWP; George Washington to Landon Carter, 25 March 1776, GWP.

17. Boatner, *Encyclopedia of the American Revolution* 262–64; Freeman, *George Washington* 4: 564; DAB 19: 514.

18. Evening Orders, 2 July 1776, GWP.

19. Trevelyan, *American Revolution* 4: 17; Joshua 1: 6; Boatner, *Encyclopedia of the American Revolution* 1121; DAB 19: 15–17.

20. Reed, *Life and Correspondence of Joseph Reed* 1: 131; WGW 3: 240.

21. Boatner, *Encyclopedia of the American Revolution* 97; General Orders, 15 May 1776, GWP.

22. Boatner, *Encyclopedia of the American Revolution* 97–98, 335–36; General Orders, 15 May 1776, GWP.

23. Boatner, *Encyclopedia of the American Revolution* 97–98, 156; DAB 19: 514; Freeman, *George Washington* 4: 50–53; Frank Moore, *Diary of the American Revolution*, New York: Charles Scribner, 1850: 1: 222–23.

24. Boatner, *Encyclopedia of the American Revolution* 97, 98, 156; DAB 19: 514; Freeman, *George Washington* 4: 50–53; Moore, *Diary of the American Revolution* 1: 222–23; Exodus 14:25.

25. William L. Clowes, *The Royal Navy: A History*, London: Sampson, Low & Marston, 1898: 3: 373–79; Boatner, *Encyclopedia of the American Revolution* 199–200; Walter Edgar, *South Carolina: A History*, Columbia: University of South Carolina Press, 1998: 227–28.

26. Clowes, *Royal Navy* 3: 373–79; Boatner, *Encyclopedia of the American Revolution* 199–200.

27. Clowes, *Royal Navy* 3: 378–79; Boatner, *Encyclopedia of the American Revolution* 199–200; Edgar, *South Carolina* 228.

28. Boatner, *Encyclopedia of the American Revolution* 797; DAB 19: 515; Middlekauff, *Glorious Cause* 340–45; George Washington to Continental Congress, 8 September 1776, GWP.

29. General Orders, 15 May 1776, GWP.

30. General Orders, 9 July 1776, GWP.

31. Freeman, *George Washington* 4: 174; DAB 19: 515; Boatner, *Encyclopedia of the American Revolution* 523.

32. Freeman, *George Washington* 4: 174, 209–31; Boatner, *Encyclopedia of the American Revolution* 522–23; 797–801.

33. Freeman, *George Washington* 4: 174; Boatner, *Encyclopedia of the American Revolution* 522–23; 797–801.

34. Freeman, *George Washington* 4: 174; Boatner, *Encyclopedia of the American Revolution* 438, 522–23, 534–35, 652–57, 797–801; Thomas W. Field, "The Battle of Long Island," *Memoirs of the Long Island Historical Society*, Brooklyn: Long Island Historical Society, 1869: 2: 458, 523.

35. Freeman, *George Washington* 4: 174; Boatner, *Encyclopedia of the American Revolution* 522–23, 652–57, 797–801; Field, "Battle of Long Island" 2: 458, 523; Larkin Spivey, *Miracles of the American Revolution*, Fairfax: Allegiance Press, 2004: 146–48.

36. Boatner, *Encyclopedia of the American Revolution* 797–801; Freeman, *George Washington* 4: 209–31; DAB 19: 515.

37. Boatner, *Encyclopedia of the American Revolution* 782–83, 797–801; Freeman, *George Washington* 4: 209–31; DAB 19: 515.

5. "THE SACRED CAUSE OF FREEDOM"

1. DAB 13: 312; Henry Augustus Muhlenberg, *The Life of Major General Peter Muhlenberg of the Revolutionary Army*, Philadelphia: Carey & Hart, 1849: 50–53; Thomas Emanuel Schmauk, *The Lutheran Church in Pennsylvania, 1638–1820*, Philadelphia: General Council Publications, 1902: 1: 392–93.

2. DAB 13: 312; Muhlenberg, *Life of Major General Muhlenberg* 50–53; Schmauk, *Lutheran Church in Pennsylvania* 1: 392–93.

3. DAB 13: 312; "Life of Major General Mulhenberg," *Littell's Living Age*, January–March 1849: 20: 418; Muhlenberg, *Life of Major General Muhlenberg* 50–53; Freeman, *George Washington* 4: 463; Frederic Klees, *The Pennsylvania Dutch*, New York: Macmillan, 1950: 176; Otto A. Rothert, *A History of Muhlenberg County*, Louisville: John P. Morton, 1913: 4–6.

4. Bonomi, *Under the Cope of Heaven* 3; Heimert, *Religion and the American Mind* 480, 501–3; Stout, *New England Soul* 283, 286–87; Moore, *Patriot Preachers of the Revolution* 228.

5. *Revolutionary Virginia: The Road to Independence*, edited by William J. Van Schreevan and Robert L. Scribner, Charlottesville: University of Virginia Press, 1973: 1: 265 and 7: 164; Bonomi, *Under the Cope of Heaven* 212; David Hein and Gardiner H. Shattuck, Jr., *The Episcopalians*, New York: Church, 2004: 37–43; James B. Bell, *A War of Religion: Dissenters, Anglicans and the American Revolution*, New York: Palgrave Macmillan, 2008: 164.

6. Trevelyan, *American Revolution* 2: 284; Thomas Hamm, *The Quakers in America*, New York: Columbia University Press, 2003: 35–36: Bonomi, *Under the Cope of Heaven* 3–5; Caroline McKean, "Domestic Life Among the Quakers of Philadelphia in the War of the American Revolution," *American Monthly Magazine* (September 1899) 15: 3: 287–89; Isaac Sharpless, *Political Leaders of Provincial Pennsylvania*, New York: Macmillan, 1919: 224–25; Trevelyan, *American Revolution* 2: 284; DAB 5: 299–300; Boatner, *Encyclopedia of the American Revolution* 454; Christopher Marshall, *Extracts from the Diary of Christopher Marshall, 1774–1781*, edited by William Duane, Albany: Joel Munsell, 1877:144; Carla Gerona, *Night Journeys: The Power of Dreams in Transatlantic Quaker Culture*, Charlottesville: University of Virginia Press, 2004, 188.

7. Martin I. Griffin, *Catholics and the American Revolution*, Philadelphia: Martin Griffin, 1907: 1: 281, 2: 164–66; JCC 1: 88; John C. Rager, "Catholic Sources and the Declaration of Independence," *Catholic Mind*, 28: 13: 258–63; Daniel Dorchester, *Christianity in the United States*, New York: Hunt & Eaton, 1895: 25, 250, 266–68; Davis, *Religion and the Continental Congress* 271; DAB 3: 522–23.

8. Frederic C. Jaher, *The Jews and the Nation: Revolution, Emancipation, State Formation, and the Liberal Paradigm in America and France*, Princeton: Princeton University Press, 1960: 138–45; Jeffrey S. Gurock, *American Jewish History*, New York: Taylor & Francis, 1998: 1: 1–20, 81; "Haym

Solomon," *Information Annual 1916,* New York: Cumulative Digest Corporation, 1917: 545; DAB 16: 313–14; Bonomi, *Under the Cope of Heaven* 222; Stout, *New England Soul* 286–87; Heimert, *Religion and the American Mind* 487–91; Katsh, *The Biblical Heritage of American Democracy* 116; Middlekauff, *Glorious Cause* 46; Perry Miller, *The New England Mind: The Seventeenth Century,* Cambridge: Harvard University Press, 1954: 1: 480; Hutson, "Religion and the Founding of the American Republic."

9. Davis, *Religion and the Continental Congress* 43–46; *Calvinism and the Political Order* 38–40; Acts 5:29; John 3:16; Romans 10:9–11; Habakkuk 2:4b; Ephesians 2:8–9.

10. *Calvinism and the Political Order* 38–40; John Calvin, *Institutes of the Christian Religion,* Philadelphia: Westminster Press, 1960: 4: 20, 29–30.

11. Trevelyan, *American Revolution* 3: 287–88; William S. Browning, *A History of the Huguenots,* London: Whitaker, 1843: 8–14; Jon Butler, *The Huguenots in America: A Refugee People in a New World Society,* Cambridge: Harvard University Press, 1983: 26–31; Peter Ross, *The Scot in America,* New York: Raeburn, 1896: 104–8.

12. Charles A. Hanna, *The Scotch-Irish: The Scot in North Britain, North Ireland and North America,* New York: G. P. Putnam's Sons, 1902: 2: 2–6; Trevelyan, *American Revolution* 3: 287–88; Ross, *Scotch-Irish* 104–8; Bonomi, *Under the Cope of Heaven* 206–11; Keith L. Griffin, *Revolution and Religion: The American Revolutionary War and the Reformed Clergy,* New York: Paragon House, 1994: 76–84.

13. *Ireland: From Independence to Occupation, 1641–1670,* edited by Jane H. Ohlmeyer, Cambridge: Cambridge University Press, 1995: 24–28; Sean Connolly, *Divided Kingdom: Ireland—1630–1800,* Oxford: Oxford University Press, 2008: 45–46; Hanna, *Scotch-Irish* 2: 2; Trevelyan, *American Revolution* 3: 287–88, 301–3; Bonomi, *Under the Cope of Heaven* 206–11.

14. Griffin, *Revolution and Religion* 76–84; 2 Corinthians 3:17; Bonomi, *Under the Cope of Heaven* 206–11; Frances E. Marston, "The Scotch-Irish," *New York Times,* 3 May 1902; John Witherspoon, *A Sermon Preached at Princeton, May 17, 1776,* Philadelphia: n.p., 1777: 27–28; *The Diary of the Revolution: From Newspaper and Original Documents,* edited by Frank Moore, Hartford: J. B. Burr, 1876, 1: 125.

15. Bonomi, *Under the Cope of Heaven* 3; Clarence B. Carson, *The Rebirth of Freedom: The Founding of the American Republic 1760–1800,* New Rochelle: Arlington House, 1973: 35.

16. Bonomi, *Under the Cope of Heaven* 3–5; Thomas L. Purvis, *Colonial America to 1763,* New York: Facts on File, 1999: 253–53; Julie Hedgepeth Williams, *The Significance of the Printed Word in Early America,* Westport: Greenwood Press, 1999: 58, 69, 93.

17. Heimert, *Religion and the American Mind* 480, 501–3; Stout, *New England Soul* 283, 286–87; Griffin, *Revolution and Religion* 62.

18. Bonomi, *Under the Cope of Heaven* 210–11, 277; LDC 1: 602; Heimert, *Religion and the American Mind* 480–91; LDC 2: 460–61; Adamses, *Letters of John and Abigail Adams* 75; Stout, *New England Soul* 283.

19. Bonomi, *Under the Cope of Heaven* 215–22; Heimert, *Religion and the American Mind* 446–47; J. C. D. Clark, *The Language of Liberty 1660–1783*, Cambridge: Cambridge University Press, 1994: 301; Charles Royster, *A Revolutionary People at War: The Continental Army and Character 1775–1783*, Chapel Hill: University of North Carolina Press, 1980: 19; E. Brooks Holifield, *God's Ambassadors: A History of the Christian Clergy in America*, Grand Rapids: William B. Eerdmans, 2007: 101.

20. Dorchester, *Christianity in the United States* 266–68; Middlekauff, *Glorious Cause* 49.

21. Bonomi, *Under the Cope of Heaven* 211, 215–22; Heimert, *Religion and the American Mind* 446–47; Clark, *Language of Liberty* 301; Holifield, *God's Ambassadors* 101; Dorchester, *Christianity in the United States* 269–70.

22. Heimert, *Religion and the American Mind* 480–91; Bonomi, *Under the Cope of Heaven* 215–22; Stout, *New England Soul* 283; Holifield, *God's Ambassadors* 101; Ellis Sandoz, *Political Sermons of America's Founding Era, 1730–1805*, Indianapolis: Liberty Fund, 1998: 1: 595–98; Abraham Keteltas, *God Arising and Pleading His People's Cause; or, the American War in Favor of Liberty, Against the Measures and Arms of Great Britain, Shewn to be the Cause of God*, Newbury: John Mycall, 1777: 29–31.

23. Stout, *New England Soul* 3–4, 285–87; Heimert, *Religion and the American Mind* 488–89; Winthrop S. Hudson, *Nationalism and Religion in America*, New York: Harper & Row, 1970: 31.

24. Heimert, *Religion and the American Mind* 489; Peter Whitney, *American Intendance Vindicated: A Sermon Delivered September 12, 1776*, Boston: n.p., 1777; Bonomi, *Under the Cope of Heaven* 125–16.

25. Stout, *New England Soul* 283–87; Holifield, *God's Ambassadors* 100–101; Jonathan Edwards, *Selected Sermons of Jonathan Edwards*, edited by H. Norman Gardiner, New York: Macmillan, 1904: 101–4; Heimert, *Religion and the American Mind* 308, 410–11.

26. Edwards, *Selected Sermons* 101–4; Heimert, *Religion and the American Mind* 308, 410–11, 416, 423.

27. J. I. Mombert, *An Authentic History of Lancaster County*, Lancaster: J. E. Barr, 1869: 247; Wellenreuther, *Revolution of the People* 91–96; Stout, *New England Soul* 299; Romans 8:31; Ephesians 6:10–18.

28. Trevelyan, *American Revolution* 3: 294–96; Bonomi, *Under the Cope of Heaven* 210–11.

29. Hamilton A. Hill, *History of the Old South Church, 1669–1884*, Boston: Houghton Mifflin, 1890: 2: 176–77, 185.

30. Heimert, *Religion and the American Mind* 475, 555, 560; *Diary of the American Revolution* 1:414; John Frost, *Heroes and Battles of the American Revolution*, Philadelphia: W. P. Hazard, 1845: 134.

31. Dorchester, *Christianity in the United States* 265; Frost, *Heroes and Battles* 134; Joel T. Headley, *The Chaplains and Clergy of the Revolution*, New York: Charles Scribner, 1864: 107–9; Hill, *History of Old South Church*, 2: 176, 185; William B. Sprague, *Annals of the American Pulpit*, New York: Robert Carter, 1860: 3: 320–21; Headley, *Chaplains and Clergy* 227.

32. Sprague, *Annals of the American Pulpit* 3: 320–21, 1: 335–40, 5: 254–57; Headley, *Chaplains and Clergy* 227; Thomas J. Fleming, *The Battle of Springfield*, Trenton: New Jersey Historical Commission, 1975: 21–22; George H. Ingram, "The Presbytery of New Brunswick in the Struggle for Independence," *Journal of the Presbyterian Historical Society* (June 1917) 9: 2: 60–62.

33. Sprague, *Annals of the American Pulpit* 3: 320–21, 1: 335–40, 5: 254–57; Headley, *Chaplains and Clergy* 227; Ingram, "Presbytery of New Brunswick in the Struggle for Independence" 9: 2: 60–62.

34. Richardson, *Standards and Colors of the American Revolution* 17; Bonomi, *Under the Cope of Heaven* 215; Lossing, *Field Book of the Revolution* 1: 542; Lucius R. Paige, *Commentary on the New Testament*, Boston: A. Tompkins, 1857: 324; Acts 5:29.

35. Samuel White Patterson, *The Spirit of the American Revolution: As Revealed in the Poetry of the Period*, New York: Badger, 1915: 26; Frank Moore, *Songs and Ballads of the American Revolution*, New York: Hunt, 1905: 13, 38, 71, 86, 181, 278; Thomas H. Gill, *Songs of the Revolution*, London: C. E. Mudie, 1848: 6.

36. Moore, *Songs and Ballads of the American Revolution*, 71, 86, 181, 278; Gill, *Songs of the Revolution* 6.

37. Moore, *Songs and Ballads of the American Revolution*, 71, 86, 181, 278; Gill, *Songs of the Revolution* 6.

38. Michael L. Mark, *A Concise History of American Music Education*, New York: Roman and Littlefield, 2008: 24. Moore, *Songs and Ballads of the American Revolution*, 71, 86, 181, 278; Gill, *Songs of the Revolution* 6.

39. Ellen Chase, *The Beginnings of the American Revolution: Based on Contemporary Letters, Diaries and Other Documents*, New York: Baker & Taylor, 1910: 3: 376–77; Trevelyan, *American Revolution* 3: 294–95.

40. *Extracts from the Journals of the Provincial Congresses of South Carolina, 1775–1776*, edited by William Edward Hemphill, Columbia: South Carolina Archives Department, 1960: 30; William Moultrie, *Memoirs of the American Revolution*, New York: David Longworth, 1802: 1: 55–56.

41. *The Birth of the Republic: The Resolutions, Declarations and Addresses Adopted by the Continental Congress, the Provincial Congresses, Conventions and Assemblies of the County and Town Meetings, and the Committees of Safety in all the Colonies from the Year 1765 to 1776*, edited by Daniel R. Godloe, New York: Belford & Clark, 1889: 159, 350, 173, 282.

42. *The Creeds of Christendom*, edited by Philip Schaft, Grand Rapids: Baker Book House, 1983: 3: 513; Griffin, *Revolution and Religion* 18–29, 40, 62; Aurelius Augustinus, *On Christian Doctrine*, edited by Robert Shaw, Lon-

donderry: Mobile Reference, n.d.: 3: 1: 1; *The Westminster Confession of Faith*, Edinburgh: T. and T. Clark, 1881: 135.

43. Morton White, *The Philosophy of the American Revolution*, New York: Oxford University Press, 1978: 229–56; Bonomi, *Under the Cope of Heaven* 216.

44. Georges Lefebvre, *The French Revolution*, New York: Columbia University Press, 1964: 2: 60, 78–79, 125, 138, 203–5, 270; Charles E. Mallet, *The French Revolution*, London: John Murray, 1892: 222–28; Bonomi, *Under the Cope of Heaven* 214–16.

45. White, *Philosophy of the American Revolution* 244–51; Bonomi, *Under the Cope of Heaven* 216; General Orders, 28 November 1775, 5 May 1778, GWP.

6. "A SIGNAL STROKE OF PROVIDENCE"

1. George Washington to Fisher Gay, 4 September 1776, GWP; Claude H. Van Tyne, *The War of Independence: American Phase*, Boston: Houghton Mifflin, 1929: 258–62; Trevelyan, *American Revolution* 1: 6–11.

2. Van Tyne, *War of Independence* 258–62; Trevelyan, *American Revolution* 1: 6–11; Thomas Rodney, "Diary of Captain Thomas Rodney, 1776–1777," *Papers of the Historical Society of Delaware*, edited by Charles P. Mallery, Wilmington: Historical Society of Delaware, 1888: 7: 13; William M. Dwyer, *The Day Is Ours! An Inside View of the Battles of Trenton and Princeton*, New York: Viking, 1983: 191.

3. Boatner, *Dictionary of the American Revolution* 797–801; Freeman, *George Washington* 4: 209–31; DAB 19: 515.

4. Morris, *Encyclopedia of American History* 105; Boatner, *Encyclopedia of the American Revolution* 784–86, 891–95; 1112; Freeman, *George Washington* 4: 322–24; James Wilkinson, *Memoirs of My Own Time*, Philadelphia: Abraham Small, 1816: 1: 126.

5. WGW 3: 500; Hill, *History of the Old South Church* 2: 186; Arthur B. Ellis, *History of the First Church in Boston, 1630–1880*, Boston: Hall & Whiting, 1881: 172, 240; Freeman, *George Washington* 4: 61–63.

6. Sprague, *Annals of the American Pulpit* 1: 417–20; WGW 3: 500.

7. Sprague, *Annals of the American Pulpit* 1: 418; WGW 3: 499–500; Bonomi, *Under the Cope of Heaven* 16; Isaiah 33:20–22.

8. WGW 3: 499–500.

9. Freeman, *George Washington* 4: 61–62; WGW 3: 499–500.

10. Van Tyne, *War of Independence* 258–62; Trevelyan, *American Revolution* 3: 99–100; George A. Billias, *General John Glover and His Marblehead Mariners*, New York: Henry Holt, 1960: 69; Boatner, *Dictionary of the American Revolution* 797–801; Freeman, *George Washington* 4: 209–31; DAB 19: 515.

11. Van Tyne, *War of Independence* 258–62; Trevelyan, *American Revolution* 3: 90, 99–100; David Hackett Fischer, *Washington's Crossing*, New York: Oxford University Press, 2004: 242; Boatner, *Encyclopedia of the American Revolution* 1112–14.

12. Fischer, *Washington's Crossing* 311; Ferling, *Almost a Miracle* 176–78; Boatner, *Encyclopedia of the American Revolution* 784–86, 891–95; Freeman, *George Washington* 4: 322–24.

13. Fischer, *Washington's Crossing* 239–44; Ferling, *Almost a Miracle* 184.

14. Fischer, *Washington's Crossing* 259; Boatner, *Encyclopedia of the American Revolution* 786; Christopher Ward, *The War of the Revolution*, New York: Macmillan, 1952: 2: 318; Fortescue, *History of the British Army* 3: 202.

15. WGW 3: 240; WGW 5: 188; General Orders, 14 November 1775, GWP.

16. George Washington Resignation Address, 23 December 1783, GWP; Freeman, *George Washington*, 4: 353–54.

17. Boatner, *Encyclopedia of the American Revolution* 132.

18. Middlekauff, *Glorious Cause* 391–95; Trevelyan, *American Revolution* 4: 242–49; Burnett, *Continental Congress* 662.

19. Francis Heyl, *The Battle of Germantown*, Philadelphia: City History Society of Philadelphia, 1908: 58–62; Fortescue, *History of the British Army* 3: 202–3; Middlekauff, *Glorious Cause* 391–95; Trevelyan, *American Revolution* 4: 242–49.

20. Heyl, *Battle of Germantown* 62; Middlekauff, *Glorious Cause* 391–95; Trevelyan, *American Revolution* 4: 242–49.

21. DAB 6: 331–32; Anne Ousterhout, *The Most Learned Woman in America: A Life of Elizabeth Graeme Fergusson*, University Park: Penn State University Press, 2003: 115, 118, 203–7; Freeman, *George Washington* 4: 541; William B. Bigelow, "The Country Church in America," *Scribner's Magazine* (July–December 1897) 22: 606.

22. DAB 6: 331–32; Ousterhout, *Most Learned Woman in America* 115, 118, 242–49; Freeman, *George Washington* 4: 541.

23. WJA 2: 368–73, 386; JCC 1: 25–28; LDC 1: 31, 35–36, 45, 55; Jacob Duché to George Washington, 8 October, 1777, Portfolio 40, Folder 13, Printed Ephemera Collection, Rare Book and Special Collections Division, Library of Congress; Freeman, *George Washington* 4: 541–42.

24. Edward D. Neil, "Rev. Jacob Duché: First Chaplain of Congress," *Pennsylvania Magazine of History and Biography* (1878) 2: 1: 70–78; Francis V. Cabeen, "The Society of the Sons of Tammany of Philadelphia," *Pennsylvania Magazine of History and Biography*, 1901: 25: 1: 447; Ousterhout, *Most Learned Woman in America* 203–7; Freeman, *George Washington* 4: 541–43.

25. Neil, "Rev. Jacob Duché" 2: 70–78; Cabeen, "Society of the Sons of Tammany" 25: 1: 447; Ousterhout, *Most Learned Woman in America* 203–7; Freeman, *George Washington* 4: 541–43.

26. George Washington to the President of Congress, 16 October 1777, GWP; Freeman, *George Washington* 4: 452; WGW 6: 115–17; General Orders, 5 May 1778, GWP; General Orders, 2 May 1778, GWP.

27. Freeman, *George Washington* 4: 452; WGW 6: 115–17; General Orders, 2 May 1778, GWP.

28. Freeman, *George Washington* 4: 522, 544–45; Boatner, *Encyclopedia of the American Revolution* 130–35; Richard M. Ketchum, *Saratoga: Turning Point of America's Revolutionary War*, New York: Henry Holt, 1997: 77.

29. Boatner, *Encyclopedia of the American Revolution* 971–74, 991; Ketchum, *Saratoga* 249–60.

30. Boatner, *Encyclopedia of the American Revolution* 971–78; Ketchum, *Saratoga* 399–405.

31. Boatner, *Encyclopedia of the American Revolution* 971–78; Ketchum, *Saratoga* 435–39.

32. Freeman, *George Washington* 4: 522, 544–45; George Washington to Kings County, New York Citizens, 1 December 1783, GWP; *Diary of the American Revolution* 1: 481; Fortescue, *History of the British Army* 1: 242–43.

33. General Orders, 18 October 1777, and George Washington to John A. Washington, 18 October 1777, GWP.

34. Boatner, *Encyclopedia of the American Revolution* 977–79; Ketchum, *Saratoga* 77, 135–39, 249–60; GWB 4: 522; Psalm 91:2–3; *Connecticut Courant*, 25 August 1777.

35. General Orders, 18 October 1777, and George Washington to John A. Washington, 18 October 1777, GWP.

7. "BY THE HAND OF PROVIDENCE"

1. Albigence Waldo, "Diary of Surgeon Albigence Waldo, of the Connecticut Line," *Pennsylvania Magazine of History and Biography*, edited by Charles J. Stille, Philadelphia: Historical Society of Pennsylvania, 1897: 21: 1: 309; Freeman, *George Washington* 4: 564.

2. George F. Scheer and Hugh F. Rankin, *Rebels and Redcoats*, New York: World, 1957: 289; Freeman, *George Washington* 4: 564; "Diary of Surgeon Waldo" 21: 308–20; Boatner, *Encyclopedia of the American Revolution* 1136–37; JCC 9: 855.

3. General Orders, 30 November 1777, GWP; Freeman, *George Washington* 4: 564.

4. Henry Dearborn, *Journals of Henry Dearborn 1776–1783*, Cambridge: John Wilson & Sons University Press, 1887: 13; Freeman, *George Washington* 4: 522.

5. Boatner, *Encyclopedia of the American Revolution* 1136–37; General Orders, 17 December 1777, GWP.

6. Boatner, *Encyclopedia of the American Revolution* 1136–37; George Weedon, *Valley Forge Orderly Book of General George Weedon of the Continental Army under Gen'l George Washington, in the Campaign of 1777–1778*, New York: Dodd, Mead, 1902: 161; Scheer and Rankin, *Rebels and Redcoats* 303–9.

7. Philip Van Cortlandt, *Revolutionary War Memoir and Selected Correspondence of Philip Van Cortlandt*, edited by Jacob Judd, Tarrytown: Sleepy Hollow Restorations, 1976: 119; Freeman, *George Washington* 4: 575–77.

8. "Diary of Surgeon Waldo" 21: 310; John Ferling, *A Leap in the Dark: The Struggle to Create the American Republic*, New York: Oxford University

Press: 2003: 204; William Shepard to David Mosely, 25 January 1778, as quoted in Freeman, *George Washington* 4: 579.

9. Henry F. Thompson, "A Letter of Miss Rebecca Franks, 1778," *Pennsylvania Magazine of History and Biography*, Philadelphia: Historical Society of Pennsylvania, 1892: 16: 1; 216; Scheer and Rankin, *Rebels and Redcoats* 318.

10. George Washington to the President of the Congress, 23 December 1777, GWP; Freeman, *George Washington* 4: 576–77.

11. Boatner, *Encyclopedia of the American Revolution* 1136–37; William S. Baker, "Itinerary of General Washington, 1777," *Pennsylvania Magazine of History and Biography*, Philadelphia: Historical Society of Pennsylvania, 1890: 14: 1: 279.

12. DAB 19: 518; Boatner, *Encyclopedia of the American Revolution* 1167; Ferling, *Almost a Miracle* 288–89; Scheer and Rankin, *Rebels and Redcoats* 303; "Six Letters of 'Signers' in 'Active Service,' " *Pennsylvania Magazine of History and Biography*, Philadelphia: Historical Society of Pennsylvania, 1916: 40: 1: 487.

13. Boatner, *Encyclopedia of the American Revolution* 278–79; Freeman, *George Washington* 4: 550–52; Henry Laurens, *The Papers of Henry Laurens, November 1, 1777–March 15, 1778*, edited by David R. Chestnutt and Peggy J. Clark, Columbia: University of South Carolina Press, 1990: 12: 285.

14. WGW 5: 329; Freeman, *George Washington* 4: 583–86; Boatner, *Encyclopedia of the American Revolution* 454–56.

15. "Autobiographical Letters of Peter Duponceau," *Pennsylvania Magazine of History and Biography*, Philadelphia: Historical Society of Pennsylvania, January 1912: 40: 157; 179; John Laurens, *The Army Correspondence of Colonel John Laurens in the Years 1777–1778*, edited by William Gilmore Simms, New York: Bedford Club, 1867: 136; Tench Tilghman, *Memoir of Lieut. Col. Tench Tilghman, Secretary and Aid to Washington*, edited by Samuel A. Harrison and Oswald Tilghman, Albany: Joel Munsell, 1876, 153; Freeman, *George Washington* 4: 564–66, 581; General Orders, 17 December 1777, GWP; WGW 11: 252.

16. Sparks, *Life of George Washington* 522; George Washington to John Armstrong, 11 March 1792, GWP; George Washington to John Armstrong, 26 March 1781; Freeman, *George Washington* 5: 493; Esther 4:14.

17. WGW 5: 194; Scheer and Rankin, *Rebels and Redcoats* 316–20; Weedon, *Valley Forge Orderly Book* 95, 168–69, 175, 177, 186.

18. WGW 5: 194, 329; Scheer and Rankin, *Rebels and Redcoats* 316–20; Weedon, *Valley Forge Orderly Book* 95, 168–69, 175, 177, 186.

19. Freeman, *George Washington* 4: 575–75; Ferling, *Almost a Miracle* 281; Matthew 7:12; Trevelyan, *American Revolution* 3: 31–33; Tilghman, *Memoir of Lt. Col. Tench Tilghman* 155.

20. WGW 5: 329; Freeman, *George Washington* 4: 583–86; Boatner, *Encyclopedia of the American Revolution* 454–56.

21. "Diary of Surgeon Waldo" 21:319; Scheer and Rankin, *Rebels and Redcoats* 201; George Washington Greene, *The Life of Nathanael Greene*, Boston: Houghton Mifflin, 1900: 1: 545; WGW 11: 252; JCC 10: 229.

22. WGW 11: 291–92.

23. "Washington's Respect for Ministers," *The Guardian: A Monthly Magazine,* edited by H. Harbaugh, July 1857: 8: 7: 221; Headley, *Chaplains and Clergy of the Revolution* 300–3; John Calvin Thorne, *A Monograph of the Rev. Israel Evans,* New York: William Abbatt, 1907: 7–14.

24. Headley, *Chaplains and Clergy of the Revolution,* 300–3; Thorne, *Monograph of the Rev. Israel Evans,* 7–14; WGW 11: 78.

25. "Washington's Respect for Ministers" 8: 221.

26. DAB 13: 309–11; Freeman, *George Washington* 4: 463; Henry Melchior Muhlenberg, *The Journals of Henry Melchior Muhlenberg,* edited by Theodore Gerhardt, Philadelphia: Evangelical Lutheran Ministerium of Pennsylvania, 1942: 3: 149; George Washington, *Washington's Inaugural Address of 1789,* Washington, DC: National Archives and Records Administration, 1986.

27. Muhlenberg, *Journals of Henry Melchior Muhlenberg* 3: 149.

28. Mrs. Thomas Potts James, *Memorial of Thomas Potts Junior,* Cambridge: n.p., 1874: 220; "Washington's Prayer at Valley Forge," *The Friend: A Religious and Literary Journal,* 25 March 1907: 80: 46, 363; Freeman, *George Washington* 4: 572; Mason Locke Weems, *A History of the Life and Death, Virtues and Exploits of General George Washington,* Philadelphia: J. B. Lippincott, 1918: 234; DAB 19: 604–5.

29. General Orders, 2 May 1778, GWP; Weedon, *Valley Forge Orderly Book* 303; WGW 11: 342–43.

30. WGW 5: 247; Romans 8:28.

31. Freeman, *George Washington* 4: 616–19; Boatner, *Encyclopedia of the American Revolution* 1055–58.

32. Boatner, *Encyclopedia of the American Revolution* 1137; LDC 9: 700; Page Smith, *A People's History of the American Revolution,* New York: McGraw-Hill, 1976: 2: 1016; WGW 12: 343.

33. Hoffman Nickerson, *The Turning Point of the Revolution,* Cambridge: Riverside Press, 1928: 410–17; Boatner, *Encyclopedia of the Revolution,* 400–401.

34. Freeman, *George Washington* 5: 1–2; General Orders, 5 May 1778, GWP; *Valley Forge Orderly Book* 307; Hampton Carson, "Washington at Valley Forge," *Pennsylvania Magazine of History and Biography,* 1919: 43: 1: 115.

35. General Orders, 5 May 1778, GWP; *Valley Forge Orderly Book* 307; Freeman, *George Washington* 5: 2.

36. Boatner, *Encyclopedia of the American Revolution* 236–38, 524–25, 844–45; Freeman, *George Washington* 5: 10; Carson, "Washington at Valley Forge" 43: 113: WGW 11: 3–4.

37. Trevelyan, *American Revolution* 4: 341–44; "Notices of New Works," *Metropolitan Magazine* (February 1838) 21: 44; Robert Leckie, *George Washington's War: The Saga of the American Revolution,* New York: HarperCollins, 1992: 146–47; Charles Lee, *Memoirs of the Life of the Late Charles Lee,* edited by Edward Langworthy, London: J. S. Jordan, 1792: 424; Ketchum, *Sara-*

toga 78; Boatner, *Encyclopedia of the American Revolution* 524–26; "Original Letters," *Collections of the New Hampshire Historical Society*, (1827) 2: 166–67.

38. Leckie, *George Washington's War* 146–47; Lee, *Memoirs of the Life of the Late Charles Lee* 424; Boatner, *Encyclopedia of the American Revolution* 524–26; "Original Letters" 2: 166–67.

39. WGW 3: 504; George Washington to John A. Washington, 31 March 1776, PGW; Van Tyne, *War for Independence* 2: 432; George Washington to Annapolis Officials, 22 December 1783, PGW.

40. Henry Clinton, *The American Rebellion: Sir Henry Clinton's Narrative of His Campaigns 1775–1782*, edited by William B. Willcox, New York: Archon Books, 1971: 21: 87–90; Van Tyne, *War for Independence* 2: 432; Trevelyan, *American Revolution* 4: 376–79; Freeman, *George Washington* 5: 27–30; Boatner, *Encyclopedia of the American Revolution* 718–19.

41. Van Tyne, *War for Independence* 2: 432; Trevelyan, *American Revolution* 4: 376–79; Freeman, *George Washington* 5: 27–30; Boatner, *Encyclopedia of the American Revolution* 718–19.

42. Trevelyan, *American Revolution* 4: 378–79; General Orders, 30 June 1778, GWP.

43. Trevelyan, *American Revolution* 4: 385–87; Freeman, *George Washington* 5: 37–46; Middlekauff, *Glorious Cause* 429.

44. Trevelyan, *American Revolution* 4: 385–87; Morris, *Encyclopedia of American History* 103–11; WGW 7: 161; George Washington to Thomas Nelson, Jr., 20 August 1778, GWP.

8. "UNDER THE SMILES OF HEAVEN"

1. Samuel Holten, "Journal of Samuel Holten, M.D., While in the Continental Congress, May 1778 to August 1780," *Historical Collection of the Essex Institute*, 1919: 55: 166; JCC 11: 641; Burnett, *Continental Congress* 340: John W. Jordan, "Sessions of the Continental Congress Held in the College of Philadelphia in July 1778," *Pennsylvania Magazine of History and Biography*, Philadelphia: Historical Society of Philadelphia, 1898: 22: 114–15.

2. Holten, "Journal of Samuel Holten" 55: 166; JCC 11: 641; Jordan, "Sessions of the Continental Congress Held in the College of Philadelphia" 22: 114–15.

3. JCC 11: 641; LDC 10: 165.3; JCC 22: 137; LDC 9: 562; 632.

4. James H. Hutson, *Forgotten Features of the Founding: The Recovery of Religious Themes in the Early American Republic*, Lanham: Lexington Books, 2003: 1; James H. Hutson, *Religion and the Founding of the American Republic*, Washington, DC: Library of Congress, 1988: 50–52.

5. Katsh, *Biblical Heritage of American Democracy* 115; JCC 11: 657.

6. Moses Coit Tyler, *The Literary History of the American Revolution 1763–1783*, New York: G. P. Putnam's Sons, 1897: 2: 284–86; JCC 4: 208–9; JCC 2: 192; 2 Chronicles 7:14.

7. Bonomi, *Under the Cope of Heaven* 69, 211; John 3:16; William D. Love, *The Fast and Thanksgiving Days of New England*, Boston: Houghton Mifflin, 1895: 345; *Religion and the Law: A Handbook of Suggestions for Laymen and Clergy Preparing Law Day Addresses*, Chicago: American Bar Association, 1975: 48; Caleb Haskell, *Caleb Haskell's Diary, May 5, 1775–May 30, 1776*, edited by Lothrop Withington, Newburyport: William H. Huse: 1881: 8.

8. *Diary of the Revolution* 1: 86–87, 118; "Yesterday," *New York Gazette*, 24 July 1775; "At New Castle, Delaware," *Pennsylvania Packet*, 24 July 1775.

9. Christopher Marshall, *Passages from the Diary of Christopher Marshall*, edited by William Duane, Philadelphia: Hazard & Mitchell, 1849: 1: 71; *Diary of the Revolution* 1: 53.

10. JCC 2: 87–88; Love, *Fast and Thanksgiving Days* 442; "Chronological Table," *Collections of the Massachusetts Historical Society*, Boston: Munroe, Francis & Parker, 1809: 10: 217; Adamses, *Letters of John and Abigail Adams* 64.

11. *Journals of Each Provincial Congress in Massachusetts 1774 and 1775*, edited by William Lincoln, Boston: Dutton & Wentworth, 1839: 383–85.

12. *Records of the Presbyterian Church in the United States, 1706–1788*, edited by William Engles, Philadelphia: Presbyterian Board of Publications, 1841: 466–67; Job 11:13–14.

13. JCC 6: 1022–23.

14. Ibid.; JCC 8: 453.

15. JCC 9: 854–55; 907; Davis, *Religion and the Continental Congress* 87.

16. JCC 9: 854–55.

17. JCC 10: 229–30.

18. Ibid.

19. JCC 15: 1192; JCC 9: 855; JCC 6: 1022.

20. JCC 11: 474–81.

21. Ibid.

22. Ibid.; Micah 4:4.

23. LDC 10: 165, 317; LDC 6: 209; LDC 1: 599; LDC 9: 631.

24. LDC 3: 320; LDC 9: 562; JCC 10: 229–30; Davis, *Religion and the Continental Congress* 68; JCC 12: 1138–39.

25. LDC 8: 186–87; 506; LDC 6: 269–70; LDC 10: 325–26; JCC 11: 474–81; George Clinton, *Public Papers of George Clinton, First Governor of New York*, Albany, James B. Lyon, 1900: 3: 303; *Documents from the Revolutionary History of the State of New Jersey*, edited by William S. Stryker, Trenton: John I. Murphy, 1901: 1: 528.

26. JCC 5: 510–15; JCC 12: 1080–83; William V. Wells, *The Life and Public Service of Samuel Adams*, Boston: Little & Brown, 1865: 3: 413; Charles Stedman, *The History of the Origin, Progress and Termination of the American War*, London: J. Murray, 1794: 2: 58–63.

27. Middlekauff, *Glorious Cause* 407–8; Boatner, *Encyclopedia of the American Revolution* 844; Stedman, *History of the American War* 2: 58–63.

28. Middlekauff, *Glorious Cause* 407–8; Stedman, *History of the American War* 2: 58–63.

29. *The Parliamentary History of England,* edited by T. C. Hansard, London: T. C. Hansard, 1814: 19: 1391; *Annals of the American Revolution,* edited by Jedediah Morse, Hartford: J. Morse, 1824: 298–302; Middlekauff, *Glorious Cause* 407–8; Boatner, *Encyclopedia of the Revolution* 844; LCC 4: 144.

30. JCC 12: 1080–83; *Annals of the American Revolution* 298–302.

31. JCC 12: 1081–83, 1139; Wells, *Life and Public Service of Samuel Adams* 3: 17.

32. JCC 12: 138–39; *Proclamations for Thanksgiving Issued by the Continental Congress,* edited by Benjamin Franklin Hough, Albany: Munsell & Rowland, 1858: 8.

33. JCC 12: 138–39.

34. Ibid.

35. Ibid.; LCC 1: 20; Bruce Chadwick, *George Washington's War: The Forging of a Revolutionary Leader and the American Presidency,* Naperville: Sourcebooks, 2005: 161; Middlekauff, *Glorious Cause* 434–35.

9. "GRACE TO REPENT OF OUR SINS"

1. Elijah Fisher, *Elijah Fisher's Journal While in the War for Independence,* Augusta: Badger & Manley, 1880: 29; Freeman, *George Washington* 5: 90–92; Henry Dearborn, *Revolutionary War Journals of Henry Dearborn 1775–1783,* edited by Lloyd A. Brown and Howard A. Peckham, Westminster: Heritage Books, 2007: 143; General Orders, 22 December 1788, GWP; WGW 7: 300–3; JCC 12: 1250, 1264.

2. Fisher, *Elijah Fisher's Journal* 29; Dearborn, *Revolutionary War Journals of Henry Dearborn* 143; JCC 12: 1250; WGW 7: 299–302; Freeman, *George Washington* 5: 90–92.

3. Freeman, *George Washington* 5: 90–92; Esther 5:14; WGW 7: 282, 299–303.

4. WGW 7: 282–83, 299–303.

5. WGW 7: 300–3; George Washington to Benjamin Harrison, 18 December 1778, GWP; Freeman, *George Washington* 5: 92–94.

6. WGW 4: 385; WGW 7: 282, 300–3; Boatner, *Encyclopedia of the American Revolution* 980–88, 1033–36.

7. Nat and Sam Hilborn, *Battleground of Freedom: South Carolina in the Revolution,* Columbia: Sandlapper Press, 1970: 85; Boatner, *Encyclopedia of the American Revolution* 987–89, 1035–36.

8. Hilborn, *Battleground of Freedom* 85; Boatner, *Encyclopedia of the American Revolution* 987–89, 1035–36.

9. Freeman, *George Washington* 5: 98; Claude H. Van Tyne, *The American Revolution 1776–1783,* New York: Harper & Brothers, 1905: 250.

10. WGW 8: 493; JCC 13: 342–44; Hebrews 12:6.

11. JCC 13: 342–44.

12. Ibid.

13. Ibid.; Proverbs 14:34; Psalms 10:17; Hebrews 12:6, 11; Psalms 146:9; James 1:27.

14. JCC 13: 342–44; James 1:3–5; Philippians 4:6–7.

15. JCC 14: 553; Hugh McLellan, *History of Gorham, Maine,* Portland: Smith & Sale, 1903: 191; Reuben A. Guild, *Life, Times and Correspondence of James Manning,* Boston: Gould & Lincoln, 1864: 267; General Orders, 12 April 1779, GWP; Fisher, *Elijah Fisher's Journal* 79–80; F. R. Brace, "New Jersey Chaplains in the Army of the Revolution," *Proceedings of the New Jersey Historical Society* (January 1921) 6: 1: 6–7.

16. George Washington, *The Glorious Struggle: George Washington's Revolutionary War Letters,* edited by Edward G. Lengel, Washington, DC: Smithsonian Books, 2007: 179; *Frontier Advance on the Upper Ohio, 1778–1779,* edited by Louise Phelps Kellogg, Madison: Wisconsin Historical Society, 1916: 23: 40, 323; Freeman, *George Washington* 5: 105.

17. DAB 19: 518–19; Ferling, *Almost a Miracle* 571–73; Freeman, *George Washington* 5: 92–98.

18. DAB 19: 518–19; Ferling, *Almost a Miracle* 571–73; Freeman, *George Washington* 5: 92–98; LDC 25: 74, 552; *A Compilation of the Messages and Papers of the Presidents,* edited by James D. Richardson, New York: Bureau of National Literature, 1897: 1: 56.

19. JCC 14: 649–58; 1 Samuel 17:40–51.

20. JCC 14: 649–58; 2 Chronicles 7:14; Acts 5:29; Philippians 4:6–8.

21. JCC 14: 764; Samuel Holten Diary, 4 July 1779; LDC 13: 145; Laurens, *Papers of Henry Laurens* 126; JCC 12: 1029; Bird Wilson, *Memoir of the Life of the Right Reverend William White,* Philadelphia: James Kay, 1839: 51; DAB 20: 121–22.

22. Bird, *Memoir of Reverend White* 51–55; DAB 4: 489–90; JCC 12: 1029.

23. DAB 20: 121–22; Bird, *Memoirs of Reverend White* 51–55.

24. Holten Diary, 4 July 1779, LDC 13: 145; Laurens, *Papers of Henry Laurens* 126; Romans 12:1–3.

25. Martin I. Griffin, "The Continental Congress at Mass," *The American Catholic Historical Researches,* edited by Martin I. Griffin (April 1889) 6: 2: 56–59; Griffin, *Catholics and the American Revolution* 1: 316–19; Ruth Strong Hudson, "The Minister from France: Conrad-Alexandre Gérard," *Pennsylvania Magazine of History and Biography* (January–April 1907) 21: 1: 136–37.

26. Griffin, "Continental Congress at Mass," 6: 2: 56–59.

27. Holten Diary, 4 July 1779, LDC 13: 145; Laurens, *Papers of Henry Laurens* 126; DAB 5: 489–90; Alice L. George, *Philadelphia: A Pictorial Celebration,* New York: Sterling, 2006: 26.

28. Herbert A. Gibbons, "Old Pine Street Presbyterian Church, Philadelphia, in the Revolutionary War," *Journal of the Presbyterian Historical Society,* Philadelphia: Presbyterian Historical Society, 1906: 3: 72–74; DAB 5: 489–90; Holten Diary, 4 July 1779, LDC 13: 145; Romans 13:1–2.

29. *The Siege of Savannah in 1779*, edited by Charles C. Jones, Albany: Joel Munsell, 1874: 30–39; Boatner, *Encyclopedia of the American Revolution* 984–87; Hilborn, *Battleground of Freedom* 96.

30. *Siege of Savannah* 39; Boatner, *Encyclopedia of the American Revolution* 984–87, 1036.

31. WGW 8: 98–99; George Washington to Edmund Pendleton, 1 November 1779, GWP; Freeman, *George Washington* 5: 92–94.

32. JCC 15: 1192–93; Burnett, *Continental Congress* 422; DAB 16: 148.

33. JCC 15: 1192–93.

34. Ibid.

35. Ibid; Boatner, *Encyclopedia of the American Revolution* 984.

10. "FIGHT AGAINST THEM THAT FIGHT AGAINST ME"

1. Freeman, *George Washington* 5: 166–67; *Cyclopaedia of American Literature*, edited by Evert A. Duyckinck and George L. Duyckinck, New York: Charles Scribner, 1856: 1: 279–83; Cyrus R. Edmunds, *The Life and Times of General Washington*, London: Thomas Tegg, 1836: 2: 25; Burnett, *Continental Congress* 456.

2. Edward McCrady, *The History of South Carolina in the Revolution 1775–1780*, New York: Macmillan, 1901: 445–55; Hilborn, *Battleground of Freedom* 97–114; Boatner, *Encyclopedia of the American Revolution* 205–12.

3. Hilborn, *Battleground of Freedom* 97–114; Boatner, *Encyclopedia of the American Revolution* 212–13; McCrady, *South Carolina in the Revolution* 504–15.

4. Freeman, *George Washington* 5: 165–68; Burnett, *Continental Congress* 454–56; Edmunds, *Life and Times of Washington* 2: 25.

5. WGW 8: 186; Freeman, *George Washington* 5: 165–68; Burnett, *Continental Congress* 454–56.

6. Burnett, *Continental Congress* 444–47; JCC 16: 252–53.

7. JCC 16: 225, 252–53.

8. Ibid.; Freeman, *George Washington* 5: 171; Burnett, *Continental Congress* 444–47.

9. Freeman, *George Washington* 5: 171; WGW 8: 304.

10. McCrady, *South Carolina in the Revolution* 518–25; Hilborn, *Battleground of Freedom* 119–20; Boatner, *Encyclopedia of the Revolution* 1036–37; Robert Bass, *The Green Dragoon: The Lives of Banastre Tarleton and Mary Robinson*, New York: Henry Holt, 1957: 260.

11. Hilborn, *Battleground of Freedom* 131–38; McCrady, *South Carolina in the Revolution* 671–74; Boatner, *Encyclopedia of the Revolution* 165–68.

12. McCrady, *South Carolina in the Revolution* 671–74; Boatner, *Encyclopedia of the Revolution* 571; Hilborn, *Battleground of Freedom* 131–38.

13. McCrady, *South Carolina in the Revolution* 525, 595, 610, 645, 747, 817; Daniel W. Barefoot, *Touring South Carolina Revolutionary War Sites*,

Winston-Salem: John F. Blair, 1999: 9, 29, 93; Hilborn, *Battleground of Freedom* 138–46; Bass, *Green Dragoon* 110–11.

14. Van Tyne, *American Revolution* 320–23; Freeman, *George Washington* 5: 200–10.

15. Boatner, *Encyclopedia of the Revolution* 25–42; Van Tyne, *American Revolution* 306–8; Freeman, *George Washington* 5: 205–9.

16. Boatner, *Encyclopedia of the Revolution* 25–42; Van Tyne, *American Revolution* 306–8; WGW 3: 499, 493.

17. JCC 18: 950–51; Burnett, *Continental Congress* 470.

18. Burnett, *Continental Congress* 470; Boatner, *Encyclopedia of the Revolution* 1038–39; McCrady, *South Carolina in the Revolution* 740–46.

19. *The Correspondence of King George the Third with Lord North from 1768 to 1783*, edited by W. Bodham Dunne, London: John Murray, 1867: 2: 336; Van Tyne, *American Revolution* 301.

20. Boatner, *Encyclopedia of the Revolution* 676, 576; DAB 12: 283; Robert Bass, *Swamp Fox*, New York: Henry Holt, 1959: 82; Trevelyan, *George the Third and Charles Fox* 2: 102; Yates Snowden, *History of South Carolina*, Chicago: Lewis, 1920: 1: 387.

21. Hilborn, *Battleground of Freedom* 145–55; McCrady, *South Carolina in the Revolution* 782–92; Van Tyne, *American Revolution* 301–2.

22. Hilborn, *Battleground of Freedom* 145–55; McCrady, *South Carolina in the Revolution* 782–92; "Monument at Sycamore Shoals," *Journal of the Presbyterian Historical Society* (1909–1910) 5: 352; Boatner, *Encyclopedia of the Revolution* 578–81; J. David Dameron, *King's Mountain: The Defeat of the Loyalists, October 7, 1780*, Cambridge: Da Capo Press, 2003: 41; Lyman C. Draper, *King's Mountain and Its Heroes*, Cincinnati: Peter G. Thompson, 1881: 175–77, 216–18.

23. Hilborn, *Battleground of Freedom* 145–55; McCrady, *South Carolina in the Revolution* 782–92; Dameron, *King's Mountain* 41; "Monument at Sycamore Shoals," 5: 352; Judges 7: 12–22; Draper, *King's Mountain* 175–77, 216–18.

24. Hilborn, *Battleground of Freedom* 153–55; Boatner, *Encyclopedia of the Revolution* 577–82; Freeman, *George Washington* 5: 227; George Washington, *The Revolutionary Orders of General Washington*, edited by Henry Whiting, New York: Wiley & Putnam, 1844: 123.

25. WGW 12: 111; Van Tyne, *American Revolution* 323; Boatner, *Encyclopedia of the Revolution* 453–56; Clinton, *American Rebellion* 228.

26. Freeman, *George Washington* 4: 367; Boatner, *Encyclopedia of the American Revolution* 453–56.

27. Van Tyne, *American Revolution* 323; Boatner, *Encyclopedia of the Revolution* 453–56; George Washington to Nathanael Greene, 27 February 1781, GWP; Trevelyan, *American Revolution* 4: 188; Freeman, *George Washington* 4: 367.

28. William Johnson, *Sketches of the Life and Correspondence of Nathanael Greene*, Charleston: A. E. Miller, 1822: 1: 19, 35, 216; Greene, *Life of Nathanael*

Greene 1: 5; Trevelyan, *George the Third and Charles Fox* 2: 172; Charles Caldwell, *Memoirs of the Life and Campaigns of the Hon. Nathanael Greene*, Philadelphia: Robert DeSilver, 1819: 30; DAB 7: 569.

29. DAB 7: 572; Edgar, *South Carolina* 235–36; Johnson, *Sketches of Nathanael Greene* 1: 97; Boatner, *Encyclopedia of the Revolution* 454–56; Judges 7:12–22.

30. Banastre Tarleton, *History of the Campaigns of 1780 and 1781 in the Southern Provinces of North America*, Dublin: Coles, Exshaw & White, 1787: 222–24; DAB 13: 166–67; Daniel Morgan, *The Cowpens Papers: Being Correspondence of General Morgan and Prominent Actors*, edited by Theodorus B. Myers, Charleston: News & Courier, 1881: 24–26; Don Higginbotham, *Daniel Morgan: Revolutionary Rifleman*, Chapel Hill: University of North Carolina Press, 1961: 1–2, 213–14; R. T. Roberts, "Welsh Presbyterian Church in America," *Schaff-Herzog Encyclopedia of Religious Knowledge*, edited by Samuel M. Jackson, New York: Funk & Wagnall, 1911: 9: 236; Owen M. Edwards, *A Short History of Wales*, Chicago: University of Chicago, Press, 1907: 44.

31. James Graham, *The Life of Daniel Morgan*, New York: Derby Jackson, 1856: 446–48, 460; Morgan, *Cowpens Papers* 26; DAB 13: 167; Hilborn, *Battleground of Freedom* 174–82; Walter Edgar, *Partisans and Redcoats: The Southern Conflict that Turned the Tide of the American Revolution*, New York: William Morrow, 2001: 66; Snowden, *History of South Carolina* 1: 387.

32. Freeman, *George Washington* 5: 256; WGW 9: 125.

33. JCC 19: 208; JCC 11: 657; Burnett, *Continental Congress* 500–2.

34. LCC 6: 1; JCC 11: 657; Burnett, *Continental Congress* 500–2; JCC 14: 649; George Washington to William Fitzhugh, 25 March 1781, GWP.

35. Van Tyne, *American Revolution* 324–25; Middlekauff, *Glorious Cause* 478–87; Boatner, *Encyclopedia of the Revolution* 461–70.

36. George W. Kyte, "A Projected British Attack Upon Philadelphia in 1781," *Pennsylvania Magazine of History and Biography* (October 1952) 74: 4: 381; Van Tyne, *American Revolution* 324–25; Middlekauff, *Glorious Cause* 478–87; Boatner, *Encyclopedia of the Revolution* 461–70.

37. Van Tyne, *American Revolution* 324–25; Middlekauff, *Glorious Cause* 478–87; Boatner, *Encyclopedia of the Revolution* 461–70; Kyte, "Attack Upon Philadelphia in 1781" 74: 4: 381.

38. JCC 19: 284–86.

39. Ibid.

40. Kyte, "Attack Upon Philadelphia in 1781," 74: 4: 381–90; Trevelyan, *American Revolution* 2: 360.

41. Fortescue, *History of the British Army* 3: 393; Middlekauff, *Glorious Cause* 559–63; Kyte, "Attack Upon Philadelphia in 1781" 74: 4: 381–90; Trevelyan, *American Revolution* 2: 360.

42. JCC 1: 26; Middlekauff, *Glorious Cause* 562; Kyte, "Attack Upon Philadelphia in 1781" 74: 4: 381–90.

43. Middlekauff, *Glorious Cause* 562; Kyte, "Attack Upon Philadelphia in 1781" 74: 4: 381–90; Fortescue, *History of the British Army* 3: 393.

ii. "SUCH ASTONISHING INTERPOSITIONS OF PROVIDENCE"

1. Baker, *Itinerary of General Washington* 219–20; Fortescue, *History of the British Army* 3: 393–94; Aaron Chester Adams, *Historic Sketch of the First Church of Christ in Wethersfield*, Wethersfield: n.p., 1876: 16; Charles Albert Wight, *Some Old Time Meeting Houses of the Connecticut Valley*, Chicopee Falls: Rich Printing, 1911: 133–36; Mabel Cassine Holman, "Along the Connecticut River," *Connecticut Magazine*, 1907: 11: 1: 561; Freeman, *George Washington* 5: 286; Matthew 5: 3.

2. WGW 9: 125; Middlekauff, *Glorious Cause* 552.

3. Freeman, *George Washington* 5: 302–7; Middlekauff, *Glorious Cause* 562–65; Fortescue, *History of the British Army* 3: 397–98; Trevelyan, *George the Third and Charles Fox* 2: 365.

4. WGW 9: 192–93; Middlekauff, *Glorious Cause* 552.

5. Freeman, *George Washington* 5: 302–7; Middlekauff, *Glorious Cause* 562–65; Fortescue, *History of the British Army* 3: 397–98; Trevelyan, *George the Third and Charles Fox* 2: 366.

6. Freeman, *George Washington* 5: 309; Van Tyne, *American Revolution* 325–27; Fortescue, *History of the British Army* 3: 397–98; Boatner, *Encyclopedia of the American Revolution* 225–26, 398–402; Trevelyan, *George the Third and Charles Fox* 2: 372.

7. Fortescue, *History of the British Army* 3: 397–98; Boatner, *Encyclopedia of the American Revolution* 225–26, 398–402; William Heath, *Heath's Memoirs of the American War*, edited by Rufus R. Wilson, New York: A. Wessels, 1904: 316; Van Tyne, *American Revolution* 325–27.

8. Fortescue, *History of the British Army* 3: 397–98; Boatner, *Encyclopedia of the American Revolution* 225–26, 398–402; Van Tyne, *American Revolution* 325–27.

9. Fortescue, *History of the British Army* 3: 401–2; Boatner, *Encyclopedia of the American Revolution* 1236–44, 1248.

10. Van Tyne, *American Revolution* 325–27; Boatner, *Encyclopedia of the American Revolution* 1244–48; Freeman, *George Washington* 5: 378–84.

11. WGW 23: 247; Freeman, *George Washington* 5: 380–84, 388; Boatner, *Encyclopedia of the American Revolution* 1244–46, 1248; Henry Phelps Johnston, *The Yorktown Campaign and the Surrender of Cornwallis 1781*, New York: Harper & Brothers, 1881: 155, 183.

12. Freeman, *George Washington* 5: 380–84, 388; Richard M. Ketchum, *Victory at Yorktown: The Campaign That Won the Revolution*, New York: Henry Holt, 2004: 247–48: Scheer and Rankin, *Rebels and Redcoats* 490; Boatner, *Encyclopedia of the American Revolution* 1244–46, 1248; Johnston, *Yorktown Campaign* 155.

13. Fortescue, *History of the British Army* 3: 413; Trevelyan, *George the Third and Charles Fox* 2: 387; Johnston, *Yorktown Campaign* 176; Sheer and Rankin, *Rebels and Redcoats* 490; Freeman, *George Washington* 5: 388.

14. Fortescue, *History of the British Army* 3: 413; Trevelyan, *George the Third and Charles Fox* 2: 387; *Spirit of 'Seventy-Six'* 1243; Edward S. Dundas, "Battle-Grounds of America—Yorktown," *Graham's Lady's and Gentleman's Magazine*, June 1844–January 1845: 25: 135; Boatner, *Encyclopedia of the American Revolution* 421–22, 812, 849–50, 1248; Ketchum, *Victory at Yorktown* 251; Johnston, *Yorktown Campaign* 176; Freeman, *George Washington* 5: 388.

15. *Spirit of 'Seventy-Six'* 1243; Dundas, "Battle-Grounds" 25: 135; Boatner, *Encyclopedia of the Revolution* 421–22, 812, 849–50, 1248; Sidney J. Low and F. S. Pulling, *The Dictionary of English History*, London: Castle, 1910, 496.

16. General Orders, 20 October 1781, GWP; George Washington, *Writings of George Washington, Correspondence and Other Papers: Correspondence, Addresses, Messages, and Other Papers, Official and Private*, edited by Jared Sparks, Boston: Little & Brown, 1855: 12: 402.

17. Freeman, *George Washington* 5: 460–61; George Washington to Continental Congress, 19 October 1781, GWP; General Orders, 20 October 1781, GWP.

18. Freeman, *George Washington*, 5: 460–61; General Orders, 20 October 1781, GWP; Dundas, "Battle-Grounds" 25: 135; Middlekauff, *Glorious Cause* 570–71.

19. "Surrender of Lord Cornwallis," *Donahoe's Magazine*, July 1881–January 1882: 6: 388; Abram E. Brown, *History of the Town of Bedford*, Bedford: A. Brown, 1891: 13; Anna Rawle, "Occurrences in Philadelphia after Cornwallis's Surrender," *Philadelphia Magazine of History and Biography* (1892) 16: 103; Jacob H. Patton, *Yorktown*, New York: Fords, Howard & Hulbert, 1882: 33; Johnston, *Yorktown Campaign* 11; F. T. Wilson, *Official Programme of the Yorktown Centennial Celebration*, Washington, DC: Judd & Detweiler, 1881: 110; JCC 21: 1071.

20. Charles and Mary Beard, *History of the United States*, New York: Macmillan, 1921: 1: 186; JCC 1: 26–27; JCC 21: 1071; Rawle, "Occurrences in Philadelphia" 103.

21. JCC 21: 1071; Jonathan Trumbull, "The Trumbull Papers," *Collections of the Massachusetts Historical Society*, Boston: Wilson & Son, 1902: 3: 298; Rawle, "Occurrences in Philadelphia" 103–4; J. Thomas Scharf and Thompson Westcott, *History of Philadelphia from 1609 to 1884*, Philadelphia: L. H. Everts, 1884, 2: 1421; Robert F. Looney, *Old Philadelphia in Early Photographs*, Philadelphia: Free Library of Philadelphia, 1976: 103; *Appleton's Cyclopaedia of American Biography*, New York: D. Appleton, 1897: 3: 578; William J. Finck, *Lutheran Landmarks and Pioneers in America*, Philadelphia: General Council Publication House, 1913: 103; Johnston, *Yorktown Campaign* 158.

22. JCC 18: 151; DAB 2: 477–78; Trumbull, "Trumbull Papers" 3: 441, 343.

23. JCC 18: 151; DAB 2: 477–78; Trumbull, "Trumbull Papers" 3: 441, 343.

24. Wilson, *Official Programme of the Yorktown Centennial Celebration*: 110; DAB 18: 20; Trumbull, "Trumbull Papers" 3: 306.

25. JCC 21: 1074–76.
26. Ibid.
27. Ibid.
28. Robert Morris, *The Papers of Robert Morris, 1781–1784*, edited by Elmer J. Ferguson, Pittsburgh: University of Pittsburgh Press, 1977: 1: 131; William Gordon, *The History of the Rise, Progress and Establishment of the Independence of the United States of America*, London: Charles Dilly, 1778, 4: 203–7; Griffin, *Catholics in the American Revolution* 1: 311–14; E. Pruente, "The Continental Congress at Mass," *The Christian Family: An Illustrated Magazine for the Catholic Home* (1907) 2: 294–95; A. A. Lamb, "Replies," *American Catholic Historical Researches* (July 1885) 2: 1: 101.
29. Gordon, *History of the United States* 4: 203–7; Griffin, *Catholics in the American Revolution* 1: 311–14; Pruente, "Continental Congress at Mass" 2: 294–95; Morris, *Papers of Robert Morris* 1: 131.
30. JCC 21: 1099; Morris, *Papers of Robert Morris* 1: 131–32; DAB 9: 373–74.
31. JCC 21: 1166; Gordon, *History of the United States* 4: 202; Charles A. Goodrich, *A History of the United States of America*, Boston: Brewer & Tileston, 1852: 200; Gordon, *History of the Independence of the United States* 3: 264; *Broadsides and Ballads Printed in Massachusetts*, edited by Worthington C. Ford, Boston: Massachusetts Historical Society, 1922: 75: 318; "Archives of New Jersey," *Proceedings of the New Jersey Historical Society* (1917) 2: 318; David L. Pierson, *History of the Oranges*, New York: Lewis Historical Publishing, 1922: 1: 163; Thomas Smith and Samuel Deane, *Journals of the Rev. Thomas Smith and the Rev. Samuel Deane*, edited by William Willis, Portland: Joseph Bailey, 1819: 348; Jacob N. Beam, "Dr. Robert Smith's Academy at Pequea, Pennsylvania," *Journal of the Presbyterian Historical Society* (December 1915) 8: 4: 156–60; Exodus 15:1.
32. Robert Smith, *The Obligations of the Confederate States of North America to Praise God: Preached at Pequea, December 13, 1781*, Philadelphia: Francis Bailey, 1782; Psalms 67:5.
33. DAB 17: 355–57; William Smith, *The Works of William Smith: Late Provost of the College and Academy of Philadelphia*, Philadelphia: Maxwell & Fry, 1803: 2: 146–48.

12. "HE HAS APPROVED OUR BEGINNINGS"

1. WGW 9: 417, 415; Freeman, *George Washington* 5: 326, 403–4.
2. JCC 21: 1080; WGW 9: 409.
3. Freeman, *George Washington* 5: 400–8; WGW 9: 417; John T. Faris, *The Romance of Old Philadelphia*, Philadelphia: J. B. Lippincott, 1918: 187.
4. JCC 21: 1143–44; Freeman, *George Washington* 5: 400–4; WGW 9: 417.
5. Van Tyne, *American Revolution* 329, 333; Johnston, *Yorktown Campaign* 161; *The Diplomatic Correspondence of the American Revolution*, edited by Jared

Sparks, Boston: Hale, Gray & Bowen, 1829: 1: 204; *Annual Statistician for 1877*, edited by John P. Mains, San Francisco: L. P. McCarty, 1877: 145; George C. Rogers, Jr., *Charleston in the Age of the Pinckneys*, Columbia: University of South Carolina Press, 1980: 169.

6. Freeman, *George Washington* 5: 417–18.

7. WGW 10: 22.

8. George Washington to Albany, New York, Reformed Dutch Church, 28 June 1782, GWP; George Washington to Magistrates and Military Officers of Schenectady, New York, 30 June 1782, GWP; George Washington to Schenectady, New York, Reform Church, June 30, 1782, GWP.

9. Burnett, *Continental Congress* 561–69; JCC 5: 689–90.

10. Galliard Hunt, *The Seal of the United States: How It Was Developed and Adopted*, Washington, DC: U.S. Department of State, 1892: 5–7; JCC 5: 690.

11. JCC 22: 338–39; Hunt, *Seal of the United States* 10–25; *Harper's Encyclopedia of United States History*, edited by Benson J. Lossing, New York: Harper & Brothers, 1906: 8: 101–2.

12. JCC 22: 339–40; Hunt, *Seal of the United States* 24–25.

13. JCC 18: 979–80; JCC 19: 91; JCC 23: 573–74; William H. Gaines, "The Continental Congress Considers Publication of a Bible," *Studies in Bibliography*, edited by Fredson Bowers, Charlottesville: Bibliographical Society of the University of Virginia, 1951: 41: 274–78; Thomas C. Pears, "The Story of the Aitken Bible," *Journal of the Presbyterian Historical Society* (June 1939) 18: 225–41; JCC 8: 536; LDC 7: 312–13.

14. DAB 1: 181–82; DAB 6: 236–37; James Price, "Memorable Places Within the Bounds of the United Presbyterian Presbytery," *Journal of Presbyterian History* (1911–12) 6: 236; Scharf, *History of Philadelphia* 2: 1274–75; Benjamin Franklin, *The Writings of Benjamin Franklin*, edited by Albert H. Smyth, New York: Macmillan, 1907: 6: 15; "Abstract of Church Records," Collection Box 3031, Scots Presbyterian Church Records, Historical Society of Pennsylvania.

15. JCC 8: 536; LDC 7: 312–13; PCC 42: 1: 34.

16. JCC 8: 536; PCC 42: 1: 35; "Daniel Roberdeau," Fort Roberdeau website, www.fortroberdeau.org; WJA 2: 6–7, 22–23; WJA 10: 104–5; DAB 15: 646–47; DAB 17: 308–9.

17. JCC 8: 734; PCC 1: 163–64; LDC 7: 312–13; Gaines, "Continental Congress Considers Publication of a Bible" 3: 274–76, 280–81.

18. JCC 8: 734; PCC 1: 163–64; Gaines, "Continental Congress Considers Publication of a Bible," 3: 274–76.

19. JCC 8: 536, 734; LDC 1: 34–36, 75; LDC 7: 312–13; LDC 8: 536; PCC 1: 163–64; Gaines, "Continental Congress Considers Publication of a Bible," 3: 274–78, 280–81.

20. JCC 8: 536, 743, 739–42; LDC 1: 34–36, 75; LDC 7: 312–13; PCC 1: 163–64; Gaines, "Continental Congress Considers Publication of a Bible," 3: 274–76, 280–81.

21. JCC 8: 536, 743, 739–42; LDC 1: 34–36, 75; LDC 7: 312–13; PCC 1: 163–64; Gaines, "Continental Congress Considers Publication of a Bible," 3: 274–76, 280–81.

22. JCC 8: 536, 743, 739–42; LDC 1: 34–36, 75; LDC 7: 312–13; PCC 1: 163–64; Gaines, "Continental Congress Considers Publication of a Bible," 3: 274–76, 280–81.

23. JCC 23: 573–74; JCC 18: 979; LDC 19: 119; Gaines, "Continental Congress Considers Publication of a Bible" 3: 275–83; Pears, "Story of the Aitken Bible" 18: 225–41.

24. JCC 23: 573–74; Pears, "Story of the Aitken Bible" 18: 225–41; Gaines, "Congress Considers Publication of a Bible" 3: 275–83.

25. JCC 22: 137–38; William H. Egle, "Joseph H. Montgomery," *Pennsylvania Magazine of History and Biography*, Philadelphia: Pennsylvania Historical Society, 1877: 1:217–18; *The Twentieth Century Biographical Dictionary of Notable Americans*, edited by Rossiter Johnson and John Howard Brown, Boston: Biographical Society, 1904; 1; DAB 20: 442–43; *Proceedings of the American Philosophical Society*, edited by Edgar F. Smith, Philadelphia: American Philosophical Society, 1904: 45: 50; DAB 16: 495–96.

26. JCC 22: 137–38.

27. Ibid.

28. Van Tyne, *American Revolution* 329–33; DAB 20: 298–300, 435–37 JCC 23: 647;

29. JCC 23: 647.

30. JCC 24: 238–40; JCC 27:617; Van Tyne, *American Revolution* 330; Burnett, *Continental Congress* 563–64; DAB 19: 520, 616–25; Boatner, *Encyclopedia of the American Revolution* 847–49.

31. JCC 27: 617.

32. General Orders, 18 April 1783, GWP.

33. George Washington to Massachusetts Senate and House of Representatives, 10 August 1783, GWP; George Washington to Albany, New York, Mayor, Aldermen, Citizens, and Officials, 4 August 1783, GWP; George Washington to Israel Putnam, 2 June 1783, GWP; George Washington to Continental Congress, 26 August 1783, GWP; JCC 24: 523.

34. George Washington to Meshech Weare et al., 18 June 1783, GWP.

35. George Washington Farewell Orders to the Continental Armies, 1 November 1783, GWP.

36. Freeman, *George Washington* 5: 460–68; Johnston, *Yorktown Campaign* 161; James Riker, *Evacuation Day 1783*, New York: Crichton, 1883: 5–20; Henry P. Johnston, "Evacuation of New York City by the British, 1783," *Harper's Magazine* (June–November 1883) 67: 919–23.

37. Freeman, *George Washington* 5: 467–68; Johnston, *Yorktown Campaign* 161; Riker, *Evacuation Day* 5–20; Johnston, "Evacuation of New York City" 67: 919–23.

38. Freeman, *George Washington* 5: 467–68; Johnston, *Yorktown Campaign* 161; Riker, *Evacuation Day* 5–20; Johnston, "Evacuation of New York City," 67: 919–23.

39. Freeman, *George Washington* 5: 467–68.

40. JCC 25: 700–1; Freeman, *George Washington* 5: 470–71; Mary V. Thompson, *In the Hands of a Good Providence: Religion in the Life of George Washington*, Charlottesville: University of Virginia Press, 2008: 113.

41. JCC 25: 699–701.

42. Jonathan D. Sassi, *A Republic of Righteousness: The Public Christianity of the Post-Revolution New England Clergy*, New York: Oxford University Press, 2001: 213–14; Joann Calhoun, *The Circular Church: Three Centuries of Charleston History*, Charleston: History Press, 2008: 59; Love, *Fast and Thanksgiving Days of New England* 552; Johnston, "Evacuation of New York City" 67; 921; Tyler, *Literary History of the American Revolution* 1: 315; Riker, *Evacuation Day* 20.

43. George Duffield, *A Sermon Preached in the Third Presbyterian Church, in Philadelphia, on Thursday, December 11, 1783*, Philadelphia: F. Bailey, 1784: 1–25; Madison C. Peters, *Justice to the Jew: The Story of What He Has Done for the World*, New York: Trow Press, 1910: 18–19; Tyler, *Literary History of the American Revolution* 1: 315; George Washington to Lucretia Van Winter, 30 March 1785, GWP.

44. JCC 25: 819–20; Burnett, *Continental Congress* 76; Freeman, *George Washington* 5: 474–75.

45. JCC 25: 819–20; Burnett, *Continental Congress* 76; Freeman, *George Washington* 5: 474–75.

46. Burnett, *Continental Congress* 76; Freeman, *George Washington* 5: 474–75.

47. JCC 25: 701–2, 818–19; JCC 24: 521–23; JCC 5: 510; Burnett, *Continental Congress* 76; Freeman, *George Washington* 5: 474–75.

48. JCC: 25: 818–19; 837; Freeman, *George Washington* 5: 446, 449, 452–53, 474–75; JCC 25: 818–19; Burnett, *Continental Congress* 591; LDC 1: 498; Bernard Christian Steiner, *The Life and Correspondence of James McHenry*, Cleveland: Burrows Brothers, 1907: 69.

49. Freeman, *George Washington* 3: 446, 449, 452–53; Ibid. 5: 474–75; JCC 25: 818–19; Burnett, *Continental Congress* 591; LDC 1: 498; Steiner, *Life and Correspondence of James McHenry* 69.

50. DAB 19: 509–22; Freeman, *George Washington* 5: 474–76.

51. DAB 19: 518–22; Freeman, *George Washington* 5: 474–76.

52. DAB 19: 509–22; George Washington to William Gordon, 23 December 1788, GWP; Freeman, *George Washington* 5: 474–76.

53. JCC 24: 521–22; JCC 5: 510; WGW 14: 369.

54. DAB 19: 509–22; Sparks, *Life of Washington* 1: 398–440; *Compilation of the Messages and Papers of the Presidents* 1: 50; George Washington to Lucretia Van Winter, 30 March 1785, GWP; George Washington to John Armstrong, 11 March 1792, GWP.

55. Freeman, *George Washington* 6: 191–92; Sparks, *Life of Washington* 1: 440; *Compilation of Messages and Papers of the Presidents* 1: 50; William MacLay and George W. Harris, *Sketches of Debate in the First Senate of the United States*, Harrisburg, PA: Lane Hart, 1880: 16–17; Gordon DenBoer, *The Documentary History of the First Federal Elections 1778–1790*, Madison: University of Wisconsin Press, 1989: 4: 268–69.

BIBLIOGRAPHY

Abbot, Jacob. *Makers of History: Charles I.* New York: Harper Brothers, 1876.

"Abstract of Church Records." Collection Box 3031 of the Scots Presbyterian Church Records. Historical Society of Pennsylvania.

Acton, G. W., A. W. Ward, and Stanley Prothero. *Cambridge Modern History of the United States.* Cambridge: Cambridge University Press, 1970.

Adams, Aaron Chester. *Historic Sketch of the First Church of Christ in Wethersfield.* Wethersfield: n.p., 1876.

Adams, John. *The Adams Papers Digital Edition.* C. James Taylor, editor. Charlottesville: University of Virginia Press, Rotunda, 2008.

———. *The Works of John Adams: Second President of the United States.* Charles Francis Adams, editor. Boston: Little, Brown, 1850–56.

Adams, John, and Abigail Adams. *The Letters of John and Abigail Adams.* Frank Shuffleton, editor. New York: Penguin Books, 2004.

Allen, Alexander. *Jonathan Edwards.* Boston: Houghton Mifflin, 1890.

Amos, Gary, and Richard Gardiner. *Never Before in History: America's Inspired Birth.* Dallas: Haughton, 1998.

Anderson, Christopher. *Annals of the English Bible.* London: Jackson, Walford & Hodder, 1862.

Anderson, Fred. *Crucible of War: The Seven Years' War and the Face of Empire in British North America, 1754–1766.* New York: Alfred A. Knopf, 2000.

Annals of the American Revolution. Jedediah Morse, editor. Hartford: J. Morse, 1824.

Annual Statistician for 1877. John P. Mains, editor. San Francisco: L. P. McCarty, 1877.

Appleton's Cyclopaedia of American Biography. New York: D. Appleton, 1897.

"Archives of New Jersey." *Proceedings of the New Jersey Historical Society.* Vol. 2 (1917).

"At New Castle, Delaware." *Pennsylvania Packet,* July 24, 1775.

Atkinson, Roger. "Letters of Roger Atkinson, 1769–1776." A. J. Morrison, editor. *Virginia Magazine of History and Biography.* Vol. 15 (1908).

Augustinus, Aurelius. *On Christian Doctrine.* Robert J. F. Shaw. Londonderry: Mobile Reference. n.d.

Austin, Bill R. *Austin's Topical History of Christianity.* Wheaton, IL: Tyndale House, 1983.

"Autobiographical Letters of Peter Duponceau." *Pennsylvania Magazine of History and Biography.* Vol. 40, no. 157 (January 1912).

Baker, William S. "Itinerary of General Washington, 1777." *Pennsylvania Magazine of History and Biography.* Vol. 14, no. 1 (1890).

———. *Itinerary of General Washington from June 15, 1775 to December 23, 1783.* Philadelphia: J.B. Lippincott, 1892.

Baldwin, Alice Mary. *The New England Clergy and the American Revolution.* New York: Ungar, 1928.

Bancroft, George. *History of the Colonization of America.* New York: Julius Hart, 1886.

———. *History of the United States.* New York: D. Appleton, 1884.

Barefoot, Daniel W. *Touring South Carolina Revolutionary War Sites.* Winston-Salem: John F. Blair, 1999.

Bass, Robert D. *The Green Dragoon: The Lives of Banastre Tarleton and Mary Robinson.* New York: Henry Holt, 1957.

———. *Swamp Fox.* New York: Henry Holt, 1959.

Beam, Jacob N. "Dr. Robert Smith's Academy at Pequea, Pennsylvania." *Journal of the Presbyterian Historical Society.* Vol. 8 (December 1915).

Beard, Charles, and Mary Beard. *History of the United States.* New York: Macmillan, 1921.

Becker, Carl. *Eve of Revolution.* New Haven: Yale University Press, 1920.

Bell, James B. *A War of Religion: Dissenters, Anglicans and the American Revolution.* New York: Palgrave Macmillan, 2008.

Bigelow, William B. "The Country Church in America." *Scribner's Magazine.* Vol. 22 (July–December 1897).

Billias, George A. *General John Glover and His Marblehead Mariners.* New York: Henry Holt, 1960.

Biographical Dictionary of the United States Congress, 1774–2005. Andrew Dodge, editor. Washington: U.S. Government Printing Office, 2005.

The Birth of the Republic: The Resolutions, Declarations and Addresses Adopted by the Continental Congress, the Provincial Congresses, Conventions and Assemblies of the County and Town Meetings, and the Committees of Safety in all the Colonies from the Year 1765 to 1776. Daniel R. Godloe, editor. New York: Belford & Clark, 1889.

Boatner, Mark Mayo. *Encyclopedia of the American Revolution.* New York: David MacKay, 1966.

Bonomi, Patricia U. *Under the Cope of Heaven: Religion, Society and Culture in Colonial America.* New York: Oxford University Press, 1986.

Book of Days: A Miscellany of Popular Antiquities. R. Chambers, editor. Detroit: Gale Research, 1967.

Brace, F. R. "New Jersey Chaplains in the Army of the Revolution." *Proceedings of the New Jersey Historical Society.* Vol. 6, no. 1 (January 1921).

Bradford, William. *Bradford's History of Plimoth Plantation.* Boston: Wright & Potter, 1899.

Bridenbaugh, Carl. *Cities in Revolt: Urban Life in America 1743–1776.* New York: Capricorn, 1964.

Brinton, Crane, John B. Christopher, and Robert Lee Wolff. *A History of Civilization.* Saddle River: Prentice Hall, 1976.

Broadsides and Ballads Printed in Massachusetts. Worthington Chauncey Ford, editor. Boston: Massachusetts Historical Society, 1922.

Brown, Abram E. *History of the Town of Bedford.* Bedford: A. Brown, 1891.

Brown, Alexander. *Genesis of the United States.* Boston: Houghton Mifflin, 1890.

Browning, William S. *A History of the Huguenots.* London: Whitaker, 1843.

Bruce, F. F. *The Books and the Parchment.* Westwood: Fleming H. Revell, 1963.

Burke, Edmund. *Edmund Burke's Speech in the House of Commons, Mary 22, 1775, on Moving His Resolutions for Conciliation with the Colonies.* Frances R. Lange, editor. New York: Silver, Burdett, 1897.

Burnett, Edmund Cody. *The Continental Congress: A Definitive History of the Continental Congress from Its Inception in 1774 to March, 1789.* New York: W. W. Norton, 1941.

Burns, James MacGregor, Susan Dunn, and Arthur M. Schlesinger Jr. *George Washington.* New York: Macmillan, 2004.

Butler, Jon. *The Huguenots in America: A Refugee People in a New World Society.* Cambridge: Harvard University Press, 1983.

Cabeen, Francis V. "The Society of the Sons of Tammany of Philadelphia." *Pennsylvania Magazine of History and Biography.* Vol. 25, no. 1 (1901).

Cadwalader, Richard McCall. *Observance of the 123rd Anniversary of the Evacuation of Philadelphia by the British Army.* Lancaster: New Era, 1901.

Caldwell, Charles. *Memoirs of the Life and Campaigns of the Hon. Nathanael Greene.* Philadelphia: Robert DeSilver, 1819.

Calhoun, Joann. *The Circular Church: Three Centuries of Charleston History.* Charleston: History Press, 2008.

Calvin, John. *Institutes of the Christian Religion.* Philadelphia: Westminster Press, 1960.

Calvinism and the Political Order. George L. Hunt, editor. Philadelphia: Westminster, 1965.

Carson, Clarence B. *The Rebirth of Freedom: The Founding of the American Republic 1760–1800*. New Rochelle: Arlington House, 1973.

Carson, Hampton. "Washington at Valley Forge." *Pennsylvania Magazine of History and Biography*. Vol. 43, no. 1 (1919).

Chadwick, Bruce. *George Washington's War: The Forging of a Revolutionary Leader and the American Presidency*. Naperville: Sourcebooks, 2005.

Chamberlain, Mellen. *John Adams, The Statesman of the Revolution: With Other Essays and Addresses, Historical and Literary*. Boston: Houghton Mifflin, 1898.

Chase, Ellen. *The Beginnings of the American Revolution: Based on Contemporary Letters, Diaries and Other Documents*. New York: Baker & Taylor, 1910.

"Chronological Table." *Collections of the Massachusetts Historical Society*. Vol. 10 (1849).

Clark, J. C. D. *The Language of Liberty 1660–1783*. Cambridge: Cambridge University Press, 1994.

Clinton, George. *Public Papers of George Clinton, First Governor of New York*. Albany: James B. Lyon, 1900.

Clinton, Henry. *The American Rebellion: Sir Henry Clinton's Narrative of His Campaigns 1775–1782*. William B. Willcox, editor. New York: Archon Books, 1971.

Clowes, William L. *The Royal Navy: A History*. London: Sampson, Low & Marston, 1898.

A Compilation of the Messages and Papers of the Presidents. James D. Richardson, editor. New York: Bureau of National Literature, 1897.

Connolly, Sean. *Divided Kingdom: Ireland—1630–1800*. Oxford: Oxford University Press, 2008.

Cooke, John Esten. *Virginia: A History of Its People*. Boston: Houghton Mifflin, 1903.

The Correspondence of King George the Third with Lord North from 1768 to 1783. W. Bodham Dunne, editor. London: John Murray, 1867.

The Creeds of Christendom. Philip Schaft, editor. Grand Rapids: Baker Book House, 1983.

Curti, Merle. *The Growth of American Thought*. New York: Harper & Row, 1943.

Custis, George Washington Parke, Mary Randolph Custis Lee, and Benson John Lossing. *Recollections and Private Memoirs of George Washington*. Philadelphia: J. W. Bradley, 1861.

Cyclopaedia of American Literature. Evert and George Duyckinck, editors. New York: Charles Scribner, 1856.

Dameron, J. David. *King's Mountain: The Defeat of the Loyalists, October 7, 1780*. Cambridge: Da Capo Press, 2003.

"Daniel Roberdeau." Official Website, Fort Roberdeau Historic Site. Altoona, Pennsylvania. www.fortroberdeau.org.

Davis, Derek H. *Religion and the Continental Congress 1774–1789.* New York: Oxford University Press, 2000.

Dearborn, Henry. *Journals of Henry Dearborn 1776–1783.* Cambridge: John Wilson & Son University Press, 1887.

———. *Revolutionary War Journals of Henry Dearborn 1775–1783.* Lloyd A. Brown and Howard A. Peckham, editors. Westminster: Heritage Books, 2007.

DenBoer, Gordon. *The Documentary History of the First Federal Elections 1778–1790.* Madison: University of Wisconsin Press, 1989.

Diary of the American Revolution: From Newspapers and Original Documents. Frank Moore, editor. New York: Charles Scribner, 1860.

Dictionary of American Biography. Allen Johnson and Dumas Malone, editors. New York: Charles Scribner's Sons, 1928–36.

Dictionary of National Biography. Leslie Stephens and Sidney Lee, editors. London: Oxford University Press, 1921.

The Diplomatic Correspondence of the American Revolution. Jared Sparks, editor. Boston: Hale, Gray & Bowen, 1829.

Documents from the Revolutionary History of the State of New Jersey. William S. Stryker, editor. Trenton: John I. Murphy, 1901.

Dorchester, Daniel. *Christianity in the United States.* New York: Hunt & Eaton, 1895.

Draper, Lyman C. *King's Mountain and Its Heroes.* Cincinnati: Peter G. Thompson, 1881.

Duffield, George. *A Sermon Preached in the Third Presbyterian Church, in Philadelphia, on Thursday, December 11, 1783.* Philadelphia: F. Bailey, 1784.

Dundas, Edward S. "Battle-Grounds of America—Yorktown." *Graham's Lady's and Gentleman's Magazine,* Vol. 25 (June 1844–January 1845).

Dwyer, William M. *The Day Is Ours! An Inside View of the Battles of Trenton and Princeton.* New York: Viking, 1983.

Edgar, Walter. *Partisans and Redcoats: The Southern Conflict That Turned the Tide of the American Revolution.* New York: William Morrow, 2001.

———. *South Carolina: A History.* Columbia: University of South Carolina Press, 1998.

Edmunds, Cyrus R. *The Life and Times of General Washington.* London: Thomas Tegg, 1836.

Edwards, Jonathan. *Selected Sermons of Jonathan Edwards.* H. Norman Gardiner, editor. New York: Macmillan, 1904.

Edwards, Owen M. *A Short History of Wales.* Chicago: University of Chicago Press, 1907.

Eerdmans' Handbook to the History of Christianity. Tim Dowley, editor. Grand Rapids: Eerdmans, 1977.

Egle, William H. "Joseph H. Montgomery." *Pennsylvania Magazine of History and Biography.* Philadelphia: Pennsylvania Historical Society, 1877.

Ellis, Arthur B. *History of the First Church in Boston, 1630–1880.* Boston: Hall & Whiting, 1881.

Extracts from the Journals of the Provincial Congresses of South Carolina, 1775–1776. William Edward Hemphill, editor. Columbia: South Carolina Archives Department, 1960.

A Faithful Account of the Processions and Ceremonies Observed in the Coronations of the Kings and Queens of England. Richard Thomson, editor. London: John Major, 1820.

Faris, John T. *The Romance of Old Philadelphia.* Philadelphia: J. B. Lippincott, 1918.

Ferling, John E. *Almost a Miracle: The American Victory in the War of Independence.* New York: Oxford University Press, 2007.

———. *The First of Men: A Life of George Washington.* Knoxville: University of Tennessee Press, 1988.

———. *A Leap in the Dark: The Struggle to Create the American Republic.* New York: Oxford University Press: 2003.

Field, Thomas W. "The Battle of Long Island." *Memoirs of the Long Island Historical Society.* Brooklyn: Long Island Historical Society, 1869.

Finck, William J. *Lutheran Landmarks and Pioneers in America.* Philadelphia: General Council Publication House, 1913.

Findling, John, and Frank Thackery. *Events That Changed America in the Eighteenth Century.* Westport: Greenwood, 1998.

First Charter of Virginia, April 10, 1606. Avalon Project. Lillian Goldman Law Library. Yale University.

Fischer, David Hackett. *Washington's Crossing.* New York: Oxford University Press, 2004.

Fisher, Elijah. *Elijah Fisher's Journal While in the War for Independence.* Augusta: Badger & Manley, 1880.

Fisher, George. *The Reformation.* New York: Scribner & Armstrong, 1873.

Fiske, John. *The American Revolution.* Boston: Houghton Mifflin, 1902.

Fleming, Thomas J. *Affectionately Yours, George Washington: A Self Portrait in Letters of Friendship.* New York: W. W. Norton, 1967.

———. *The Battle of Springfield.* Trenton: New Jersey Historical Commission, 1975.

Ford, Daniel J. *In the Name of God, Amen: Rediscovering Biblical and Historical Covenants.* St. Louis: Lex Rex, 2003.

Fortescue, J. W. *History of the British Army.* London: Macmillan, 1902.

Franklin, Benjamin. *Memoirs of Benjamin Franklin.* William Templeton Franklin, editor. New York: Derby & Jackson, 1859.

———. *The Writings of Benjamin Franklin.* Albert H. Smyth, editor. New York: Macmillan, 1907.

Freeman, Douglas Southall. *George Washington: A Biography.* New York: Charles Scribner's Sons, 1948.

Frontier Advance on the Upper Ohio, 1778–1779. Louise Phelps Kellogg, editor. Madison: Wisconsin Historical Society, 1916.

Frost, John. *Heroes and Battles of the American Revolution.* Philadelphia: W. P. Hazard, 1845.

Frothingham, Richard. *History of the Siege of Boston.* Boston: Little & Brown, 1903.

Gaines, William H. "The Continental Congress Considers Publication of a Bible." *Studies in Bibliography.* Fredson Bowers, editor. Charlottesville: Bibliographical Society of the University of Virginia. Vol. 41 (1951).

George, Alice L. *Philadelphia: A Pictorial Celebration.* New York: Sterling, 2006.

Gerona, Carla. *Night Journeys: The Power of Dreams in Transatlantic Quaker Culture.* Charlottesville: University of Virginia Press, 2004.

Gibbons, Herbert A. "Old Pine Street Presbyterian Church, Philadelphia, in the Revolutionary War." *Journal of the Presbyterian Historical Society.* Philadelphia: Presbyterian Historical Society, Vol. 3 (1906).

Gill, Thomas H. *Songs of the Revolution.* London: C. E. Mudie, 1848.

Gledstone, James P. *George Whitefield: Field Preacher.* Boston: American Tract Society, 1901.

Goodrich, Charles A. *A History of the United States of America.* Boston: Brewer & Tileston, 1852.

Goodwin, A. R. *Bruton Parish Church Restored and Its Historic Environment.* Petersburg: Franklin Press, 1907.

Gordon, William. *The History of the Rise, Progress and Establishment of the Independence of the United States of America.* London: Charles Dilly, 1778.

Gragg, Rod. *Forged in Faith: How Faith Shaped the Birth of the Nation, 1607–1776.* New York: Simon & Schuster, 2010.

Graham, James. *The Life of Daniel Morgan.* New York: Derby Jackson, 1856.

Grant, Neil. *Kings & Queens.* Glasgow: HarperCollins, 1996.

Green, Evarts B. *The American Nation: A History.* New York: Harper Brothers, 1905.

Green, John Richard. *History of the English People.* London: Macmillan, 1885.

Greene, George Washington. *The Life of Nathanael Greene.* Boston: Houghton Mifflin, 1900.

Griffin, Keith L. *Revolution and Religion: The American Revolutionary War and the Reformed Clergy.* New York: Paragon House, 1994.

Griffin, Martin I. *Catholics and the American Revolution.* Philadelphia: Martin Griffin, 1907.

———. "The Continental Congress at Mass." *The American Catholic Historical Researches.* Martin I. Griffin, editor. Vol. 6, no. 2 (April 1889).

Grizzard, Frank E., Jr. *The Ways of Providence: Religion and George Washington.* Charlottesville: Mariner, 2005.

Guild, Reuben A. *Life, Times and Correspondence of James Manning.* Boston: Gould & Lincoln, 1864.

Gurock, Jeffrey S. *American Jewish History.* New York: Taylor & Francis, 1998.

Hall, David W. *The Genevan Reformation and the American Founding.* Lanham: Lexington, 2003.

Hall, John. *History of the Presbyterian Church in Trenton, New Jersey.* New York: Anson Randolph, 1859.

Hamm, Thomas. *The Quakers in America.* New York: Columbia University Press, 2003.

Hanna, Charles A. *The Scotch-Irish: The Scot in North Britain, North Ireland and North America.* New York: G. P. Putnam's Sons, 1902.

Harland, Marion. *The Story of Mary Washington.* Boston: Houghton Mifflin, 1892.

Harper's Encyclopedia of United States History. Benson J. Lossing, editor. New York: Harper & Brothers, 1906.

Haskell, Caleb. *Caleb Haskell's Diary, May 5, 1775–May 30, 1776.* Lothrop Withington, editor. Newburyport: William H. Huse, 1881.

Hayes, Kevin J. *The Road to Monticello: The Life and Mind of Thomas Jefferson.* New York: Oxford University Press, 2008.

"Haym Solomon." *Information Annual 1916.* New York: Cumulative Digest Corporation, 1917.

Haynes, Henry Williamson. *Memoir of Mellen Chamberlain.* Cambridge: John Wilson, 1906.

Headley, Joel T. *The Chaplains and Clergy of the Revolution.* New York: Charles Scribner, 1864.

Heath, William. *Heath's Memoirs of the American War.* Rufus R. Wilson, editor. New York: A. Wessels, 1904.

Heimert, Alan. *Religion and the American Mind: From the Great Awakening to the Revolution.* Cambridge: Harvard University Press, 1966.

Hein, David and Gardiner H. Shattuck Jr. *The Episcopalians.* New York: Church, 2004.

Heyl, Francis. *The Battle of Germantown.* Philadelphia: City History Society of Philadelphia, 1908.

Hibbert, Christopher. *George III: A Personal History.* New York: Basic Books, 1998.

———. *The Tower of London.* New York: Newsweek Books, 1981.

Higginbotham, Don. *Daniel Morgan: Revolutionary Rifleman.* Chapel Hill: University of North Carolina Press, 1961.

Hilborn, Nat, and Sam Hilborn. *Battleground of Freedom: South Carolina in the Revolution.* Columbia: Sandlapper, 1970.

Hill, Hamilton Andrew. *History of the Old South Church, 1669–1884.* Boston: Houghton Mifflin, 1890.

Holifield, E. Brooks. *God's Ambassadors: A History of the Christian Clergy in America.* Grand Rapids: William B. Eerdmans, 2007.

Holman, Mabel Cassine. "Along the Connecticut River." *Connecticut Magazine.* Vol. 11, no. 1 (1907).

Holmes, Abiel. *The Annals of America*. Cambridge: Hilliard & Brown, 1929.

Holten, Samuel. "Journal of Samuel Holten, M.D., While in the Continental Congress, May 1778 to August 1780." *Historical Collection of the Essex Institute*. Vol. 55 (1919).

The Holy Bible: Containing the Old and New Testaments, Translated Out of the Original Tongues. Walpole: Anson Whipple, 1815.

Hopkins, Donald R. *The Greatest Killer: Smallpox in History*. Chicago: University of Chicago Press, 2002.

Hudson, Ruth Strong. "The Minister from France: Conrad-Alexandre Gérard." *Pennsylvania Magazine of History and Biography*. Vol. 21, no. 1 (January–April 1907).

Hudson, Winthrop S. *Nationalism and Religion in America*. New York: Harper & Row, 1970.

Humphreys, David. *Life of George Washington*. Athens: University of Georgia Press, 1991.

Hunt, Gaillard. *The Seal of the United States: How It Was Developed and Adopted*. Washington, DC: U.S. Department of State, 1892.

Hutson, James H. *Forgotten Features of the Founding: The Recovery of Religious Themes in the Early American Republic*. Lanham: Lexington Books, 2003.

———. "Religion and the Founding of the American Republic." Exhibition website, Library of Congress, 1988.

Ingram, George H. "The Presbytery of New Brunswick in the Struggle for Independence." *Journal of the Presbyterian Historical Society*. Vol. 9 (June 1917).

Ireland: From Independence to Occupation, 1641–1670. Jane H. Ohlmeyer, editor. Cambridge: Cambridge University Press, 1995.

Jaher, Frederic C. *The Jews and the Nation: Revolution, Emancipation, State Formation, and the Liberal Paradigm in America and France*. Princeton: Princeton University Press, 1960.

James, Mrs. Thomas Potts. *Memorial of Thomas Potts Junior*. Cambridge: n.p., 1874.

Jefferson, Thomas. Thomas Jefferson Papers. Manuscript Division. Library of Congress.

———. *The Works of Thomas Jefferson*. Paul Leicester Ford, editor. New York: G. P. Putnam's Sons, 1905.

Johnson, Samuel. *A Dictionary of the English Language*. Dublin: Thomas Ewing, 1768.

Johnson, William. *Sketches of the Life and Correspondence of Nathaael Greene*. Charleston: A. E. Miller, 1822.

Johnston, Henry P. "Evacuation of New York City by the British, 1783." *Harper's Magazine*. Vol. 67 (June–November 1883).

———. *The Yorktown Campaign and the Surrender of Cornwallis 1781*. New York: Harper & Brothers, 1881.

Jordan, John W. "Sessions of the Continental Congress Held in the College of Philadelphia in July 1778." *Pennsylvania Magazine of History and Biography.* Vol. 22, no. 1 (1898).

Journals of the Continental Congress, 1774–1789. Worthington C. Ford, editor. Washington, DC: U.S. Government Printing Office, 1906.

The Journals of Each Provincial Congress in Massachusetts 1774 and 1775. William Lincoln, editor. Boston: Dutton & Wentworth, 1839.

Journals of the House of Burgesses of Virginia, 1761–1765. John Pendleton Kennedy, editor. Richmond: Virginia State Library, 1907.

Katsh, Abraham Isaac. *The Biblical Heritage of American Democracy.* New York: KTAV, 1977.

Ketchum, Richard M. *The Battle for Bunker Hill.* New York: Doubleday, 1962.

———. *Saratoga: Turning Point of America's Revolutionary War.* New York: Henry Holt, 1997.

———. *Victory at Yorktown: The Campaign That Won the Revolution.* New York: Henry Holt, 2004.

Keteltas, Abraham. *God Arising and Pleading His People's Cause; or, the American War in Favor of Liberty, Against the Measures and Arms of Great Britain, Shewn to be the Cause of God.* Newbury: John Mycall, 1777.

Klees, Frederic. *The Pennsylvania Dutch.* New York: Macmillan, 1950.

Kumpa, Peter. "Robert Hanson Harrison: Lost Hero of the Revolutionary Era." *Baltimore Sun,* December 31, 1990.

Kyte, George W. "A Projected British Attack Upon Philadelphia in 1781." *Pennsylvania Magazine of History and Biography.* Vol. 74, no. 4 (October 1952).

Lamb, A. A. "Replies." *Catholic Historical Researches.* Vol. 2, no. 1 (July 1885).

Laurens, Henry. *The Papers of Henry Laurens, November 1, 1777—March 15, 1778.* David R. Chestnutt and Peggy J. Clark, editors. Columbia: University of South Carolina Press, 1990.

Laurens, John. *The Army Correspondence of Colonel John Laurens in the Years 1777–1778.* William Gilmore Simms, editor. New York: Bedford Club, 1867.

Leckey, William E. *A History of England in the Eighteenth Century.* London: Longmans & Green, 1906.

Leckie, Robert. *George Washington's War: The Saga of the American Revolution.* New York: HarperCollins, 1992.

Lee, Charles. *Memoirs of the Life of the Late Charles Lee.* Edward Langworthy, editor. London: J. S. Jordan, 1792.

Lefebvre, Georges. *The French Revolution.* New York: Columbia University Press, 1964.

Letters of Delegates to Congress, 1774–1789. Paul H. Smith, editor. Washington, DC: Library of Congress, 1976–2000.

"Life of Major General Muhlenberg." *Littell's Living Age.* Vol. 20 (January–March 1849).

Lillback, Peter A. *George Washington's Sacred Fire.* Bryn Mawr: Providence Forum Press, 2006.

Lindsey, Thomas. *A History of the Reformation.* New York: Charles Scribner's Sons, 1906.

Looney, Robert F. *Old Philadelphia in Early Photographs.* Philadelphia: Free Library of Philadelphia, 1976.

Lossing, Benjamin J. *Pictorial Field-Book of the American Revolution.* New York: Harper's, 1850.

Love, William D. *The Fast and Thanksgiving Days of New England.* Boston: Houghton Mifflin, 1895.

Low, Sidney J., and F. S. Pulling. *The Dictionary of English History.* London: Castle, 1910.

Luther, Martin. *The Works of Martin Luther.* Adolph Spaeth, L. D. Reed, and Henry Jacobs, editors. Philadelphia: J. Holman: 1915.

Maclay, William, and George W. Harris. *Sketches of Debate in the First Senate of the United States.* Harrisburg: Lane Hart, 1880.

Mallet, Charles E. *The French Revolution.* London: John Murray, 1892.

Mark, Michael. *A Concise History of American Music Education.* New York: Roman and Littlefield, 2008.

Marshall, Christopher. *Extracts from the Diary of Christopher Marshall, 1774–1781.* William Duane, editor. Albany: Joel Munsell, 1877.

Marston, Frances E. "The Scotch-Irish." *New York Times,* May 3, 1902.

Marston, Jerrilyn Green. *King and Congress: The Transfer of Political Legitimacy, 1774–1776.* Princeton: Princeton University Press, 1987.

"Mayflower Compact, 1620." Avalon Project. Lillian Goldman Law Library. Yale University.

McCrady, Edward. *The History of South Carolina in the Revolution 1775–1780.* New York: Macmillan, 1901.

McCullough, David. *John Adams.* New York: Simon & Schuster, 2001.

McKean, Caroline. "Domestic Life Among the Quakers of Philadelphia in the War of the American Revolution." *American Monthly Magazine.* Vol. 15, no. 3 (September 1899).

McLellan, Hugh. *History of Gorham, Maine.* Portland: Smith & Sale, 1903.

Means, Oliver William. *A Sketch of the Strict Congregational Church of Enfield Connecticut.* Boston: Harvard Seminary Press, 1899.

Melville, Lewis. *Farmer George.* London: Pittman & Sons, 1907.

Middlekauff, Robert. *The Glorious Cause: The American Revolution, 1763–1789.* New York: Oxford University Press, 1982.

Miller, Perry. *The New England Mind: The Seventeenth Century.* Cambridge: Harvard University Press, 1954.

Miller, Perry, and Thomas H. Johnson. *The Puritans: A Sourcebook of Their Writings.* New York: Harper & Row, 1963.

"Miscellaneous Colonial Documents." *Virginia Magazine of History and Biography.* Vol. 18 (July 1910–July 1911).

Mode, Peter G. *Sourcebook and Bibliographical Guide for American Church History.* Menasha: Collegiate Press, 1921.

Mombert, J. I. *An Authentic History of Lancaster County*. Lancaster: J. E. Barr, 1869.

Montresor, John. "Journal of Captain John Montresor, July 1, 1777 to July 1, 1778." G.D. Scull, editor. *Pennsylvania Magazine of History and Biography*. Vol. 6, no. 1 (1882).

"Monument at Sycamore Shoals." *Journal of the Presbyterian Historical Society*. Vol. 5 (1909–10).

Moore, Frank. *Diary of the American Revolution*. New York: Charles Scribner, 1850.

———. *Songs and Ballads of the American Revolution*. New York: Hunt, 1905.

Morgan, Daniel. *The Cowpens Papers: Being Correspondence of General Morgan and Prominent Actors*. Theodorus B. Myers, editor. Charleston: News & Courier, 1881.

Morison, Samuel Eliot. *Oxford History of the American People*. New York: Oxford University Press, 1965.

Morris, Richard B. *Encyclopedia of American History*. New York: Harper & Row, 1961.

Morris, Robert. *The Papers of Robert Morris, 1781–1784*. Elmer J. Ferguson, editor. Pittsburgh: University of Pittsburgh Press, 1977.

Moultrie, William. *Memoirs of the American Revolution*. New York: David Longworth, 1802.

Muhlenberg, Henry Augustus. *The Life of Major General Peter Muhlenberg of the Revolutionary Army*. Philadelphia: Carey & Hart, 1849.

Muhlenberg, Henry Melchior. "Extracts from the Rev. Dr. Muhlenberg's Journals of 1776 and 1777." *Collections of the Historical Society of Pennsylvania*. Vol. 1 (1853).

———. *The Journals of Henry Melchior Muhlenberg*. Theodore Gerhardt, editor. Philadelphia: Evangelical Lutheran Ministerium of Pennsylvania, 1942.

Mumby, Frank Arthur. *George III and the American Revolution*. London: Constable, 1924.

Neil, Edward D. "Rev. Jacob Duché: First Chaplain of Congress." *Pennsylvania Magazine of History and Biography*. Vol. 2, no. 1 (1878).

Newling, Dan. "Did George III's Powdered Wig Send Him Mad?" London *Daily Mail*, July 15, 2004.

Nickerson, Hoffman. *The Turning Point of the Revolution*. Cambridge: Riverside Press, 1928.

Noll, Mark A. *A History of Christianity in the United States and Canada*. Grand Rapids: William B. Eerdmans, 1992.

"Notices of New Works." *Métropolitain Magazine*. Vol. 21, no. 44 (February 1838).

Novak, Michael, and Jane Novak. *Washington's God: Religion, Liberty and the Father of Our Country*. New York: Basic Books, 2006.

"Original Letters." *Collections of the New Hampshire Historical Society*. Vol. 2 (1827).

Ousterhout, Anne. *The Most Learned Woman in America: A Life of Elizabeth Graeme Fergusson.* University Park: Penn State University Press, 2003.

The Oxford Companion to American Military History. John Whiteclay Chambers II, editor. New York: Oxford University Press, 1999.

The Oxford Dictionary of the Christian Church. F. L. Cross and E. A. Livingstone, editors. Oxford: Oxford University Press, 1953.

The Oxford Encyclopedia of the Reformation. Hans J. Hillerbrand, editor. New York: Oxford University Press, 1996.

Paige, Lucius R. *Commentary on the New Testament.* Boston: A. Tompkins, 1857.

Papers of the Continental Congress, 1774–1789. Washington, DC, National Archives and Records Administration.

The Parliamentary History of England. T. C. Hansard, editor. London: T. C. Hansard, 1814.

The Patriot Preachers of the American Revolution. Frank Moore, editor. New York: Charles T. Evans, 1862.

Patterson, Samuel White. *The Spirit of the American Revolution: As Revealed in the Poetry of the Period.* New York: Badger, 1915.

Patton, Jacob H. *Yorktown:* New York: Fords, Howard & Hulbert, 1882.

Pears, Thomas C. "The Story of the Aitken Bible." *Journal of the Presbyterian Historical Society.* Vol. 18 (June 1939).

Percy, George. "A Trewe Relacyon: Virginia from 1609–1612." *Tyler's Historical and Genealogical Magazine.* Leon G. Tyler, editor. Vol. 3 (1922).

Perspectives on Church Government: Five Views of Church Polity. Chad Owen Brand and R. Stanton Norman, editors. Nashville: Broadman & Holman, 2004.

Peters, Madison C. *Justice to the Jew: The Story of What He Has Done for the World.* New York: Trow Press, 1910.

Pierson, David L. *History of the Oranges.* New York: Lewis Historical Publishing, 1922.

"The Pilgrim Fathers." *Westminster and Foreign Quarterly Review.* London: Trubner. Vol. 40 (1871).

Price, Ira M. *The Ancestry of the English Bible: An Account of Manuscripts, Texts and Versions of the Bible.* Philadelphia: Times Company, 1906.

Price, James. "Memorable Places within the Bounds of the United Presbyterian Presbytery." *Journal of Presbyterian History.* Vol. 6 (1911–12).

Printed Ephemera Collection. Rare Book and Special Collections Division. Library of Congress.

Proceedings of the American Philosophical Society. Edgar F. Smith, editor. Philadelphia: American Philosophical Society, 1904.

Proclamations for Thanksgiving Issued by the Continental Congress. Benjamin Franklin Hough, editor. Albany: Munsell and Rowland, 1858.

Pruente, E. "The Continental Congress at Mass." *The Christian Family: An Illustrated Magazine for the Catholic Home.* Vol. 2 (1907).

Purvis, Thomas L. *Colonial America to 1763.* New York: Facts on File, 1999.

Rager, John C. "Catholic Sources and the Declaration of Independence." *Catholic Mind*. Vol. 28, no. 13 (July 8, 1930).

Ramsay, David. *The History of the American Revolution*. Trenton: James J. Wilson, 1811.

Rawle, Anna. "Occurrences in Philadelphia after Cornwallis's Surrender." *Philadelphia Magazine of History and Biography*. Vol. 16 (1892).

Records of the Presbyterian Church in the United States, 1706–1788. William Engles, editor. Philadelphia: Presbyterian Board of Publications, 1841.

Reed, William B. *Life and Correspondence of Joseph Reed*. Philadelphia: Lindsay & Blakeston, 1847.

Religion and the Law: A Handbook of Suggestions for Laymen and Clergy Preparing Law Day Addresses. Chicago: American Bar Association, 1975.

Revolutionary Virginia: The Road to Independence. William J. Van Schreevan and Robert L. Scribner, editors. Charlottesville: University of Virginia Press, 1973.

Richardson, Edward W. *Standards and Colors of the American Revolution*. Philadelphia: University of Pennsylvania Press, 1982.

Riker, James. *Evacuation Day 1783*. New York: Crichton, 1883.

Roberts, R. T. "Welsh Presbyterian Church in America." *Schaff-Herzog Encyclopedia of Religious Knowledge*. Samuel M. Jackson, editor. New York: Funk & Wagnall, 1911.

Rodney, Thomas. "Diary of Captain Thomas Rodney, 1776–1777." *Papers of the Historical Society of Delaware*. Charles P. Mallery, editor. Wilmington: Historical Society of Delaware, 1888.

Rogers, George C., Jr. *Charleston in the Age of the Pinckneys*. Columbia: University of South Carolina Press, 1980.

Rogers, Robert. *Diary of the Siege of Detroit in the War with Pontiac*. Franklin B. Hough, editor. Albany: Joel Munsell, 1860.

Ross, Peter. *The Scot in America*. New York: Raeburn Books, 1896.

Rothert, Otto A. *A History of Muhlenberg County*. Louisville: John P. Morton, 1913.

Royster, Charles. *A Revolutionary People at War: The Continental Army and Character 1775–1783*. Chapel Hill: University of North Carolina Press, 1980.

Sandoz, Ellis. *Political Sermons of America's Founding Era 1730–1805*. Indianapolis: Liberty Fund, 1998.

Sassi, Jonathan D. *A Republic of Righteousness: The Public Christianity of the Post-Revolution New England Clergy*. New York: Oxford University Press, 2001.

Saul, David, "The Disorder Responsible for George III's 'Madness' Also Affected Many of His Descendants." London: *Sunday Telegraph*, 19 July 1998.

Scharf, J. Thomas, and Thompson Westcott. *History of Philadelphia from 1609 to 1884*. Philadelphia: L. H. Everts, 1884.

Scheer, George F. and Hugh F. Rankin. *Rebels and Redcoats*. New York: World, 1957.

Schmauk, Thomas Emanuel. *The Lutheran Church in Pennsylvania, 1638–1820.* Philadelphia: General Council Publications, 1902.

Sharpless, Isaac. *Political Leaders of Provincial Pennsylvania,* New York: Macmillan, 1919.

The Siege of Savannah in 1779. Charles C. Jones, editor. Albany: Joel Munsell, 1874.

"Six Letters of 'Signers' in 'Active Service.' " *Pennsylvania Magazine of History and Biography.* Philadelphia: Historical Society of Pennsylvania. Vol. 40, no. 1 (1916).

Smith, John. *Travels and Works of Captain John Smith, President of Virginia and Admiral of New England, 1580–1631.* Edward Arber, editor. Edinburgh: John Grant, 1910.

Smith, Page. *A People's History of the American Revolution.* New York: McGraw-Hill, 1976.

Smith, Robert. *The Obligations of the Confederate State of North America to Praise God: Preached at Pequea, December 13, 1781.* Philadelphia: Francis Bailey, 1782.

Smith, Thomas, and Samuel Deane. *Journals of the Rev. Thomas Smith and the Rev. Samuel Deane.* William Willis, editor. Portland: Joseph Bailey, 1819.

Smith, William. *History of the First Discovery and Settlement of Virginia.* New York: Joseph Sabin, 1865.

Smith, William. *The Works of William Smith: Late Provost of the College and Academy of Philadelphia.* Philadelphia: Maxwell & Fry, 1803.

Snowden, Yates. *History of South Carolina.* Chicago: Lewis, 1920.

Solberg, Winton U. *Redeem the Time: The Puritan Sabbath in Early America.* Cambridge: Harvard University Press, 1977.

Sparks, Jared. *The Life of George Washington.* London: Henry Colburn, 1839.

Spirit of Seventy-Six: The Story of the American Revolution as Told by Participants. Henry Steele Commager and Richard B. Morris, editors. New York: Da Capo, 1975.

Spivey, Larkin. *Miracles of the American Revolution.* Fairfax: Allegiance Press, 2004.

Sprague, William B. *Annals of the American Pulpit.* New York: Robert Carter, 1860.

Stedman, Charles. *The History of the Origin, Progress and Termination of the American War.* London: J. Murray, 1794.

Steiner, Bernard Christian. *The Life and Correspondence of James McHenry.* Cleveland: Burrows Brothers, 1907.

Stout, Harry S. *The New England Soul: Preaching and Religious Culture in Colonial New England.* New York: Oxford University Press, 1986.

Stowell, William Henry. *History of the Puritans in England.* London: Thomas Nelson, 1878.

"Surrender of Lord Cornwallis." *Donahoe's Magazine*, Vol. 6 (July 1881–January 1882).

Tarleton, Banastre. *History of the Campaigns of 1780 and 1781 in the Southern Provinces of North America*. Dublin: Coles, Exshaw & White, 1787.

Thackeray, William Makepeace. *The Four Georges: Sketches of Manners, Morals, Court and Town Life*. London: John Long, 1905.

Thompson, Henry F. "A Letter of Miss Rebecca Franks, 1778." *Pennsylvania Magazine of History and Biography*. Vol. 16, no. 1 (1892).

Thompson, Mary V. *In the Hands of a Good Providence: Religion in the Life of George Washington*. Charlottesville: University of Virginia Press, 2008.

Thorne, John Calvin. *A Monograph of the Rev. Israel Evans*. New York: William Abbatt, 1907.

Thornton, John Wingate. *The Pulpit of the American Revolution*. Boston: Gould & Lincoln, 1860.

Thorpe, Francis Newton. *The Federal and State Constitutions, Colonial Charters, and Other Organic Laws of the States, Territories and Colonies Now or Heretofore Forming the United States of America*. Washington, DC: U.S. Government Printing Office, 1877.

Tilghman, Tench. *Memoir of Lieut. Col. Tench Tilghman, Secretary and Aide to Washington*. Samuel A. Harrison and Oswald Tilghman, editors. Albany: Joel Munsell, 1876.

Tocqueville de, Alexis. *Democracy in America*. New York: George Adlard, 1839.

Toner, J. M. *Washington's Rules of Civility and Decent Behavior in Company and Conversation*. Washington, DC: W. H. Morrison, 1888.

Tracy, Joseph. *The Great Awakening: A History of the Revival of Religion in the Time of Edwards and Whitefield*. Boston: Charles Tappan, 1845.

Trevelyan, George Otto. *The American Revolution*. New York: Longmans & Green, 1922.

———. *George the Third and Charles Fox: The Concluding Part of the American Revolution*. London: Longmans & Green, 1916.

Trumbull, Jonathan. "The Trumbull Papers." *Collections of the Massachusetts Historical Society*. Boston: Wilson & Son, 1902.

The Twentieth Century Biographical Dictionary of Notable Americans. Rossiter Johnson and John Howard Brown, editors. Boston: Biographical Society, 1904.

Tyler, Moses Coit. *The Literary History of the American Revolution, 1763–1783*. New York: G. P. Putnam's Sons, 1897.

———. *Patrick Henry*. Boston: Houghton Mifflin, 1899.

Usher, Roland G. *The Pilgrims and Their History*. New York: Macmillan, 1918.

Van Cortlandt, Philip. *Revolutionary War Memoir and Selected Correspondence of Philip Van Cortlandt*. Jacob Judd, editor. Tarrytown: Sleepy Hollow Restorations, 1976.

Van Schreeven, William James. *Revolutionary Virginia: The Road to Independence*. Robert Scribner, editor. Charlottesville: University Press of Virginia, 1977.

Van Tyne, Claude H. *The American Nation: A History*. New York: Harper Brothers, 1905.

———. *The American Revolution 1776–1783*. New York: Harper Brothers, 1905.

———. "Influence of the Clergy and of Religious and Sectarian Forces on the American Revolution." *American Historical Review*. Vol. 19, no. 1 (October 1913).

———. *The War of Independence: American Phase*. Boston: Houghton Mifflin, 1929.

Ver Steeg, Clarence L. *The Formative Years 1607–1763*. New York: Hill & Wang, 1965.

Waldo, Albigence. "Diary of Surgeon Albigence Waldo, of the Connecticut Line." *Pennsylvania Magazine of History and Biography*. Charles J. Stille, editor. Vol. 21, no. 1 (1897).

Ward, Christopher. *The War of the Revolution*. New York: Macmillan, 1952.

Washington, George. *The Daily Journal of Major George Washington 1751–1752*. J. M. Toner, editor. Albany: Joel Munsell's Sons, 1892.

———. *The Diaries of George Washington, 1741–1799*. Donald Jackson and Dorothy Twohig, editors. Charlottesville: University Press of Virginia, 1986.

———. *Diary of George Washington from 1789 to 1791*. Richmond: Historical Society Press, 1861.

———. The George Washington Papers, 1741–1799. Washington, DC: Manuscript Division, Library of Congress.

———. *The Glorious Struggle: George Washington's Revolutionary War Letters*. Edward G. Lengel, editor. Washington, DC: Smithsonian Books, 2007.

———. *The Orderly Book of General George Washington, Commander in Chief of the American Armies, Kept at Valley Forge 18 May—11 June 1778*. New York: Lamson & Wolf, 1898.

———. *The Papers of George Washington, Revolutionary War Series*. Philander D. Chase, editor. Charlottesville: University Press of Virginia, 1985.

———. *The Revolutionary Orders of General Washington*. Henry Whiting, editor. New York: Wiley & Putnam, 1844.

———. *Washington's Inaugural Address of 1789*. Washington, DC: National Archives and Records Administration, 1986.

———. *Writings of George Washington, Correspondence and Other Papers: Correspondence, Addresses, Messages, and Other Papers, Official and Private*. Jared Sparks, editor. Boston: Little & Brown, 1855.

———. *Writings of George Washington from the Original Manuscript Sources, 1745–1799*. John Clement Fitzpatrick, editor. Washington, DC: U.S. Government Printing Office, 1944.

"Washington's Prayer at Valley Forge." *The Friend: A Religious and Literary Journal*. Vol. 80, no. 46 (March 25, 1907).

"Washington's Respect for Ministers." *The Guardian: A Monthly Magazine*. H. Harbaugh, editor. Vol. 8, no. 7 (July 1857).

Weedon, George. *Valley Forge Orderly Book of General George Weedon of the Continental Army under Gen'l George Washington, in the Campaign of 1777–1778.* New York: Dodd, Mead, 1902.

Weems, Mason Locke. *A History of the Life and Death, Virtues and Exploits of General George Washington.* Philadelphia: J. B. Lippincott, 1918.

Wellenreuther, Herman. *The Revolution of the People: Thoughts and Documents on the Revolutionary Process in North America 1774–1776.* Gottingen: University of Gottingen, 2006.

Wells, William V. *The Life and Public Service of Samuel Adams.* Boston: Little & Brown, 1865.

Westminster Confession of Faith. Edinburgh: T. and T. Clark, 1881.

White, Morton. *The Philosophy of the American Revolution.* New York: Oxford University Press, 1978.

Whitney, Peter. *American Intendance Vindicated: A Sermon Delivered September 12, 1776.* Boston: n.p., 1777.

Wight, Charles Albert. *Some Old Time Meeting Houses of the Connecticut Valley.* Chicopee Falls: Rich Printing, 1911.

Wilkinson, James. *Memoirs of My Own Time.* Philadelphia: Abraham Small, 1816.

Williams, Julie Hedgepeth. *The Significance of the Printed Word in Early America.* Westport: Greenwood Press, 1999.

Wilson, Bird. *Memoir of the Life of the Right Reverend William White.* Philadelphia: James Kay, 1839.

Wilson, F. T. *Official Programme of the Yorktown Centennial Celebration.* Washington, DC: Judd & Detweiler, 1881.

Wineke, William R. "Modern Medicine Studies the Madness of King George." *Wisconsin State Journal*, April 15, 1996.

Wirt, William. *Sketches of the Life and Character of Patrick Henry.* Ithaca: Andrus & Gauntlett, 1850.

Witherspoon, John. *A Sermon Preached at Princeton, May 17, 1776.* Philadelphia: n.p., 1777.

"Yesterday." *New York Gazette*, July 24, 1775.

INDEX

Act of Settlement (1701), 41
Adams, Abigail, 16, 40, 99, 129
Adams, John, 16, 38, 40, 47, 75, 99, 129, 140, 152, 158, 195, 197, 198, 200–202
Adams, Samuel, 40, 131, 135, 136, 138
Age of Reason, 15
Aitken, Robert, 198, 202–3
Albemarle County, Virginia: prayer/ thanksgiving days in, 86
Alison, Francis, 199
Allen, Moses, 81
Allen, Thomas, 80
American Bible Society, 186
American cause. *See* independence, American
"American Hearts of Oak" (song), 83
American Revenue Act (1764). *See* Sugar Act
American Revolution: American motivation for, 3–4; American turnaround in, 165–66; American victory in, 207–8, 213–14; as biblically justified war, 82–83, 136; British lack of understanding of reasons behind, 136–37; British perplexity about American survival in, 7–8; brutality during, 86–87; as David and Goliath battle, 149, 173;

end of, 206; European views about, 98; French Revolution compared with, 87; God/Providence role in, 1–4, 7–8, 62–63, 211, 215; inalienable rights as basis for, 136; Judeo-Christian worldview and, 70–71, 82–83, 85, 87; as just war, 86, 130, 131, 133, 139; Kings Mountain battle as turning point in, 168, 169; Lexington as beginning of, 39; low point in, 165; motivation for, 70–71, 82–83, 85, 87; official end to fighting in, 207; peace negotiations/ treaty in, 183, 195, 203, 205, 206–7, 209; as "religious war," 75–76; revolt against abuse of law, 87; as self-defense action, 86; slogan of, 2; uniqueness of, 87; unofficial end of, 183; Washington's role in, 215; worst calamity during, 157, 158. *See also* independence, American; *specific person or battle*
Anglican Church: clergy of, 69; divisions within, 69; post-revolutionary, 150; Scots-Irish as members of, 72; transformation of American, 150; Washington as member of, 19. *See also* Church of England; *specific church or person*

275